SPHERES OF EXISTENCE

Also by C. L. R. James

C. L. R. James

SPHERES OF EXISTENCE

Selected Writings

Allison & Busby

This selection first published 1980
by Allison and Busby Limited
6a Noel Street, London W1V 3RB

ISBN 0 85031 298 1 (hardback)
ISBN 0 85031 299 X (paperback)

The publishers gratefully acknowledge the invaluable help
they have received in compiling this selection from
C. L. R. James, David Cork, Michael Dibb, Robert A. Hill,
Selma James, John LaRose, Alan J. MacKenzie, Reinhard
Sander, Richard Small.

Set in Times by Malvern Typesetting Services
and printed in Great Britain by
Redwood Burn Ltd, Trowbridge & Esher

Contents

Here the impossible union
Of spheres of existence is actual,
Here the past and the future
Are conquered, and reconciled,
Where action were otherwise movement
Of that which is only moved
And has in it no source of movement—

T. S. Eliot
The Dry Salvages

C. L. R. JAMES: A BIOGRAPHICAL INTRODUCTION

C. L. R. James—the author of historical studies, a novel, short stories, a play; a seminal figure in black politics on three continents; writer on Hegel and philosophy, and a major innovator in marxist theory and working-class organisation; the author of books and essays on literature, art and sport; and above all a participant, teacher and activist in the events of his time—was born in Tunapuna, near Port of Spain, Trinidad, in 1901, the son of a schoolteacher. He attended Queen's Royal College, the island's major government secondary school, as a scholarship boy, and in the 1920s became a teacher there himself; during this time he played club cricket and began writing fiction.

In 1932 he came to England with the encouragement of an old acquaintance and cricketing opponent, Learie Constantine, whom he was to help to write his autobiography; for a while James lived in Constantine's adopted town of Nelson, Lancashire. He had brought with him his first political book, *The Life of Captain Cipriani*, a pioneer work arguing the case for West Indian self-government which was published that year in Nelson with Constantine's assistance, and later in a shortened version by Leonard Woolf's Hogarth Press in London.

An article by James on cricket in the *Daily Telegraph* brought him to the attention of Neville Cardus, and as a result of this meeting James began to write as cricket correspondent for the *Manchester Guardian*. This, followed by similar employment with the *Glasgow Herald*, was to provide him with a living throughout his first stay in the country. Meanwhile he had become active in British politics and society. Until 1936 he was a member of the Independent Labour Party and chairman of its Finchley branch, and he wrote regularly for the ILP papers *Controversy* and the *New Leader*. In that year he left to help form the Revolutionary Socialist League, along with other trotskyists who had left the ILP, and he was editor of its newspaper *Fight*. At the same time he was editor of *International African Opinion*, the journal of the International African Service Bureau; the members of this organisation included Jomo Kenyatta, and its founder and chairman was George Padmore, whom James had known from childhood and whom he was later to introduce to Kwame Nkrumah. (James was to write in a letter to Padmore in 1945: "George, this young man [Nkrumah] is coming to you . . . do what you can for him because he's determined to throw the Europeans out of Africa.''

It was under the auspices of the Bureau that Nkrumah was to go from London to the Gold Coast in 1947 to begin his preparations for the revolution which was to initiate a new Africa.) James participated in the movement of the unemployed, and made speaking tours in England, Scotland and Wales. He was chairman of the International African Friends of Abyssinia during the Italian invasion, writing many articles on this issue for *The Keys* (the journal of the League of Coloured Peoples) and agitating among British workers for solidarity actions. He also played a part in the growth of the trotskyist movement in France, and was one of the British delegates to the founding conference of the Fourth International in 1938. During this period he wrote his famous history of the Haitian revolution, *The Black Jacobins* (1938), an extensive history of the Third International, *World Revolution* (1937), and *A History of Negro Revolt* (1938), as well as publishing a novel, *Minty Alley* (1936). He translated Boris Souvarine's *Stalin* (1939), the first major exposé of its subject, from the French. He also wrote and acted in a play, *Toussaint L'Ouverture* (1936), in which he and Paul Robeson appeared together at the Westminster Theatre.

At the end of 1938 James went to the United States of America on a lecture tour, and stayed there for the next fifteen years. In this period his activity developed in two main directions. First of all, he pioneered the idea of an autonomous black movement which would be socialist but not subject to control by the leaderships of white-majority parties and trade unions. The record of his 1938 discussions with Trotsky, in which he laid the basis of this principle, is still one of the fundamental texts establishing a black marxism. James took part in wartime sharecroppers' strikes in the South, and agitated among blacks to oppose the world war. In the course of this activity he came to the conclusion that not only did the black movement have autonomy, it was also more advanced than the rest of the labour movement and would act as its detonator: this view is summed up in the programme entitled *The Revolutionary Answer to the Negro Problem in the US* (1948). His other main activity (and in fact they interacted) was in the Socialist Workers' Party, where together with Raya Dunayevskaya he led a tendency that gradually elaborated an independent marxism, breaking with its trotskyist background. It extended to women and youth its idea of the special role of the black movement (this was still the 1940s) and later began to criticise the traditional "democratic centralist" version of the marxist organisation. This rethinking is recorded in various political documents of the tendency and in articles in *The New International* during the 1940s; it culminates in two full-length works, *Notes on Dialectics* (1948), a study of Hegel's *Science of Logic* and the development of the dialectic in Marx and his continuators, and *State Capitalism and World*

Revolution (1950). During this period, James had also helped to initiate the first English translation of Marx's *Economic and Philosophic Manuscripts of 1844*. In 1952 he was interned on Ellis Island, and was expelled from the USA in the following year. It was during his internment that he wrote *Mariners, Renegades and Castaways*, a study of the work of Herman Melville.

James spent the next five years in England. He continued to contribute to the political debate in the US through the pages of the Detroit-based journal *Correspondence*. In 1958 he published *Facing Reality*, which presented the ideas worked through in the forties in the light of the Hungarian revolution and the growth of rank-and-file shop stewards'-type movements in Europe and North America. But at the same time he embarked upon a long programme of writing in which he was to re-examine the basis of his assumptions about human culture, and it was with this purpose that on his return to England he began his now classic book on cricket, *Beyond a Boundary* (1963).

The struggle for colonial emancipation in which James had continuously been involved was by now showing some results. In the years before the second world war he had been among the very few who not only foresaw but worked for the independence of Africa, and he maintained and strengthened his links with the Pan-Africanist movement, and with Nkrumah, during his visits to Ghana during the early years of the new régime. *Nkrumah and the Ghana Revolution* (1977) chronicles the events that led up to and ensued from Ghana becoming the first African country to win independence in 1957.

In 1958 James returned to Trinidad, in the run-up to the West Indian independence which he had already been advocating when he left a quarter of a century earlier. He became Secretary of the Federal Labour Party, the governing party of the embryonic West Indies Federation, and he worked with Dr Eric Williams in the Trinidad PNM (People's National Movement), editing and contributing copiously to its newspaper *The Nation*. Over the next three years he wrote two books, *Modern Politics* and *Party Politics in the West Indies*, as well as writing and lecturing on West Indian culture. His partnership with his former student and friend Williams came to an end as a result of the break-up of the West Indies Federation, and more particularly as a result of Williams's rejection of a non-aligned position in favour of the USA and its retention of the Chaguaramas Naval Base. *Modern Politics* was banned, and James returned to England in 1962, a few days before Trinidad's independence. He continued to publish from a distance in the Trinidadian press, and returned in 1965 as a cricket correspondent to report the Test series. He was immediately put under house arrest, but his status as one of the founding fathers of West Indian independence ensured an outcry that led to his release.

4 C. L. R. JAMES

He stayed for several months, during which he founded and edited a newspaper, *We the People*, and initiated the formation of the Workers' and Peasants' Party.

James returned to England in the same year. He has continued to write prolifically on the variety of matters which have concerned him throughout his life, and to take an active part in political life. He initiated the 6th Pan-African Congress in Dares-Salaam in 1974, but because of a decision to exclude certain dissident Caribbean movements he declined to attend himself. He has contributed to a number of journals spanning three continents. These include *New Society*, *New Left Review*, *Race Today* in Britain; *Black World*, *Freedomways*, *Radical America* and *Amistad* in the USA; *Transition* in Africa; *New World* and many occasional publications in the Caribbean. He has been Visiting Professor of Political Science at Northwestern University, Illinois, and most recently Professor of Humanities at Federal City College, Washington; the rest of his time is divided between London and the West Indies. He continues to write on cricket, and is completing his autobiography.

(The Selected Writings of C. L. R. James are being published in three volumes: *The Future in the Present*, *Spheres of Existence* and *At the Rendezvous of Victory*.)

1

La Divina Pastora

*[James wrote several pieces of fiction before he left Trinidad for
the first time; this short story which was published in* The
Saturday Review *in October 1927, and reappeared in* Best Short
Stories, *edited by E. J. O'Brien, in 1928, predates the better-
known "Triumph" (included in the* The Future in the Present)
*which is credited with being the earliest literary piece in the
Caribbean depicting "yard life".]*

Of my own belief in this story I shall say nothing. What I have
done is to put it down as far as possible just as it was told to me,
in my own style, but with no addition to or subtraction from the
essential facts.

Anita Perez lived with her mother at Bande l'Est Road, just
at the corner where North Trace joins the Main Road. She had
one earthly aim. She considered it her duty and business to be
married as quickly as possible, first because in that retired spot it
marked the sweet perfection of a woman's existence, and
secondly, because feminine youth and beauty, if they exist, fade
early in the hard work on the cocoa plantations. Every morning
of the week, Sundays excepted, she banded down her hair, and
donned a skirt which reached to her knees, not with any
pretensions to fashion, but so that from seven till five she might
pick cocoa, or cut cocoa, or dry cocoa, or in some other way
assist in the working of Mr Kayle-Smith's cocoa estate. She did
this for thirty cents a day, and did it uncomplainingly, because
her mother and father had done it before her, and had thriven
on it. On Sundays she dressed herself in one of her few dresses,
put on a little gold chain, her only ornament, and went to Mass.
She had no thought of woman's rights, nor any Ibsenic theories
of morality. All she knew was that it was her duty to get
married, when, if she was lucky, this hard life in the cocoa
would cease.

Every night for the past two years Sebastian Montagnio came
down from his four-roomed mansion, half a mile up the trace,
and spent about an hour, sometimes much more, with the Perez
family. Always he sat on a bench by the door, rolling cheap
cigarettes and half-hiding himself in smoke. He was not fair to
outward view, but yet Anita loved him. Frequently half an hour
would elapse without a word from either, she knitting or sewing
steadily, Sebastian watching her contentedly and Mrs Perez
sitting on the ground just outside the door, smoking one of
Sebastian's cigarettes and carrying on a ceaseless monologue in
the local patois. Always when Sebastian left, the good woman

rated Anita for not being kinder to him. Sebastian owned a few acres of cocoa and a large provision garden, and Mrs Perez had an idea that Anita's marriage would mean relief from the cocoa-work, not only for Anita, but also for her.

Anita herself said nothing. She was not the talking kind. At much expense and trouble, Sebastian sent her a greeting card each Christmas. On them were beautiful words which Anita spelt through so often that in time she got to know them by heart. Otherwise nothing passed between the two. That he loved no one else she was sure. It was a great consolation; but did he love her? Or was it only because his home was dull and lonely, and theirs was just at the corner, that he came down every night?

As the months slipped by, Anita anxiously watched her naturally pale face in the little broken mirror. It was haggard and drawn with watching and waiting for Sebastian to speak. She was not young and her manner was not attractive. The gossiping neighbours looked upon her as Sebastian's property. Even in the little cocoa-house dances (Sebastian never went because he did not dance) she was left to herself most of the time. And then, she loved him.

It came about that Anita's aunt, who lived at Siparia, paid her a surprise visit on Sunday. She had not visited North Trace for years, and might never come back again. Consequently there were many things to be talked about. Also the good lady wanted to know what Anita was doing for herself.

"And when will you be married, *ma chère*?" she asked, secure in the possession of three children and a husband. Anita, aching for a confidante, poured forth her simple troubles into the married lady's sympathetic ear. Mrs Perez expatiated on Sebastian's worldly goods. Mrs Reis, you remember, came from Siparia. "Pack your clothes at once, girl," she said, "you will have to miss this week in the cocoa. But don't mind, I know someone who can help you. And that is La Divina."

Of La Divina Pastora, the Siparia saint, many things can be written, but here only this much need be said. It is a small image of some two feet in height which stands in the Roman Catholic Church at Siparia. To it go pilgrims from all parts of the island, at all times of the year: this one with an incurable malady, that one with a long succession of business misfortunes, the other with a private grudge against some fellow-creature to be satisfied, some out of mere curiosity. Once a year there used to be a special festival, the Siparia fête, when, besides the wor-shippers, many hundreds of sightseers and gamblers gathered at the little village, and for a week there were wild Bacchanalian carouses going on side by side with the religious celebrations. This has been modified, but still the pilgrims go. To many the saint is nothing more than a symbol of the divine. To more—like the Perez family—it possesses limitless powers of its own to help the importunate. From both parties it receives presents of all descriptions, money frequently, but oft-times a gift from the suppliant—a gold ring, perhaps, or a brooch, or some other article of jewellery. Anita had no money; her aunt had to pay her passage. But she carried the little gold chain with her, the maiden's mite, for it was all that she had. It was not fête time, and quietly and by herself, with the quiet hum of the little country village in her ears, Anita placed the chain around the neck of the saint and prayed—prayed for what perhaps every woman except Eve has prayed for, the love of the man she loved.

That Sunday night when Sebastian reached Madame Perez's house, the even tenor of his way sustained a rude shock. Anita was not there, she had gone to Siparia, and was not coming back till next Sunday, by the last train. Wouldn't he come in and sit down? Sebastian came in and sat down, on his old seat, near the door. Mrs Perez sat outside commenting on the high price of shop goods generally, especially tobacco. But Sebastian did not answer; he was experiencing new sensations. He missed Anita's quiet face, her steady, nimble fingers, her glance at him and then away, whenever he spoke. He felt ill at ease, somehow disturbed, troubled, and it is probable that he recognised the cause of his trouble. For when Anita landed at Princes' Town the next Sunday, Tony the cabman came up to her and said: "Sebastian told me to bring you up alone, Anita." And he had to say it again before she could understand. During the six-mile drive, Anita sat in a corner of the cab, awed and expectant. Faith she had had, but for this she was not prepared. It was too sudden, as if the Saint had had nothing to do with it.

They met Sebastian walking slowly down the road to meet them. For an hour he had been standing by her house, and as soon as the first cab passed started, in his impatience, to meet her on the way. The cab stopped, and he was courageous enough to help her down. The cabman jumped down to light one of his lamps and the two stood waiting hand in hand. As he drove off Sebastian turned to her. "Nita," he said, shortening her name for the first time, "I missed you, Nita. God, how I missed you!"

Anita was happy, very happy indeed. In her new-found happiness she came near to forgetting the saint, whose answer had come so quickly. Sebastian himself was very little changed. Still he came every night, still Mrs Perez smoked his cigarettes, ruminating now on her blissful future. But things were different. So different in fact that Sebastian proposed taking her to the little cocoa-house dance which was to come off in a day or two. It was the first time that they were going out together since that Sunday. Everybody who did not know before would know now, when they saw Sebastian taking her to a dance, a thing he had never done before. So she dressed herself with great care in the blue muslin dress, and what with happiness and excitement looked more beautiful than she had ever seen herself. Then, as she cast another last look in the mirror, she missed something.

"How I wish," she said with a genuine note of regret in her voice, "how I wish I had my little gold chain." Here her mother, determined not to jeopardise her future, called sharply to her, and she came out, radiant.

The dance continued till long after five o'clock, but Anita had to leave at three. Sebastian got tired of sitting down in a corner of the room while she whisked around. He felt just a trifle sulky, for he had wanted to leave an hour before, but she, drinking of an intoxicating mixture of admiration, success and excitement, had implored him to stay a little longer. They went home almost in silence, he sleepy, she tired, each thinking the other offended. It was the first little cloud between them.

"It is nothing," thought Anita, "we shall make it up tomorrow night." She thought of something and smiled, but as she peeped at Sebastian and saw him peeping at her, she assumed a more serious expression. Tomorrow, not tonight.

Once inside the bedroom she started to undress quickly, took out a few pins and went to the table to put them down in the cigarette tin in which she kept her knick-knacks. Her mother, who was lying on the bed and listening with half-closed eyes to Anita's account of the dance, was startled by a sudden silence, followed by the sound of a heavy fall. She sprang down quickly, bent over the prostrate form of Anita, and turned to the little table to get the smelling-salts. Then she herself stood motionless, as if stricken, her senseless daughter lying unheeded on the floor. There, in its old place in the cigarette tin, lay a little chain of gold.

1927

2

Turner's Prosperity

[*The literary journal* Trinidad, *in the first issue of which this story was originally published (Christmas, 1929), was, with* The Beacon, *one of the two earliest magazines closely related to the emergence of West Indian fiction. James was co-editor, with Alfred Mendes, of the first issue of* Trinidad, *of which in fact only one other edition appeared, at Easter, 1930.*]

The pay envelopes were sent round at three o'clock exactly, and Turner's creditors began to congregate from about half past two. Some of them, like Mills, who lent twenty-four cents for thirty cents during the week (more if you wanted, according to the same scale) had business to do also with some of Turner's fellow-clerks, but of the dozen or so people who had taken up unassuming attitudes on the pavement opposite the store or on the very pavement on which Turner was standing, nearly half of them had come to him. There was Mills himself, half East Indian, down from San Juan to collect his interest, and for the smaller amounts, interest and principal. Turner had promised faithfully to give him $5.60 that afternoon—accumulation of principal $4.00 and unpaid interest $1.60 for four weeks. He had put him off for three weeks but he had promised faithfully to pay that afternoon. He was a man to make a row which would draw such a crowd in front of the store as would stop the traffic in the street. Then there was Ellis with the bill from the grocery. If he didn't pay today they would certainly sue on Monday. Little Jane from her mother, the washerwoman, who had sent her daughter because she knew if she didn't get money on Friday there was none coming again until after seven long days. A little distance off waited two East Indian men from each of whom he had taken cloth promising to pay fifty cents a week. All were waiting to get money from him. But even if Turner gave each man who had come the very smallest that would pacify him, the twelve dollars that his envelope contained would not have sufficed to go round. And then there was money to give his wife to carry on for the week, and arrears of rent, and instalments on judgment summonses. Sometimes when he thought of his difficulties his head would swim, especially on Fridays and Saturdays when the chase was hot. Round the corner came another: Prince, the shoemaker, who had half-soled the boots of the elder of his two sons. Another seventy-two cents. As was not uncommon when brought to bay like this on a Friday he felt for a second like leaving creditors, job, family and everything, running madly down the street and jumping into the Gulf. But as usual the fit passed.

"Your envelope, Mr Turner," said the office boy.

Turner took it mechanically and put it into his hip pocket. Striving to suppress his rage at his difficulties and his impotence he took it out again and walked up to the cashier's desk, knowing that the eyes of his clients were fixed on him.

"Could you give me as much change as possible for this, Mr Thompson?" he said holding out seven dollars.

Thompson gave him dollar notes and silver which he put into his trouser pocket. The remaining five dollars were safe in the envelope in his hip pocket. He was going to hold on to that. He looked round the store to see if anything might be required of him, then passed out of the door and walked a little way down the pavement to be out of sight of his fellow-workers. They all knew everything about him but still he preferred to make his disbursements in private.

Jane came across to him with the simple directness of childhood and put in his hands a dirty piece of paper on which was written "seventy-six cents." He took forty-eight cents out of his pocket and pushed it into her hand.

"Tell your mother that's all I can manage this afternoon. Tomorrow morning she will get the rest."

"But, Mr Turner—"

He glared at her.

"Tell her tomorrow morning she will get the rest," he repeated with emphasis. "I have no more money now."

There was no possibility of his getting any more money by the next day but his chief care, as always, was to get rid at any cost of whoever might be worrying him at a particular time. He looked round for Mills next but Mills was busy with another clerk. Turner beckoned to the two Indian sellers of cloth. They were patient fellows who would stand any amount of putting off. He had promised them on the previous Friday two dollars each (he owed one eighteen dollars for nearly as many months and the other eleven dollars, a debt on which he had never paid one cent from the day he got the flannel trousers for himself and the blouse for his wife, some nine months before). He rapidly decided to offer them a dollar each. Out of the corner of his eye he could see Prince, the shoemaker, hovering round to catch his glance. . . .

Ten minutes after, by payment, promise, evasion, by supplication and bluster, by hook and by crook, Turner had got rid of all of them. His five dollars were still safe in his hip pocket but there was only one dollar and eighty-four cents of the seven dollars with which to pay Mills.

"I will pay you the interest, one-sixty," he said briskly to Mills as the latter, his other business finished, turned towards Turner who was still on the pavement outside.

"Look here, Mr Turner," said Mills in a very decided voice, "I want my money today. I want it now. I didn't want to lend it to you. I know what kind of a man you are, but you told me you had a bailiff in the house and you beg like a child and I lend you the money. Three weeks you been putting me off. I want it now. I am a man like that. I have no manners when it comes to my money." He looked coolly but sternly at Turner. He was a little fellow, but fit and hard. Turner was not too sure that he wouldn't assault him. He knew what kind of person Mills was. Gibbs his friend had warned him to do anything rather than borrow money from Mills.

"I know it's my fault and I promised you faithfully for today," said Turner, attempting to put his hand ingratiatingly on Mills's shoulder.

"Don't touch me, man, don't touch me. I am not a woman. When it comes to my money I'm not even a man, I am a wild beast."

And then Turner, badgered and desperate, lost his temper.

"Do what the hell you like then. I tell you I have only the interest."

"Do what the hell I like? So that is what—"

"What is this disturbance about, Mr Turner," said the Scotch accent of Mr McIntosh, the manager. "Why do you choose the pavement in front of the store to make a commotion, Mr Turner? You are drawing the attention of people. Go into my office and wait for me . . . Excuse me, I have overheard a little of your conversation. How much money has he got for you?"

"Five-sixty," said the unabashed Mills.

"Is that so, Turner?" said Mr McIntosh to the slowly retreating Turner.

"Yes, sir," Turner could barely quaver in reply.

His heart was quaking for his job, for Mr McIntosh was known to dislike people who owed money. He walked into the store and then into Mr McIntosh's office looking at no one. A minute after, Mr McIntosh came up to the cashier's cage followed by Mills.

"Pay this man five dollars and sixty cents please, Mr Thompson," he said to the cashier.

Mills counted his money carefully, pocketed it, handed over the note to Mr McIntosh and went his way.

Meanwhile Turner stood by Mr McIntosh's desk and watched him anxiously as he came in slowly and sat down.

"You owe a lot of money about the town I hear," he began.

Turner hesitated.

"Speak up, Mr Turner," said Mr McIntosh.

"Yes, sir," said Turner more audibly.

"People are regularly here to you every pay day . . . I can't hear you."

"Yes, sir," said Turner.

"And your name is frequently in the list of judgment debtors?"

"Yes, sir," said Turner feeling to sink into the earth and wondering what would be the outcome of all this. He was saying "yes, sir" but he felt as if all the time he were saying "guilty". How much did the old man know of his chaotic private affairs?

"You are married?" said Mr McIntosh after a time.

"Yes, sir, I am, sir." A gleam of hope.

"You have children?"

"Yes, sir. Two, sir."

Confound it! Why did he keep on saying "yes sir, yes sir," even when there was no need for it!

"It is impossible for a man to do his work properly if his chief attention is directed to evading creditors."

There was a pause.

"About how much do you owe?" asked Mr McIntosh suddenly.

Turner hesitated.

Mr McIntosh lost his temper.

"That is what I have never been able to understand in my forty years' experience with the natives of this colony. You are the most thriftless, improvident—About how much money do you owe?"

But Turner could not answer for he did not know.

Mr McIntosh must have seen his discomfiture and his genuine terror of losing his job. He relented.

"Very well then. Mr de Souza says that you do your work well and I will give you a chance. But I cannot have people coming here to you during working hours and fighting with you on the pavement just in front of the store . . . Make a list of what you owe and let me have it. Not for tomorrow, for Monday, and then we will see what can be done. But, mind you, you will have to start paying me back so much a week from next Friday."

Turner could scarcely murmur thanks.

For once on a Friday afternoon he went straight home to tell his wife the good news. On Fridays always, on other days in the week sometimes, he went to settle his bill at the rumshop and to spend the afternoon in the back-room having a few drinks with his friends. But today he surprised his wife by appearing at home at half past four.

She was not a bad-looking woman, if rather flashy, and though she and Turner used to quarrel often they got on well on the whole. She was electrified at once with hopes for the future, and from five o'clock until half past seven he was busy making a draft of the list, his wife supplementing his memory. It amounted in all to about two hundred and fifty dollars.

Late that night they were lying in bed discussing things. They had sketched out how they were going to move from where they were, take a better house, and various other ways in which they would spend the ten dollars.

"Old Mac will hardly take out more than two dollars a week," said Turner.

"And you will still be able to get things at the store on credit?"

"I suppose so," replied Turner. "That scarcely comes under Mac's notice." They were silent for a while.

"But you know, Charles," said Mrs Turner, "two hundred and fifty dollars isn't much."

"No, but if Mac didn't come to the rerrescue, I don't—Ah-ha! I forgot that seventeen dollars we owe that grocery next to where we used to live in Belmont."

"Seventeen dollars? I thought you told me you had paid half."

"Oh, oh, yes, eight-fifty, eight-fifty. Let me get up and put it down."

"Don't bother, leave that till tomorrow. As I was telling you, two hundred and fifty dollars isn't much. Not to a man like Mr McIntosh."

"Well, that's all right. So much the better. He wouldn't scruple to pay."

"Why don't you put down some more? Put down four hundred and something—four hundred and fifty. You could make out a list to suit. What about Gibbs? You and he could make a false pro note and fix up things somehow. That will leave us with something substantial in hand. We could buy up a few necessaries with some and I could do some little business to bring in something to help. Send out an ice-cream cart perhaps. That is a paying thing—or something like that at any rate."

"It's a damned good idea," said Turner slowly.

Together they elaborated the details of the plot.

Monday morning Turner presented himself to Mr McIntosh at his desk. Old Mac was not a man to waste time.

"You have the amount?"

"Yes, sir," said Turner and handed over the list.

Mac looked at the total first and then read it through. He grunted.

"Four hundred and sixty-one dollars and twenty-seven cents! Young man, what's your salary?"

"Twelve dollars a week, sir," said Turner humbly. With luck old Mac might deduct only one dollar and fifty cents a week and not two dollars.

"Twelve dollars," said Mac. Then: "Mr Thompson," he called to the cashier, "pay this man twelve dollars—one week's salary in lieu of notice."

While Mr Thompson was counting out the money Mac turned to Turner:

'You owe too much money on too small a salary. I might have been able to help you had it been about half the amount, but not four hundred and fifty dollars. I am sorry."

1929

3

"After Hitler, Our Turn"

[World Revolution 1917–36, *first published by Secker and Warburg in 1937, was a critical history of the Third International. The chapter reproduced here describes the policies of Stalin towards the rise of fascism and nazism in Europe.*]

As the stalinist régime destroyed the Bolshevik party by slander and organisational terror (not against class enemies, it must always be remembered, which all history proves to be necessary, inevitable and not in the least confined to communists, but against honest, intelligent and devoted members of its own ranks), so it automatically transferred these methods to the International.

With the final expulsion of the Opposition in 1927 went the expulsion engineered from Moscow of all Trotsky sympathisers. Souvarine had gone before; now Monatte, Loriot, Treint, in France; in Belgium Van Overstraten, in Italy Bordiga, in the United States, Cannon, Swabeck, Abern, Shachtman; in Canada, Spector, member of the Executive of the International, later MacDonald, the party secretary. The method was stalinist: lies and slander, the ideological preparation; breach of discipline, the pretext; and then ruthless expulsion of the offending trotskyists and all their followers. For example, Moscow, wishing to clear up the mess in China, published the following in the documents for the Sixth Congress:

> Owing to a wrong conception of the tasks of the United Front, the leaders of the Communist Party of China committed a series of vital errors which considerably hampered the preparation of the revolutionary organisations for the fight and which, as later experience has shown, were the beginning of a whole chain of opportunist blunders which finally resulted in the bankruptcy of the CP leaders. . . .
> They believed that Chiang Kai-shek had become a national figure, that his desertion of the revolution would weaken the revolutionary movement and that concessions must be made to him, his demands must be satisfied so that he might be preserved for the revolution.

Who didn't subscribe to this interpretation had to go. Thus by July 1928, the way was cleared for the great turn to the left inside the Soviet Union and the International.

At the Sixth Congress in July, called after four years, Bukharin, already out of favour, still played a prominent part and announced the new policy. He was mainly responsible for the programme of the International, a document based on socialism in a single country and therefore valueless. The stabilisation of capitalism was denounced as ended, which was true enough. The Opposition had been pointing out long before that the general strike in England and the revolution in China were the precursors of new upheavals. The stalinists denied it first, the proclaimed it as a new discovery. But from this they drew conclusions, based not on reality and marxist understanding but solely on the necessities of Stalin's policy and the sycophantic ignorance of men like Manuilsky and Piatnitsky. Comfortable nonentities, their only qualifications for revolutionary leadership were their support of Stalin, to whom they owed all. He, on the other hand, could be sure that their lack of distinction in the days of Lenin, and their personal mediocrity would never aspire to challenge his position as supreme leader and chief theoretician. It is this subservience among his henchmen that prevents any check on Stalin's theories, however fantastic, however ridiculous, however dangerous. The congress laid down that the world revolution was imminent, that the masses were becoming "radicalised," that they had lost faith in social democracy, and the communists should prepare to lead the masses to victory. After four years the International had met, only to be still further confused and misled. The crisis was undoubtedly coming, and the masses would ultimately seek a revolutionary solution to their difficulties. But the first stage would most certainly be a growth of the social democracy. As a crisis deepens after a period of comparative prosperity the first move of the masses is towards the trade unions and so under the political leadership of the social democracy. The recent rise in France of the unions from less than two millions to five millions is an inevitable phenomenon, predictable and predicted. The Russian masses followed Kerensky first. The Spanish masses from 1931 followed the republican leaders. Except possibly after the tortures of a fascist régime, and then not with any certainty, the masses never move straight to a communist party but rally to the mass organisations. The communist party knows this and fights for its place in the mass movement, warning the workers of the inevitable treachery of the reformist leaders, laying bare the realities of each development, and guiding the growing disillusionment of the masses towards itself. Instead of foretelling this process Stalin, through his mouthpieces, proclaimed the loss of faith of the masses all over the world in social democracy (the MacDonald government in Britain was still to come; millions stuck to the German social democracy to the end), the steady swing of the masses to communism, and the imminent revolution. It is in this way that Lenin's successor, wielding more than Lenin's power without Lenin's brains, step by step, both in broad orientation and day to day direction, wrecked every opportunity of successful revolution. A correct orientation does not mean victory. Incorrect orientations so glaringly false lead to certain defeat. Over the new turn, however, hung the previous three years of revolution with Chiang Kai-shek and Wang Chin-wei, Pilsudski and the Anglo-Russian Committee. Resourceful in falsehood, the stalinists announced that a new period in post-war history—the third period—had begun. The first period was the period which had ended in 1924, the second period had ended with the defeat in China, now had begun the third and final period. The social democracy, who had been the chief friends in the second period, were now the chief enemy in the third. The same social democracy, the same parties, the same men, were yet to become, as they still are today, even better friends than in 1925–27. But behind all this verbiage one solid reality existed—the determination of the bureaucracy to use the International for the defence of the USSR. That was openly stated to be the first aim. The conference took this to mean, by means of the revolution. Stalin and the bureaucracy, however, meant, in place of the revolution.

In addition to this ideological confusion the International, wounded already by the long series of expulsions, was now drained again by another organisational onslaught. All who would not pass immediately from the social democracy being the chief friend to the social democracy being the chief enemy were expelled as right-wing deviators with abundant personal calumny. In the USA Lovestone, Gitlow and Wolfe, with the confidence of ninety per cent of the party, were driven out by the purse-controllers in Moscow. In Italy Tasca, Feroci, Santini and Blasco; in Czechoslovakia Hais and Jilek; in Austria Strasser and Schlamm; in France Doriot, then Sellier, with all their supporters; in China Chen Diu-siu, the founder and leader of the party; in. Sweden the bulk of the party and the leader, Kilboom; in Spain Nin, Andrade and Maurín (prominent leaders of the Spanish revolution today); in Germany Brandler and Thalheimer, and many good workers. The International has been stabbed and stabbed again by Stalin so that its growth has been stunted, the education (which can come only from experience guided but independently undertaken and independently studied) denied it. And all in the name of discipline, orthodoxy, centralism, leninism; whereas Lenin, great disciplinarian as he was, understood history and men too well to expect a blind obedience even from men of his own party. If you insist on obedience, he wrote to Bukharin in 1921, about the International, you will get only obedient fools. Unshakeable on questions of principle, he allowed a wise laxity except at rare moments when a revolution was in danger. He trusted to events to prove him right, and they generally did, whereupon the offenders were always accepted back on the old terms. Witness his treatment of Zinoviev and Kamenev. If he was wrong he admitted it fully. But Stalin, incapable of correct analysis, was always wrong, had never once in the whole history of the International ever admitted it, but always put the blame for failure on subordinates and covered up the old failures and the preparations for the new by abusing his opponents and then expelling them. He wanted obedient fools, and since 1929 he has had them. The expelled members formed different small groups; a Right Opposition was added to the Left Opposition, both, but more particularly the trotskyists, being the target of the whole communist press, neither time nor money being spared to destroy them. Some, unable to find a footing in revolutionary politics, drifted back to the social democracy, others, like Souvarine, to anarchism, some like Doriot even reached fascism. Some of these men were not of the stuff of which revolutionaries are made, but many of them and their followers would, under a different régime, have added their particular gifts and experience to the revolutionary movement. That they deteriorated was triumphantly pointed out by the stalinists, though they themselves were the cause of this deterioration.

The new policy of the third period was promulgated in numerous official documents, and the attack on the social democracy was crystallised in the once famous phrase, that the stalinists would give millions to bury today—the egregious folly of social fascism. In its day Stalin had all the credit for it. But like all his theoretical essays it was stolen from his chief henchman of the time.

Summing up the German failure of 1923 and blaming equally Brandler and the social democracy, Zinoviev, deprived of Lenin and therefore theoretically helpless, declared that fascism had already conquered in Germany by the aid of the social democracy.

> What is Pilsudski and the others? Fascist social democrats. Were they this ten years ago? No. Of course at that time they were potential fascists, but it is precisely during the epoch of revolution that they have become fascists. What is Italian social democracy? It is a wing of the fascists. Turati is a fascist social democrat. Could we have said this five years ago? . . . Ten years ago we had opportunists, but could we say that they were fascist social democrats? No. It would have been absurd to say it them (*sic*). Now, however, they are fascists. . . . The international social democracy has now become a wing of fascism. [*Lessons of the German Events*]

So Zinoviev in January 1924.

When in September 1924, Stalin, still expecting immediate revolution, wrote his first article on international affairs, he merely copied Zinoviev in his own way. He paraphrased and elaborated thus:

> Firstly it is not true that fascism is only a fighting organisation of

the bourgeoisie. Fascism is not merely a military-technical matter. Fascism is a fighting organisation of the bourgeoisie dependent upon the active support of social democracy. Objectively social democracy is the moderate wing of fascism. There is no ground for supposing that a fighting organisation of the bourgeoisie can reach decisive results in its struggles, or in a government of a country, without the active support of social democracy. There is just as little ground for supposing that social democracy can achieve decisive results in the struggles or in the government of a country without active support by the fighting organisation of the bourgeoisie. These organisations do not exclude but complement one another. They are not poles apart, but immediate neighbours. Fascism is the unformed political block of these two basic organisations, which arose under the critical after-war conditions of imperialism, and is intended for the struggle against the proletarian revolution. [*International Press Correspondence*, 9 October 1924]

Fascism dependent upon the active support of the social democracy—social democracy being unable to govern without the active support of fascism. This is Stalin. We must emphasise it over and over again; no one will ever understand the history of the Soviet Union and the International since 1924 unless he can grasp (and it is a difficult thing to grasp) this unique combination of economic and political ignorance and stupidity, Tammany Hall ability and ruthless determination.

Stalin wrote this in September, but a month later he proclaimed socialism in a separate country, social democracy became the chief friend, and the stalinist paraphrase and embellishment of Zinoviev was conveniently forgotten. Now with the new policy of the third period, this discarded folly was fished out and hailed as the summit of human wisdom. The actual phrase social fascism seems to have been Stalin's own, and the stalinist gramophones at home and abroad, Pollitt, Cachin, Thorez and Thaelmann, vied with each other in bringing it in on every possible occasion and paying homage to the master.

In July 1929, the ECCI held its tenth Plenum. On page 8 the General Staff of the World Revolution analysed fascism:

In countries where there are strong social democratic parties, fascism assumes the particular form of social fascism, which to an ever-increasing extent serves the bourgeoisie as an instrument for the paralysing of the activity of the masses in the struggle against the régime of fascist dictatorship. By means of this monstrous system of political and economic oppression, the bourgeoisie, aided and abetted by international social democracy, has been attempting to crush the revolutionary class movement of the proletariat for many years.

Hypnotising themselves with words, they saw millions of workers rushing from the social democracy to communism.

Stalin had said it would be so and therefore it was so already: "As a result of their own experience, the German workers are abandoning their illusions concerning the Social Democratic Party." To be quite sure of destroying any liaisons which the leftward moving sections of the Social Democratic Party might seek to make with the Communist Party, the plenum categorically instructed all sections of the CI to pay "special attention to an energetic struggle against the 'left' wing of social democracy which retards the process of the disintegration of social democracy by creating the illusion that it—the 'Left' wing—represents an opposition to the policy of the leading social democratic bodies, whereas as a matter of fact, it wholeheartedly supports the policy of social fascism."

Page after page of the report spoke of the radicalisation of the masses, "the coming revolutionary battles," "the upward swing of the labour movement," etc. etc., while under their eyes social democracy was in full control of its millions of voters and the millions in the trade unions. The trade-union leadership was described as the "social fascist trade-union bureaucracy" nearly a dozen times in as many pages; all were warned against the ever-growing "fascisation" of the trade unions. The plenum characterised social democracy as "evolving through social imperialism to social fascism," and dismissing the trade-union leaders as "sufficiently disgraced," demanded the united front from below. The leaders were not even to be spoken to.

All over the world the obedient fools rushed to ruin themselves. Thus it was that the British Communist Party, already functioning in an atmosphere traditionally unreceptive, disgraced itself in the eyes of the British workers by reckless talk of insurrection. Pollitt and Tom Mann were charged with proclaiming the imminent revolution. Up to late 1934 the British party continued with this glaring absurdity. In Mexico, in India, in China, in Africa it was the same. The Spanish revolution broke out in 1931. For nearly four years the small communist party lost its chances by playing social fascism in every key. Revolutionary situations as in Spain, a solid bourgeois democracy as in Britain, Stalin whistled and his obedient fools danced. Ruinous as it was everywhere, in Germany it reached its highest scope and led the great German proletariat to its doom. . . .

Hitler in Germany in 1924 had aimed at doing for German capitalism what Mussolini had done for Italian. But the pusillanimous capitulation of the German Communist Party had ruined Hitler's chances. The big bourgeoisie, the militarists, have no love for these demagogic parvenus with their uncouth hordes of mercenary toughs. It is only when capitalists see that the workers, disillusioned by capitalist bankruptcy, may seize power that they turn to fascism as a last expedient. Five years passed before Hitler got another chance. But he had the first requisite of any leader—belief in his cause. He continued with his agitation and his propaganda. He attacked capitalism, but got few workers to join him. He attacked Marxian socialism and substituted his own brand which, when explained to capitalists, induced some rich and influential ones to give him millions. He could not have published dozens of daily papers and kept some half a million Brownshirts without their help. Only an economic crisis would give him his opportunity—and it came in 1929.

The world economic crisis seized Germany first in Europe, because of all the great countries of Europe Germany was the most vulnerable. Since 1924 Germany had existed and been able to pay reparations chiefly by loans from America. In addition, trustification, monopoly capitalism, which had gone further in Germany than anywhere else, the consequent domination of the government by finance capital, rationalisation, with its consequent increase of unemployment and loss of purchasing power by the masses, the whole historical development of Germany between 1914 and 1929, all these meant that in Germany terrific class battles would be fought with fateful consequences for Europe and the world. The clash had been avoided in 1924. Now nothing could stave it off.

It would be as well here to point out at once the issues at stake. If the German proletariat were victorious, it meant the almost immediate victory of the Austrian proletariat. Fascism in Italy would receive a most serious blow. In Spain the revolution which had broken out in 1931 would receive an enormous impetus and an enthusiastic ally. Most important of all, the bogey of German invasion, which is the main threat that French capitalism uses to the French workers, would disappear at a stroke, and the French bourgeoisie would be jammed between the German working-class movement and its own. The difficulties of economic construction in the Soviet Union would have been solved by the combination of Soviet natural resources and Germany's marvellous industrial organisation—that alliance which Lenin had so hoped for. There was the possibility of an invasion of a Soviet Germany by France and Poland, of an invasion of a Soviet Austria by Italy. The Soviet army, ready to oppose intervention, would be a powerful barrier to this, and (given a certain development of the national class struggle) to suppose that the working classes of Britain and France, Belgium and Holland would idly allow a Soviet Germany to be crushed by imperialists is a mirage existing only in the minds of Tory diehards and (we know it today) the rulers of the Soviet régime. If the Communist International functioned as it could on the basis of the world crisis, every development in Germany would be followed by the world working-class movement and their responsibility to a Soviet Germany put clearly before them. It will be difficult enough for the imperialists to get wholehearted participation in an ordinary imperialist war. They would imperil their own existence if they tried to interfere openly in the affairs of a Soviet Germany.

On the other hand the defeat of the German proletariat would be a catastrophe for Europe. The greatest anti-war force under capitalism was the German proletariat. As long as it was powerful the war against the Soviet Union would have to begin in Berlin. But the victory of fascism in Germany would mean (we see it today) the victory of reaction all over Central and Eastern Europe. It would weaken the Spanish revolution and the French. It would mean inevitably war against the Soviet Union, it would mean all the things that face us today. This is not wisdom after the event. In the very first stages of the struggle they were clearly set down by the expelled Left Opposition, the existing state of parties in Germany estimated, the course of action to be followed outlined.

The first intimation of danger was the Reichstag election of September 1930. In May 1924, the Nazis polled 1,918,310 votes, in May 1928, 809,541 votes. Then came the crisis. Hitler had at last persuaded important sections of German capitalism that he could be depended upon to smash the German working-class movement. Backed not only by German but by international capital, he and his party drew to it the threatened middle classes by promising them to destroy the big chain stores, etc., the lumpen proletariat by bribery, and every unattached voter by playing on nationalist sentiment and promising everything to everybody. Now in September 1930, after one year of the crisis, he gained 6,406,397 votes, an increase of over five million. The blindest of the blind could see that not only the whole world but even the builders of socialism in a single country would have to concentrate on the developments in Germany during the next few years. The workers of Germany, whom fascism was aimed against and who alone could break fascism, were organised in the Social Democratic Party and the Communist Party.

The Social Democratic Party during the stabilisation had developed a huge bureaucracy. With the failure of the Communist Party in 1923 the workers had quite inevitably gone back to the social democracy, which had strengthened itself all over Europe on the basis of the temporary stabilisation of 1924–29. The social democrats had control of the Prussian government and thousands of posts in the government service. Two thirds of the police chiefs of Prussia were social democrats. There were nearly a hundred social democratic members in the Reichstag and many in the other parliaments of Germany; they had jobs in State banks, there were thousands of trade-union officials, workers in the party press, right down to posts that were much smaller but yet, in post-war Germany, safe. It has been estimated that the Social Democracy had actually at its disposal in 1931 nearly 290,000 actual posts. Anyone with the slightest experience of workers' organisations knows that this bureaucracy, basing itself on the layers next to it, with the organisation, propaganda and finances of the party and trade unions in its hand, could exercise an enormous influence on the millions on which they rested.

But below these were nearly twenty millions of the German working people in town and country. In May 1924, the social democrats had had only six million votes, the communists 3,693,000. But by December, in spite of the imminent revolution foretold by Stalin and Zinoviev, the Communist Party had lost 974,000 of these votes, and the Social Democracy had gained 1,881,000, making them 7,881,000. The revolutionary problem is to turn enough of these away from their leaders. Wels, Leipart, Otto Braun, Severing, Noske and the large majority of the German social democrats, no more than Citrine, Bevin, Attlee, Morrison, Jouhaux, Léon Blum and the others, would not prepare workers for any sort of struggle with capitalism. Before 1933 they were willing to come to terms with fascism if allowed. Now that fascism is exposed, they pretend that capitalists faced with a choice between social revolution and fascism will choose parliamentary democracy. They can always escape abroad. But the vast millions of social democratic workers have no choice but to fight fascism or be crushed by it. They listened in Germany as they will always listen to the speeches of their leaders, they hope that these will do something, they have faith in the organisations that they have built up with so much sacrifice. Their leaders teach them to have faith in democracy, in the King of Italy, in Hindenburg, in the Popular Front, in God (Walter Citrine), in everything except their own organised strength. It is usually only when the enemy is upon them that they realise that their social democratic leaders have scattered to the four winds and never intended to fight fascism at all.* It was the business of the Communist Party of Germany to expose these social democratic leaders for what they were, and win enough of the social democratic workers, or at least neutralise the others, so as to be able to make the attack on fascism. Whatever Hitler said, Mussolini in Italy had shown that fascism aimed at destroying the workers' organisations and bourgeois parliamentary democracy, leaving the workers defenceless. The army and police cannot be trusted to do that, the bourgeoisie can no longer trust the bourgeois state, so it

---

*Under one condition only will they ever fight: if, as in Spain, the liberal bourgeois is placed in such a position that he must defend himself, and gives battle to fascists. Your social democrat will always follow a bourgeois. In Austria in 1934 Bauer was on his knees before Dollfuss to the end. The workers began the fighting; the bureaucrats could not help themselves. This does not mean that some social democrats are not phyically courageous men, as many revolutionaries, e.g. Zinoviev, are physical cowards. It is a political attitude that is in question here.

organises its bands. But it is this very factor which makes the social democratic worker under skilful leadership ready to fight. He is not a revolutionary. If he were he would join the Communist Party. But he, in certain circumstances, will fight in defence of what he considers to be his lawful constitutional rights. Whenever a ruling class has to take away by violence these rights, the revolutionary situation becomes a possibility.

The German Communist Party votes in 1930 had jumped from 3,300,000 to 4,600,000, nothing in comparison to the fascist increase. But in Germany, with twenty-five large towns of over 500,000 people, with the workers dominant in the economy of the country, the combined communist and social democratic vote represented the dominant social force in the country. In highly industrial countries like Germany and Britain the organised workers hold the fate of the country in their hands. The other political parties in Germany, Nationalists, Catholic, Centre Party, etc., might be numerically imposing, as they were in Russia even after October 1917. Lenin did not fear all their votes, contemptuously dismissed the Constituent Assembly in 1918, and held the power. The ruling class $v.$ the working class is the issue, both fighting for the lower middle classes. Even the big capitalist parties were not homogeneous. In a crisis the Catholic Party, for instance, would split, probably to the advantage of the workers, who, were their leadership strong and decisive enough, could count on drawing the bulk of the Catholic workmen to their side. In unity for action the workers in the factories, transport and other essential services would be masters of the situation. With the policy of the united front against fascism, the social democratic worker, step by step, could be led on the basis of his own experience to fight against fascism; and the victorious struggle against fascism, not in parliament, but in the streets, would lead directly to power.

That was the task in the Germany of 1930. It is the task in France today, and ultimately, excepting the complications of a war, the task in Britain tomorrow. The German Communist Party had to point out every manoeuvre of Hitler and the capitalists and at the same time prove to the workers that their leaders would not fight; not by telling them this but by challenging the leaders to fight. At the same time they had a quite special responsibility, to give the workers confidence that the Communist Party was not only willing but able to lead that fight. For a very noticeable thing in the elections of 1930 was that, though the communist vote had increased by over a million and a quarter, the membership of the party had not correspondingly increased, which meant that, though many workers believed in the necessity of revolution and accepted the line of the Communist Party, they doubted the capacity of the Communist Party to carry out that line; 1923 remained in their minds.

Trotsky, in an article ("Problems of the German Revolution") written from his exile in Prinkipo just after the elections, warned them that the situation demanded careful handling. The six million voters for the social democracy did not mean that the voters were unalterably attached to the social democracy. Millions of these could be won by the communists as the Bolsheviks had won millions for the October revolution, and the German Communist Party in 1923 had been able in a few months to get the majority of the German proletariat behind it. But the Communist Party would have to drop its exaggerations and absurdities and base itself solely on realistic estimations of the political situation. With the position as it was, to take the offensive would be disastrous. The Communist Party, with the advance-guard of the workers, would be smashed to pieces, leaving the road clear for fascism. He suggested defensive battles and an unwavering struggle for the united front. The social democratic leaders would clamour that they wanted to fight. What did they propose? The Communist Party would not ask the social democratic worker to leave his party. Let him demand of his leaders that they take joint steps for defence, each party its own banner, its own flag, but a simply defined programme. If the Social Democratic Party leaders accepted, so much the better. The fight would go on and the Communist Party would apologise for having misjudged them. But they would refuse. Then as the fascist danger grew they would have the task of explaining to their members why, in face of the growing threat, they continued to refuse the quite reasonable offers of communists who, after all, were fellow-workers and were not proposing immediate revolution, but merely common defence against an immediate danger. "There is no doubt that the leaders of the social democracy and a very small stratum of workers will prefer, in the last analysis, the victory of fascism to the revolutionary victory of the proletariat." But it was precisely this preference which gave the Communist Party an opportunity to break the ranks under the control of the social democratic bureaucracy. "We must conclude agreements against fascism with divers social democratic fractions and organisations, while placing clearly before the masses precise conditions for their leaders." This was in 1930.

So that there might be no misunderstanding of the colossal blundering and treachery which gave us a fascist instead of a Soviet Germany with all that will mean for Europe, we cannot do better for the English reader than use the example of the present tactics of the Communist Party of Great Britain in its effort to get into the Labour Party.

The gentlemanly leaders of the Labour Party do not want them, for harmless as the communists are today, the very word communism compromises the social democrats with the bourgeoisie. The communist leaders know this as well as anybody else. But they make an open application to the social democratic leaders. It is true that they want to get in merely to agitate for an alliance of the Soviet Union with Britain and France against Germany and Japan, under the guise of the League of Nations and collective security. But we can leave aside their aims, which do not concern us for the moment. Naturally Morrison, Citrine, and the other Labour Party leaders refuse. But, small as the British party is, it has, as every party always has, influence among the social democratic workers in certain districts where communists and militant social democratic workers have fought many fights together in the days when the Communist Party was a fighting party. Furthermore at the present moment the politically minded workers everywhere are profoundly stirred by the war danger and the unsettled state of Europe. The British communists are not asking for revolution. There are many good comrades among them. Why then should the social democratic leaders turn them down? In social democratic districts which are favourable to the Communist Party, resolutions are passed demanding the affiliation. Trade-union conferences do the same, social democratic intellectuals like Sir Stafford Cripps and G. D. H. Cole, who have not the typical trade-union mentality and servility to bourgeois ideas of the Labour leader risen from the ranks, are sympathetic and ask why not. The *New Statesman* comes out in support. In every section of the social democratic party on every possible occasion the Communist Party urges its claim. Certain districts not only pass resolutions, but actually begin to take joint action with the communists in defiance of headquarters. In the powerful South Wales Miners' Federation a communist, Arthur Horner, is elected president. This is a strong lever. The *Daily Worker* of 6 July 1936 reports that 121 Labour Party organisations are for affiliation. In addition in Hammersmith the South Hammersmith Co-operative Political Council, the South Hammersmith Divisional Labour Party, in all fifteen organisations in the borough, have voted for unity. This means that in that district unity for action is achieved. The Communist Party consistently offers plans for united action. The social democratic leaders consistently refuse. Yet the Communist Party is only recommending the same League of Nations, the same collective security as the Labour Party.

The pressure embarrasses men like Morrison and Citrine dreadfully. The Edinburgh conference shows a Labour Party split ideologically from top to bottom. And if suddenly the war crisis were to come nearer, and the Communist Party once more puts a concrete programme for unity before the social democratic leaders, these gentlemen have either to accept them or face the possibility of grave unrest and even a serious split in their ranks. For the Communist Party is irreproachable in its demands. It is not asking to make a revolution. It is merely taking the social democratic leaders at their word and suggesting that instead of talking they do something. In Germany by October 1923, the Social Democratic Party was breaking to pieces under similar pressure. And in the Germany of 1923, unlike the Germany of 1930, Hitler's bands did not stalk the streets. Marxism aims merely at foreseeing, foretelling, clarifying and preparing in advance for what the workers will at a high moment of history instinctively respond to. The great millions of workers in Germany wanted to unite to fight fascism and fought to do so, and if a campaign of the sort the British Communist Party is waging today had been waged in Germany, after the September election of 1930, against fascism, Hitler could not have passed. The thin layer of the Labour aristocracy would, in the moment of crisis, have been swept away like dust with a broom. How then did it happen that the German Communist Party pursued the exactly opposite policy? First, the German soil was particularly fertile for Stalin's social fascist stupidity. A bitter feud had divided the two parties since the murder of Karl Liebknecht and Rosa Luxemburg and the accumulated reacheries of the social democracy. Secondly, the expulsion from the party of all who were not prepared to accept the party-line, discipline, centralism, unity, etc., and thirdly and more important than all these, the determination of Moscow at all costs to maintain a division between France and Germany, and to sacrifice the German revolution for this end. The German Communist Party tried to break away from social fascism. Sections of the social democrats made offers for unity. That the Russian bureaucracy insisted on division, even to the extent of letting Hitler come in, is one of the most criminal blunders in history.

As far back as the middle of 1931, Trotsky, watching anxiously the tactics of the Communist Party in Germany, had seen where the stalinist policy was leading and hoped in vain for a change. Before Hitler came into power Walter Duranty, Russian correspondent, had written in the *New York Times* of 20 November 1932 that "the Bolshevist Kremlin today regards the growth of the revolutionary movement in Europe with real anxiety." He was seeing only a fraction of the whole truth—that the Kremlin was prepared to sacrifice the workers' movement thinking thereby to save itself. That the German workers went down without a struggle when they had an even chance of victory was no fault of theirs. They were ruined by the ignorant and treacherous Soviet bureaucracy.

The German social democracy had been declared the chief enemy long before the third period, since 1927.* The Soviet

---

*The Essen Conference had also to fight against right deviations. A group of comrades had set its face against the thesis adopted by the conference to the effect that the left leaders in the SDP were the chief enemy.

bureaucracy feared the German Social Democratic Party for its support of Locarno. In 1922 Germany, rebuffed by Britain and France, had signed the Treaty of Rapallo with the Soviet Union. The division between France and Germany was naturally a very good thing for Russian foreign policy. But the Treaty of Locarno in 1925 seemed to Stalin and to the world at that time the beginning of a friendship, and the German social democracy, which pressed hard for this burying of the hatchet between France and Germany, became the special enemy of the Soviet bureaucracy. Stalin's second period had prevented this antagonism developing fully. But with the break-up and final exposure of the Anglo-Russian Committee and the tardy realisation that the social democracy was no help against a war of intervention, with the imminent growth of the war danger, social fascism was directed with special ferocity against German social democracy. In the material collected for the Sixth Congress we see the stalinist bitterness against the social democracy: "On question (sic) of International policy the attitude of German social democracy is in line with that of the rest of the Second International: recognition of and collaboration with the League of Nations, and bitter denunciation of the Soviet Union. German social democracy represents the 'Western orientation,' and it takes advantage of every opportunity to extend the cleavage between the Soviet Union and Germany." Hitler proclaimed his hostility to marxism in general, but also to France, and for Stalin, therefore, concerned with socialism in a single country and not with revolution, social democracy in Germany, with its Western orientation, was the main enemy. This ruined the German revolution. Social fascism in July 1929, when a year before Hitler had lost a million votes, was merely another stalinist folly preventing the Communist Party of Germany from exercising the influence it should. But after the elections of September 1930, it was criminal. For the responsibility of leading the masses against fascism rested and will always rest with the revolutionary party. The social democratic leaders are what they are, and for the revolutionary party to lay blame on them for what it knows they will do is the merest childishness. But lacking marxist training, dead in the International since 1924, ignorant and bureaucratic, the Communist Party, under Moscow's firm guidance, professed itself quite untroubled at the results of the September elections and prophesied Hitler's early doom. On 15 September 1930, the *Rote Fahne* told the German proletariat: "Last night was Herr Hitler's greatest day, but the so-called election victory of the Nazis is the beginning of the end," and on the following day, "The 14th of September was the high point of the National Socialist movement in Germany. What comes after this can only be decline and fall."

During 1931 the crisis steadily intensified. The communists

could not see and the social democrats would not see that parliamentary government was doomed in Germany, and that this political crisis would end in a dictatorship either of the right or of the left. This had long been obvious to the shrewdest capitalists inside and outside Germany.

Germany's creditors began to call in loans, bank crisis followed bank crisis. The downward trend of production and trade was intensified, and Germany, instead of sliding, began to plunge. More and more groups of German capitalists began to see their way out in Hitler. The social democrats prated of democracy, the Communist Party redoubled their attacks upon the social fascists. The violence of the fascists grew daily with their increasing financial and popular support, and in the face of this the bewildered social democratic worker was told a dozen times a day that the Social Democratic Party, social fascism, and not fascism, was the main enemy. He was invited to form the united front only from below, in other words, an ultimatum to leave his own party simply because the communists told him so. Red trade unions, an experiment already tried and a proved failure, were started again in opposition to the social fascist unions and served only to accentuate the division between the workers.

In March Bruening tried to unite Germany and Austria in a complete customs union. This would have helped German trade, given some moral confidence to Germany, and allayed for a time the spectre of German communism. But it would have threatened the ill-gotten gains of France and the little entente. They forbade it. The Hoover moratorium on German debts could not check the disintegration. The Bruening government, armed with article 48 of the constitution, by dictatorial decree after decree made the workers and salaried employees bear the brunt of the crisis. But the social democrats clung desperately to Bruening and Hindenburg. Support Bruening against Hitler, they urged the workers. Here is the lesser evil.

The workers had organised themselves into the Reichsbanner, ready to fight for the defence of the republic. It was all that the communists needed. They, while not identifying themselves with the fight for the republic, could fight side by side with the social democrats against fascism. That road, as we see in Catalonia today, could lead only to the struggle for the dictatorship of the proletariat, the social democratic workers being driven to take it, not by propaganda but by the very logic of events. But for the communists Hitler was the lesser evil. Destroy the social democracy, the dirty social fascists. Most probably unrealised by themselves, Moscow had shifted their propaganda slogans to complete with the Nazis in inciting all Germany to an antagonism against France, just as Moscow today has the French Communist Party inciting all France to antagonism against Germany. The Nazis claimed to be fighting for the national liberation of Germany from the Treaty of Versailles by war. The communists, instead of opposing this typical imperialist slogan with the slogans of international socialism, reinforced by the whole International, were made to compete with the fascists by putting forward the slogan of a popular revolution for national emancipation from the Treaty of Versailles. Adventurers of the officer type, men like Scheringer and Count Stenbock-Fermoy, thinking of nothing else but an imperialist war with France, fraternised with the Communist Party on the basis of this fight for national emancipation, and brought only further disorder and confusion into the Communist Party without the slightest gain; in this field the Nazis were invincible. All this, however, had nothing to do with the struggle of the German workers, but with Moscow's foreign policy. Then in August 1931, came an astounding interference from Moscow in the policy of the German Communist Party.

The great stronghold of the social democrats was Prussia, where since 1919 they had ruled. They had had the uninter-rupted command of the police, and Prussia, with Berlin, was the most powerful state in the Reich. But by the middle of 1931 the Prussian government was in serious danger, for the Nazis were sweeping everything before them, and it was certain that at the coming elections they would be the largest single party in the Prussian Landtag. The social democrats, therefore, with revolutionary courage, manoeuvred and manipulated so as to continue governing if no party gained an absolute majority. The Nazis were furious and demanded a referendum, their only legal means of turning out the social democratic government.

Despite three years of social fascism the first instinctive reaction of the German Communist Party was to side with the social democrats against the fascists. The party leadership in Germany started to fight against the referendum. That, however, meant support of the social democrats with their "Western orientation". Stalin made them stop their opposition to the referendum and support the fascists against the social democrats. Luckily we have the evidence of Piatnitsky himself, secretary of the Communist International. "You know, for example, that the leadership of the party opposed taking part in the referendum on the dissolution of the Prussian Landtag. A number of party newspapers published leading articles opposing participation in that referendum. But when the central com-mittee of the party jointly with the Comintern arrived at the conclusion that it was necessary to take an active part in the referendum, the German comrades, in the course of a few days, roused the whole party. Not a single party, except the CPSU, could do that."

Thaelmann and his central committee are not entirely to blame for the German catastrophe. They meant well. The tradition of obedience and discipline, the faith of the German party leaders, were mercilessly exploited against the cause. On 21 July the Communist Party, suddenly forgetting social fascism, addressed a letter to the social democratic ministers, Braun and Severing, demanding a united front for struggle on behalf of the workers' living conditions and threatening to form a united front with the fascists against them unless they agreed. The social democratic government had shot down workers demonstrating on May day, had passed savage repressive legislation against the communists, banning the communist military organisation, the Red Fighting Front, and saying openly that these actions were directed against the communists and not against the fascists. Like Walter Citrine and Herbert Morrison, Braun and Severing did not want any united front. They therefore refused this proposal, as it was certain they would refuse. Social democrats never form united fronts because of proposals addressed to them by revolutionary parties. These proposals only assume importance when backed by the mass agitation initiated by the revolutionary party among their own party-members. On this refusal the Communist Party called on its members to support the fascists in their referendum. During the campaign there appeared in the communist journal, *Fanfare*, on 1 August, a portrait of Scheringer, the rabid nationalist, with the following message: "Whoever opposes the popular revolution, the revolutionary war of liberation, betrays the cause of those who died in the World War and gave their lives for a free Germany." The same words could have been used by Hitler in the fascist campaign. Thaelmann himself tells how workers, miserably confused, came to the Communist Party and asked if after all a Braun-Severing government was not better than a Hitler-Goebbels government. Thaelmann told them they were not class-conscious enough. Had everything depended on them the Moscow-driven communist leadership would have succeeded in getting the fascists into power in Prussia since the summer of 1931. But the common sense of the German workers revolted against the blind bureaucratic stupidity above. They refused to vote, and where twenty-five million votes were required to ratify the plebiscite, the fascists did not get half that number.

In the autumn, with the fascist danger growing every day, and Bruening mercilessly slashing at the workers, as was inevitable, a section of the social democrats began to turn tentatively to the Communist Party. Breitscheid, a social democratic leader full of revolutionary words (a kind of Stafford Cripps), proclaimed openly that if things went on as they were going (the Social Democratic Party had been trying to negotiate with the centre, which, however, was drawing to the right) the Social Democratic Party would have to form a united front with the Communist Party. Here was a chance that had come unasked, and in spite of all that had gone before. Faithful to Moscow, Thaelmann rejected the offer with scorn and warned the workers against it.

To those who suggested that the Braun-Severing government was better than a Hitler-Goebbels government he said:

> This influence exercised over revolutionary workers by the treacherous ideology of the lying social democrats, these relics of social democratic thought in our ranks, is, we declare, in full agreement with the decisions of the eleventh plenum, *the most serious danger that confronts the Communist Party.* How great that danger is, is shown at the present time, among other things, by the latest manoeuvres of social fascism. . . . It is therefore undertaking a new demagogic manoeuvre, it is "threatening" to form a united front with the Communist Party. . . . We have not conducted our fundamental struggle against social democracy with sufficient sharpness and clarity. Let us take a few examples.

And his first example was, the neglect of exposing, as the most dangerous type of reformism, some thousands of workers who, disgusted with social democracy, had decided to split off from the party and form a party of their own. It was not yet communist but was heading in that direction. Social fascism demanded that they should be violently repelled.

Moscow, seeing that the red referendum manoeuvre had failed, threw all pretence aside and came openly out for letting Hitler in.

On 14 October 1931, Remmele, one of the three official leaders of the Communist Party, with stalinist effrontery announced the policy in the Reichstag. "Herr Bruening has put it very plainly; once they (the fascists) are in power, then the united front of the proletariat will be established and it will make a clean sweep of everything. (Violent applause from the communists). . . . We are the victors of the coming day; and the question is no longer one of who shall vanquish whom. This question is already answered. (Applause from the communists). The question now reads only, 'At what moment shall we overthrow the bourgeoisie?' . . . We are not afraid of the fascist gentlemen. They will shoot their bolt quicker than any other government. (Right you are! from the communists) . . ." The fascists, so ran the argument, would introduce inflation, there would be financial chaos, and then the proletarian victory would follow. The speech was printed with a form asking for membership of the party attached, and distributed in great numbers all over Germany.

Stalinist parties are led from above. Their leaders get the line and impose it. Disobedience is labelled trotskyism, right deviation, and what not, and the dissidents expelled. But the situation in Germany was too tense, and violent protests from the left wing caused the policy to be withdrawn. But from that moment it was certain that the Communist Party leadership would never fight, and that "After Hitler, our turn" was the line on which they led the party. The German leadership did not follow blindly. Some of them carried on a ceaseless struggle to the very end. But built on Moscow they faced isolation if they broke with Moscow, and the organisational vice silenced or expelled them.

October 1931 is the actual turning-point in the history of the International and therefore in the history of post-war Europe. It is usual to date this last intense period in which we live from the early months of 1933 when fascism came to power in Germany. From October 1931, however, we can see today, is the time when it was certain that fascism would come into power. For if the revolutionary party in Germany would not give the lead to the great body of workers, then nothing could stop Hitler; the German proletariat, after the Russian the greatest anti-war force in Europe, would be stripped of its organisations and its leaders, and the greatest of imperialist wars would be unavoidable.

The question is: Why did Stalin persist in this policy? How could the Soviet bureaucracy possibly conceive that any useful purpose could be served by letting Hitler come into power? No question is more important, not only for the past but for the present. In the answer to it lies the whole complex problem of the relationship between the international working-class movement and the Soviet bureaucracy.

The root of this suicidal policy, which has had such catastrophic consequences, lies in the very nature of a workers' bureaucracy, inside as well as outside the Soviet Union. And we shall understand the Soviet bureaucracy best by noting how closely it resembles the workers' bureaucracies with which we are more familiar.

A social democratic bureaucracy believes first and foremost in a national socialism. It does not consider that the success of the workers in other countries is vital to its own. The basic doctrine of the Soviet bureaucracy, socialism in a single country, is essentially the same. Each is the ideology of a caste that is well satisfied with its own position. Each social democratic bureaucracy is far more hostile to its own left wing, the revolutionary socialists, than to its own imperialist bourgeoisie. Citrine will stand on the same platform with Winston Churchill but will not do the same with Pollitt.* The Soviet bureaucracy is today far more murderous against Trotsky, Zinoviev and Kamenev and revolutionaries in Russia, than it is to the bourgeoisie of France and Britain. The reason in both instances is the same. They wish to live on good terms with the bourgeoisie, if allowed, but the revolutionaries are enemies of their prestige, privileges and perquisites. Most important for the German policy, however is the fact that the workers' bureaucracies of Western Europe, from the very positions they

---

*Pollitt, of course, is to the right of Citrine today, but the aura of the October revolution still hangs around his party.

occupy as administrators of the affairs of millions of docile workers, are incapable of conceiving that the workers whom they dominate can achieve anything, least of all the overthrow of capitalism and the establishment of a workers' state. Today the Soviet bureaucracy believes exactly the same. For both, the revolution of October 1917 was due to exceptional circumstances. The Soviet bureaucracy has not reached this position all at once, any more than the pre-war German social democracy reached its position of 1914 other than by a gradual process. In 1923 Stalin met opposition to his policy for the German revolution. He manoeuvred by saying: let the fascists attack first, though they are weak. Two years later, China offers an opportunity for a victory of the world revolution. China seems to the Soviet bureaucracy a field where a revolution can take place without the immediate complications that would ensue in Germany. Stalin is sincerely desirous of guiding the Chinese revolution to victory. But the very qualities which make him so acceptable to the bureaucracy are the very ones which unfit him for leading a revolution. His stubborn stupidity prevents him correcting the policy, even after the disastrous experience with Chiang Kai-shek. He has to experience the defection of Wang Chin-wei before at last he turns to the workers and peasants. The failure is complete and henceforth the bureaucracy, as the Sixth Congress shows, with its defence of the USSR as the first task, has lost all hope in the world revolution. The expulsion of the Opposition, the consolidation of bureaucratic power by the administrative activity of the five-year plan, intensifies the process of ossification. By 1931 the bureaucracy is fully mature. Every shred of the revolutionary ardour of 1917 has completely disappeared, driven ruthlessly out as trotskyism. Incapable of visualising a successful revolution in Germany, the choice appears to the bureaucracy to be between fascism and the social democracy. Given Stalin's foreign policy it cannot be the social democracy, with its Western orientation and League of Nations policy. It can only be fascism.

To do Stalin justice, the leader of the world proletariat is so incapable of independent theoretical analysis that he had no idea of what a fascist régime in Germany would mean. He had decreed that fascism could not rule without the support of the social democracy. They were not antipodes but twins. It could not much matter which twin was in power. But even this apparently characteristic stalinist stupidity was shared by the social democratic bureaucracy. When Hitler came to power Wels and Leipart, the German bureaucrats, offered to support him. They thought that they could accommodate themselves somehow to fascism. Citrine, at the Brighton trade-union conference in 1933, gives us the view of the British bureaucrat not before but after the catastrophe: "All I can say is that a general strike was definitely planned and projected, but the German leaders had to give consideration to the fact that a general strike after the atmosphere created by the Reichstag fire and with $6\frac{1}{4}$ million people unemployed was an act fraught with the gravest consequences which might be described as nothing less than civil war.'' The only thing, therefore, was to let Hitler in. The attitude of the Soviet bureaucracy was exactly the same, both before and after the catastrophe. In January 1934, at the seventeenth party conference in Moscow, though Hitler had been in power one year, Stalin explained his policy. ''Of course, we are far from being enthusiastic about the fascist régime in Germany. But fascism is not the issue here, if only for the reason that fascism, for example in Italy, did not prevent the USSR establishing very good relations with that country.'' He hoped to establish good relations with a Germany hostile to France. Almost at that very moment Otto Bauer in Austria was crawling before Dollfuss, ''We declared that we would be prepared even to make concessions to the notion of a 'corporative' organisation of society and of the state, in order to make an understanding possible. It was all in vain—Dollfuss refused to enter into any negotiations.'' Bauer had to fight, but the workers forced it. ''Why wait?'' they said. ''Let us strike now, while we are still ready for battle. Otherwise we shall share the fate of our comrades in Germany.''

One year after Hitler, Stalin and Otto Bauer were still hoping to come to terms with fascism. Being what they were it is clear that before they had had actual experience of Hitler, the idea of the German workers fighting fascism would not have crossed their minds. ''After Hitler, our turn,'' is the concentrated expression of bureaucratic inertia, cowardice, ignorance and short-sightedness. Stalin could not say openly what he meant. He had to dress it up in revolutionary words, to promise the deluded German workers that the revolution would come after Hitler had come to power. The foreign policy he pursued from that same October showed that nothing was further from his mind. One final difference between 1923 and 1931 should be noted. In 1923 Stalin could almost certainly have carried the bureaucracy with him for a forward policy in Germany. In China he could have abandoned Chiang Kai-shek at any time without the slightest change in the stability of his position, except loss of prestige to trotskyism. But by 1931 it is most probable that any attempt to encourage revolution in Germany would have resulted in an internal upheaval. Not that Stalin would ever have suggested any such policy. But it is necessary to emphasise that after 1931 Stalin leads the International along a predestined and acknowledged road. To expect a change is to expect Citrine and Bevin to become revolutionary socialists.

The Left Opposition was a small group incapable of exercising influence against two such powerful bureaucracies as the Communist Party and the Social Democratic Party. Trotsky at Prinkipo, branded as a conter-revolutionary, offered directive after directive and uttered warning after warning. Handicapped as he was by being unable to keep his finger on the pulse of events from day to day, yet his collected writings on the German situation are perfect examples, forever to be studied, of marxism applied to a living situation. On 26 November 1931, he finished a pamphlet "Germany—the Key to the International Situation". He had not yet learnt of the Remmele speech, but that Moscow had been counselling retreat was already clear:

> The coming into power of the German "National Socialists" would mean above all the extermination of the flower of the German proletariat, the disruption of its organisations, the extirpation of its belief in itself and in its future. Considering the far greater maturity and acuteness of the social contradictions in Germany, the hellish work of Italian fascism would probably appear as a pale and almost humane experiment in comparison with the work of the German National Socialists.

> Retreat, you say, you who were yesterday the prophets of the "third period"? Leaders and institutions can retreat, individual persons can hide. But the working class will have no place to retreat to in the face of fascism, and no place where to hide. If one were really to assume the monstrous and improbable to happen: that the party will actually evade the struggle and thus deliver the proletariat to the mercy of its mortal enemy, this would signify only one thing; the gruesome battles would unfold not *before* the seizure of power by the fascists but *after* it, that is: under conditions ten times more favourable for fascism than those of to-day. The struggle of the proletariat, taken unawares, disorientated, disappointed and betrayed by its own leadership, against the fascist régime would be transformed into a series of frightful bloody and futile convulsions. Ten proletarian insurrections, ten defeats one on top of the other, could not debilitate and enfeeble the German working class as much as a retreat before fascism would weaken it at the given moment, when the decision is still impending as to the question of who is to become master in the German household.

Trotsky was a great executive, an organiser and administrator of the first rank. But the revolutionary temperament, fortified by intense study, is as strong as in 1917. We are in the presence of imponderables here. Some men have it and some have not. But the workers will find such leadership again. The times are propitious. It is stalinism that blocks the way.

Trotsky, in the same pamphlet, showed the relationship of forces in Germany and the overwhelming superiority of the proletarian forces to the fascist:

> In the meantime, the main strength of the fascists is their strength

in numbers. Yes, they have received many votes. But in the social struggle, votes are not decisive. The main army of fascism still consists of the petty bourgeoisie and the new middle class: the small artisans and shopkeepers of the cities, the petty officials, the employees, the technical personnel, the intelligentsia, the impoverished peasantry. On the scales of election statistics, one thousand fascist votes weigh as much as a thousand communist votes. But on the scales of the revolutionary struggle, a thousand workers in one big factory represent a force a hundred times greater than a thousand petty officials, clerks, their wives and their mothers-in-law. The great bulk of the fascists consists of human rubbish.

But the petty schemers in the Kremlin, intent on building socialism in a separate country and engaged in the life and death struggle with proletariat and peasantry, the fruit of their long neglect and terror against trotskyism, with Japan threatening them on the Eastern frontier, wanted only to be left alone. Trotsky made demand after demand for the united front. The Communist Party should cease its babble about social fascism and offer to the social democratic leaders proposals for a concrete struggle against Bruening's decrees, for united committees to sweep the fascists off the streets, and for mutual protection. *Rote Fahne*, the communist paper, and *Vorwärts*, the social democratic paper, were bitter enemies. The party should propose to every social democratic worker in his district and openly to the social democratic leaders the formation of a defence corps. Much as the communists detested *Vorwärts*, yet if the fascists attacked *Vorwärts* they would fight valiantly in its defence. Conversely they would expect help from the social democratic workers if the fascists attacked *Rote Fahne*. Every day, on every issue, in every conceivable manner, they should struggle for the united front, and agitate among the social democratic workers to demand the united front from their leaders, while themselves offering it. The communist reply was, as always, a stream of abuse against the counter-revolutionary trotskyists. The social democrats did make offers. All are not Citrines and Bevins. The communists brushed them aside. In the *Communist International* of 15 March 1932, Piatnitsky wrote: "The social democrats too sometimes put forward the slogan of unity. And in this the renegade Trotsky hastens to their aid with his proposal for a 'bloc' between the communists and the social democrats. . . . How is it possible to deduce . . . the necessity of establishing a 'bloc' with the Germans social democrats, say, for the struggle against fascism, when the social democrats are doing nothing but helping the fascists?" Today, without a tremor, the members of the International will swear that they repeatedly offered the united front to the social democracy and that the defeat was due to their refusal.

On 13 March 1932, at the first ballot for the election of

President, Hindenburg received 18,661,736 votes, Hitler 11,338,571, Thaelmann five million. The social democrats voted for Hindenburg as the lesser evil. Hindenburg had not polled a majority of the total votes and a second ballot was required. Before this second ballot the Nazis terrorised Germany. Evidence transpired that despite Hitler's repeated assertions of coming to power by constitutional means, plans had been made for a *coup d'état.* On 10 April, Hindenburg was re-elected with over nineteen million votes, Hitler's vote had increased by two million, but Thaelmann had lost a million votes. Three days after Bruening dissolved Hitler's Brownshirt organisation, but left the Nazi Party untouched, the same kind of dissolution that the Popular Front government has recently applied to the Croix de Feu in France. On 24 April the Nazis won great victories in the state parliament elections, and on 30 May Hindenburg dismissed Bruening and made Von Papen Chancellor. It was a warning that the President was going to the right. Sooner or later he would reach to Hitler. Sections of the bourgeoisie were still hoping to hold power without Hitler, or subordinate him to their own purposes. Some of them still feared the socialism in his programme. All parties were hoping for an alleviation of the crisis to fall from heaven. Ultimately the bourgeoisie would have to come to Hitler, and the whole communist agitation now could have centred on that single point: We struggle for the united front, but Hitler means the destruction of the working-class movement, and the day the bourgeoisie place him in power we shall lead our workers and call on the social democrats for a mortal struggle.

On 16 June Von Papen, the aristocratic Junker, allowed the Brownshirts once more to resume their activities, along with the Stahlhelm and the republican Reichsbanner. We do not intend to go into the intrigues between Hitler, Von Papen and afterwards Schleicher. We have no time to spare for those who were horrified at Hindenburg, the old Prussian Field-Marshal, "betraying the republic" and making Hitler chancellor. Trotsky, in the middle of 1932, summed up the situation in words that ought to be branded on the foreheads of all social democratic, liberal and other progressive persons: "A bloc of the right wing with the Centre would signify the 'legalisation' of the seizure of power by the National Socialists, that is, the most suitable cloak for the fascist *coup d'état.* What relationships would develop in the early days between Hitler, Schleicher and the Centre leaders, is more important for them than it is for the German people. Politically all the conceivable combinations with Hitler signify the dissolution of bureaucracy, courts, police and army into fascism."

By the middle of 1932, under the stress of the crisis, German production was fifty-five per cent of what it had been in 1928. Nearly seventy-five per cent of industry was at a standstill.

Between January 1930 and January 1933, imports declined by two-thirds and exports by nearly half. In three years £1,500,000,000 had been taken from the incomes of the workers. The average weekly wage in eighteen months had been reduced from £2 2s. 2d. to £1 2s. 6d. Unemployment benefit was 37s. a month. Tax after tax crippled the workers and poor, crisis tax, occupation tax, head tax, salt tax, turnover tax to the small trader. But on the other hand the big magnates had been granted financial aid amounting to £144,000,000. By this time the unemployed were nearly seven million, and there were 300 suicides per week. But with Germany breaking up under their feet the social democracy and all their kith and kin of the Second International stood firmly for their democracy; while the Third International persisted in its united front from below and assured the workers that they need not be worried about Hitler because fascism was there in Germany already.

The workers were joining the Communist Party, but the absence of discussion, the stifling of criticism, the stalinist unity of the party which had ruined the CPSU had the national communist parties in its grip. In the first quarter of 1932, 94,365 new members joined the party, but 53,879 left it.

Elections to the state parliaments took place on 14 April 1932 and gave the Nazis 162 seats in Prussia, the Socialists 93, the Centre 67, the Communists 57. The Nazis seemed all-powerful, but the workers, in the face of the opposition of both bureaucracies and the increasing terror of the Nazis, were forming battalions of proletarian defence, and wherever they were formed they drove Hitler's mercenaries off the streets. In the Prussian Diet, however, the communists joined with the fascists and other reactionary parties to pass a vote of censure on the coalition government led by Braun. This government nevertheless still continued to rule as an interregnum government. The communists, still in alliance with the fascists, called for a new government. This obviously could only be the fascists with their 162 seats. In the Reichstag Von Papen, having no power behind him, but still hoping to manoeuvre without Hitler, had only one force to fear, the working-class movement. He knew, as all the bourgeois know, the stuff of which social democratic leaders are made. Yet the unity of the workers might be achieved over the heads of the makers of speeches and passers of resolutions, under the determined leadership of the Communist Party. The workers were fighting for it. But the communists were striving to turn a social democratic government out to put a fascist government in. Von Papen's road was therefore clear and he determined to take control of Prussia before the elections of 31 July. The bitterest satirist of social democracy could not have invented what happened then.

On 20 July 1932, Von Papen sent for Severing and told him that the Prussian government would be dissolved and a Commissar of the Reich, responsible to Von Papen and Hindenburg, placed in command. Severing said grandly that only force would make him submit. Basing his action on article 48, Papen dissolved the Prussian government and proclaimed martial law in Berlin. Grezhinsky, the Berlin police president, a social democrat, was informed of his dismissal by General Stuelpnagel and refused to accept it. The German general knew the dirty cowards he was dealing with. He sent a lieutenant and four men, who arrested Grezhinsky and his assistant, and while their subordinates stood around in tears, carried them off. They had had the Prussian police under their command for twelve years; they could depend on them. Berlin was over seventy per cent red, and not only in Berlin, but in all the great towns, the industrial workers were only waiting for the word. But before these two doughty warriors (how bravely they had shot down the communists!) had spent two hours in prison they had promised in writing not to perform their duties. So much for the police. Next was the government itself. The new deputy commissioner with less than half a dozen soldiers went to Severing, who, before this manifestation of force, surrendered at once. And that was the end of the twelve years of social democratic government in Prussia.

The masses were stupefied; they could not understand it. The workers in the large works waited all night for a general strike. During the night the communists distributed an illegal leaflet calling for a general strike. But they had called for numerous general strikes before, and which social democratic worker would disobey his party and join them in a general strike for a social fascist government, which was the chief enemy, and which they had just joined with the fascists to weaken? In similar circumstances, in Russia between April and October 1917, every disillusionment of the masses with the Soviet leaders resulted in a doubling and trebling of the influence of the Bolsheviks, so close did these stand behind the Soviet leaders, kicking them forward, and ceaselessly showing the masses who were responsible for the failure to implement the workers' demands. 20 July had opened the eyes of the German workers. Say the Petroffs:

A storm of indignation raged through the masses. They felt themselves to be shamefully misled, betrayed. But having been for long years bereft of any initiative of their own, these masses could not take action without their recognised leaders. So no hand moved, no shot was fired, not a single factory closed. 20 July passed, and it had brought to the masses only a boundless discouragement. But many a fist was clenched in the pocket—it was not quite clear against whom. . . . The dismissed Prussian government later on appealed to the state court. But it aroused among the workers only a smile of contempt. [Peter and Irma Petroff, *The Secret of Hitler's Victory*]

It is at such moments that a revolutionary party which has followed a correct policy reaps its reward. That Braun and Severing had shot communists made no difference to the necessity for the united front. Lenin in hiding and Trotsky in prison offered it all the more.

With every failure of the left the right increases in audacity. The Nazi terror increased. There were twenty-five murders during the election weekend of 31 July. This violence and assurance on the one hand, the grievous failure of social democrats and communists to supply anything like a lead on the other, resulted in a great increase of Nazi votes—13,700,000 and 239 seats. The social democrats still had 7,000,000, the communists 5,300,000. In Parliament the Papen government was so openly dishonest and so reactionary that it aroused the indignation of the sorely-tried German working people, and the Nazis, by voting for it, compromised themselves in the eyes of their poorer supporters. Their violence during the election drove the proletariat still further to organise anti-fascist defence corps. Many workers, in spite of the bureaucracy, were fighting to organise themselves as workers, but social democrats and communists fought to keep these on party lines: "The workers had at last recognised that their disunity was the cause of their weakness. They energetically demanded the tearing down of all barriers. But their leaders always met their demands with dishonesty, hypocrisy, and sabotage. So it was with the social democrats; so it was with the communists" [Petroff]. One can no more quarrel with parasites for sucking the blood of the animals on which they live. That is their nature. But the communist action was unnatural. Stalin had analysed the situation. Let Hitler come in; he will soon collapse and then will be the revolution. In September 1932, the twelfth plenum of the ECCI was held, a plenum which should have had one subject on the agenda—the coming struggle in Germany. The Executive studiously avoided giving prominence to Germany: "Only by directing the main blows against Social Democracy, this social mainstay of the bourgeoisie—will it be possible to strike at and defeat the chief class enemy of the proletariat—the bourgeoisie." That the whole future fate of the International was trembling in the balance was far from the minds of these bureaucrats. One section of the report is grandiloquently headed, "The Development of the Revolutionary Upsurge and the Preparation of the Struggle for the Dictatorship of the Proletariat". But Germany is not even first among equals. China has two lines; Poland two and a half lines; Germany two and a half lines, as follows: "an increase in the mass influence of the Communist Party; social democratic workers, in spite of their leaders, have begun to resist the terror of fascist gangs"; Belgium and India have more space than Germany. On the specific tasks of the major communist parties, Germany has just one more line than France, and Germany, France and China are equally treated. The plenum was much more concerned with a resolution on the war in the Far East, and the "Tasks of the Communists in the Struggle against Imperialist War and Military Intervention against the USSR".

In the official guide to the plenum it is the same. True they say, "Of exceptional importance to the fate of revolution in Europe and the whole world is the revolutionary upsurge in Germany." But Poland has more space than Germany, and we are informed that "the growth of the revolutionary upsurge in Poland, along with the growth of the revolutionary upsurge in Germany, is *the decisive factor for preparing the revolutionary outburst in the chief capitalist countries.*"

Stalin and his minions in September 1932 put Poland on a level with Germany, and told the International that the revolutionary upsurge in these two countries was a factor for preparing outbursts elsewhere.

The guide warned against exaggerations, but explained in detail why the chief blow should be directed against social fascism, and why the united front be formed only from below. No call to the masses of the world, especially in Britain, France, Poland and Austria, to stand by in defence of the German proletariat, as had been done in the first part of 1923 and when Chiang Kai-shek was leading the Chinese workers to victory.

Independent thought having long been destroyed in the International, all its writers had developed the complementary quality of embellishing Stalin's great contribution to marxism with loving and respectful ingenuity. The MacDonald government was fascist, so was the government of Hoover, and the government of the Gaekwar of Baroda. Anarchists were anarcho-fascists, syndicalists were syndicalo-fascists, the trotskyists were trotskyo-fascists. All these puerilities, offshoots of the oriental idolatry Stalin demanded from all in the Soviet Union, could only harm the movement everywhere. In Germany, however, it was helping to push the working class into the jaws of Hitler. The German Communist Party had been calling the Bruening government fascist, the Papen government fascist, later they were to call the Schleicher government fascist also. In Germany Right Opposition and Left had been urging that this nonsense should cease; the Left Opposition wanted the various forms of government clearly analysed before the workers, always pointing out that Hitler's coming into power would mean the destruction of the movement and should therefore be the signal for a nationwide struggle beginning with the general strike and ending, come what might, in revolution. Said the guide to the twelfth plenum: "The social democrats and their Trotskyite and Brandlerite agents, while utilising this clever manoeuvring of the German bourgeoisie, deny the fascist character of the Papen-Schleicher government, attempting to

implant among the masses deceptive illusions that the victory of
the fascist dictatorship is impossible unless Hitler comes to
power, unless the fascist domination is openly proclaimed,
unless there is a German edition of the 'march on Rome'.''
From between the lines peeped hints of Stalin's curious ideas on
German class relations and international politics. The German
bourgeoisie, said the guide, were afraid of Hitler. ''In addition
they are afraid that if Hitler comes to power it will create an
extremely intense *international* situation for Germany, and will
hasten the maturing of a revolutionary crisis.'' Furthermore,
why argue about names? Hitler was already in power. ''In
Germany social democracy has called on the workers three times
in six months to smash fascism at the ballotbox. The result is
the Hitler government and the establishment of the fascist
dictatorship.''

The voice might be the voice of Manuilsky, but the ideas are
unmistakable. That is the mentality of Stalin from his very first
writings to the present day.

In that very September Trotsky finished *The Only Road*. It was
one long plea for the united front:

> How much time has been lost—aimlessly, senselessly, shamefully!
> How much could have been achieved, even in the last two years
> alone! Was it not clear in advance that monopolistic capital and its
> fascist army would drive the social democracy with fists and
> blackjacks toward the road of opposition and of self-defence? This
> prognosis should have been unfolded before the eyes of the entire
> working class, the initiative should have been retained firmly in our
> hands at every new stage. It was not necessary to shout, nor to
> scream. An open game could have been played quietly. It would
> have sufficed to formulate, in a clear-cut manner, the inevitability
> of every next step of the enemy and to set up a practical programme
> for a united front, without exaggerations and without haggling, but
> also without weakness and without concessions. How high the
> communist party would stand today if it had assimilated the ABC of
> leninist policy and applied it with the necessary perseverance!

Millions were disillusioned with the Social Democratic Party,
but for them to leave it or at least turn elsewhere there must be
another party, and every action of the Communist Party drove
them away instead of bringing them nearer. There was still time.
If, however, the party did not mend its ways, then the Third
International was doomed and the international proletarian
movement would have to begin all over again. It was then that
he forecast the new Fourth International, the very idea of which
is such a thorn in Stalin's side and which he is striving to destroy.
''Should the worst variant materialise; should the present official parties, despite all our efforts, be led to a collapse by the
stalinist bureaucracy; should it mean in a certain sense to begin

all over again, then the new International will trace its genealogy from the ideas and cadres of the communist Left Opposition." But that was still to come.

But the workers of both parties, so treacherously misled, were taking action together. Between September and November the united proletarian front in the streets grew. In September the Reichstag was dissolved. The reactionary nature of the Nazis, proved in the last Reichstag, and the instinctive strivings of the proletariat struck a great blow at fascism. In the elections of 6 November the Nazis lost nearly two million votes and thirty-four seats. The vagaries of history had given the communists one more opportunity to rally the forces of the proletariat. The right were conscious of the danger to themselves. Some of them had been opposing Hitler, but they realised that if the process of disintegration continued German capitalism would lose its only mass support, many of the lowest ranks of the Nazis would swing to the left, and capitalist Germany would be in serious danger. Hitler, playing for position, moved to the left, and Nazis and Communists led a great transport strike in Berlin, against the wishes of the social democrats. They also fought the police side by side.

At the elections in November the Communist Party increased its vote by twenty per cent, and the bourgeoisie made yet one more move. On 2 December Von Schleicher became chancellor. In addition to trying to win over the trade unions to his side, Von Schleicher was careful to give free play to the Nazis, and granted them permission to hold a demonstration in the east of Berlin, the working-class district. The social democrats asked their followers, as usual, not to take part in the resistance organised by the communists. But many of them came out, and the Nazis with all their bluff and bluster had to be heavily protected by a huge force of police, armed with machine-guns and armoured cars. The workers, aware of the danger, were getting closer and closer together on the streets. But the communists, rooted in their social fascism and the united front only from below, continued with their slogan of social democracy as the main enemy, and the social democrats were only too glad to point to the communists as the real enemy of working-class unity, and shelter their own cowardice behind it. Then on 30 January 1933, Hindenburg appointed Hitler chancellor. To the Communist Party it was not a matter of great importance; merely another fascist government. They issued one of their rhetorical appeals for a general strike. It failed, as it was bound to fail. A general strike cannot be called for at will. As a deliberate act by a revolutionary party it is the fruit of a long preparation among all classes of workers, revolutionary and otherwise. But they did not mean the general strike. Long before Hitler they had been preparing to go underground. In December, Stampfer, a social-democratic editor, had written in *Vorwärts* suggesting united action between the two parties. The Communist Party took no notice. In March Hitler burnt the Reichstag. In those desperate days Stampfer went to the Russian Embassy asking for assistance, seeking ways and means to form some sort of united front. The communist leaders ridiculed the idea. Telegrams, letters and resolutions poured in from all over the country asking them to resist. They had never had any intention of resisting. They left the masses leaderless. "After Hitler, our turn." Meanwhile the social democracy was still the chief enemy. Let the workers watch and see how the social democracy would be the chief support of Hitler. They said it when Hitler came to power and for one year afterwards. Hitler out-manoeuvred his nationalist allies, and using the Reichstag fire as the basis of his propaganda, threw the whole force of the state into a new election. The results testify as to what was the strength of the working-class movement in Germany. All Hitler's propaganda, his violence and intimidation, could not shake it. Losses were negligible. But fascism has its duty to perform. At the last election in September Hitler had had only one-third of the votes. But he was powerful enough to begin and conclude the systematic extermination of every organisation that was not Nazi. Power, it was once more proved, does not depend on an election majority.

Then began the most dreadful part of this dreadful record of stupidity and crime. The social democratic leaders, proverbially stupid, had no idea of what was about to happen to them, and even if they had it would have made no difference. They were quite prepared to serve Hitler, and in the Reichstag had declared the Hitler government to be a "constitutional and parliamentary government". Leipart, the trade-union leader, was quite prepared to hand over the trade unions to Hitler and accept their reorganisation "on the Italian model". He offered "the knowledge and experience" of himself and his colleagues to Hitler. They had sent the funds abroad. Hitler asked them to bring them back—they obligingly did so. Wels, in the Reichstag, offered to support Hitler's foreign policy—a good beginning. It should be noted that the democracy these gentlemen defend is to be defended only from the left. Given their jobs and the opportunity to "protest", they can accommodate themselves to any amount of inroads on democracy from the right. But the fascist boot they bent so dutifully to kiss was only seeking to consolidate its stance before kicking these worthless turncoats from the jobs and pensions to which they clung so desperately. On 1 May Hitler ordered a National Socialist labour demonstration. The social democratic leaders recommended the workers to go. On that night Hitler began the raids, the mass arrests, the murders, the confiscations of buildings and funds, directed especially against the trade-union movement. The bureaucrats fled for their lives.

But all through and right up to early 1935 the International learnt nothing, understood nothing, and literally sent thousands of German workers to torture, imprisonment and death. This must be traced in detail, for it shows that Stalin, working out his tortuous policies, had had no idea of what fascism meant, of what it would do in Germany. Stalin and the stalinists really and honestly thought that Hitler was just such another as Schleicher or Papen. It was not only the demoralising defeat without a struggle that has so crushed the German proletariat and broken the faith of all marxists in the International. It was the policy of the International after the defeat which ruined German socialism for perhaps a decade, and started the movement to break with the stalinists once and for all and build the new International.

On 1 April Fritz Heckert, as representative of the Communist Party of Germany, made his report to the Executive of the Communist International. Stalin's prestige came first. "As far back as 1924, the leader of the international proletariat, Comrade Stalinn gave an estimate unsurpassed in its exactness and perspicacity of the evolution of social democracy towards fascism—an estimate which lies at the basis of the progrramme of the Comintern and the policy of the Communist Party of Germany. . . . Fascism, said Comrade Stalin . . ." and Heckert quoted in full the passage in which Stalin had proved to the satisfaction of the whole International that social democracy is a wing of fascism, and they were not antipodes but twins. "Everything which has happened in Germany has fully confirmed the correctness of Comrade Stalin's prognosis. Hitler does not reject tʰe support of social democracy." Never in history has been such degrading fanaticism.

The first law of stalinism is to praise Stalin. The second is to abuse Trotsky. It was on Trotsky that Heckert's wrath chiefly fell for the heinous crime of proposing the united front, and writing in the *Manchester Guardian* that it was the refusal to form the united front on the basis of defence of parliamentary democracy and of the mass trade unions which had caused the defeat. Trotsky, said Heckert, was a "social fascist", Leipart was "Trotsky's ally", Trotsky was "the confederate of Hitler". "The Welses and Leiparts, however, do not come alone. They come to Hitler with Trotsky. It was he, Trotsky, who, carrying out the social orders of Hitler, tried to sling mud at the only party which is struggling against fascism in the most difficult conditions."

The presidiumn having heard the reportn declared "that the political line and the organisational policy pursued by the Central Committee of the Communist Party of Germanyn led by Comrade Thaelmann, before and at the time of the Hitler coupn was quite correct." Then came a typical feature of Stalin's leninism. Exactly as in Germany in 1923 and in China in 1927, having proved their previous follies, which had ruined the revolution, correct, the International called upon the German workers to prepare for the coming revolution:

> The revolutionary upsurge in Germany will inevitably grow in spite of the fascist terror. The resistance of the masses to fascism is bound to increase. The establishment of an open fascist dictatorship, by destroying all the democratic illusions among the masses and liberating them from the influence of social democracy, accelerates the rate of Germany's development towards proletarian revolution. . . . It is necessary to strengthen the party and strengthen all the mass organisations of the proletariat, to prepare the masses for decisive revolutionary battles, for the overthrow of the fascist dictatorship by an armed rebellion.

This desperate folly, approved by the Presidium and persisted in for nearly a year, cost the lives of hundreds and the imprisonment of thousands of the finest and bravest German comrades. That Stalin and Litvinov did not believe a word of all this will, however, soon be made clear.

All through that year of 1933 the ECCI led the German workers to believe that Hitler's defeat was near. The more Hitler battered the workers and concentrated power into his own hands, the more the International sent them into the open on strikes and demonstrations, delivering them to their enemies. In the middle of 1933 Piatnitsky published a document called "The Present Situation in Germany". Hitler had already launched his attack on the trade unions, and Piatnitsky, still encased in the armour-plate of social fascism, explained why. It was merely a matter of jobs. "The fascists needed for their own supporters the 400,000 soft jobs occupied by social democrats." This, however, was "no easy task. . . . In order that this might be achieved, it was necessary to implicate the social democrats in the Van der Lubbe affair, even if but for a few days, so as to provide the fascists with a pretext for closing down their press during the excitement—for they might possibly think of exposing the outrageous fascist provocation. . . . At the same time the fascists made use of the social democrats to penetrate through them into the working class, and this could be done much more easily if they thrashed them soundly first. . . ."

Until Stalin gave the word that fascism and social fascism were no longer twins his bureaucrats were physically incapable of seeing the wholesale destruction of social democracy going on before their very eyes:

> But it would be a great mistake to think that the social democratic party has already been destroyed in Germany. Gradually the fascists will let it have its press back and will then permit it to continue the demagogy which it carried on before Hitler came to power. . . . The CPG will have to put in a great deal of work to convince the social

democratic workers that the social democrats are responsible for the fact that the fascists came to power in Germany. Anyone who thinks that the objective conditions will themselves do this work without systematic, bold and self-sacrificing effort on the part of the CPG is making a great mistake.

A long experience has taught all Stalin's servants that the safest policy, the only safe policy, is to go on saying what he has said until he changes his mind. It is not facts, but what Stalin says, that matters. Piatnitsky claimed to see that the German proletariat was recovering from the fascist blows. "The German communists have shown that they know no fear. They go out into the streets. They allow their names to be openly put forward as candidates at factory committee elections in spite of fascist terror, etc." One after another, still waiting for the communist revolution, the German comrades were driven straight into the concentration camps and the torture chambers.

He admitted that there was a temporary retreat, but "that, however, did not imply the collapse of the process of the maturing of the revolutionary crisis." The German bourgeoisie was turning and twisting like an animal wounded though not yet fatally. "In proportion as the CP of Germany liberates the majority of the workers from the influence of social democracy and leads them to the struggle against the fascists, the conditions will mature under which armed insurrection will be converted from a slogan of propaganda into a slogan of action, under which the party will pass on to the direct realisation of this slogan." So it went on all through the year.

In December 1933, the thirteenth plenum of the ECCI was held. By this time the working-class organisations in Germany had been crushed except for a nucleus of communists fighting magnificently but misguidedly for revolution. In its official report the plenum still harped on social fascism: "German social democracy was and still remains the banner-bearer of all the parties of the Second International which follow the steps of German social democracy. Social democracy continues to play the role of the main social prop of the bourgeoisie also in the countries of open fascist dictatorship." In Germany, said the plenum, "enormous revolutionary energy is being accumulated among the masses and a new revolutionary upsurge is already beginning." A special section was headed: "Against social democracy and for a united front from below." The plenum confirmed that the policy had been correct. But here there was a hitch. Of the three leaders of the German Communist Party whose tactical line was held up as correct, Thaelmann was in prison, and Remmele and Neumann had escaped. These two men, less docile than the well-meaning but too loyal Thaelmann, had opposed the line before Hitler came to power. Now, their eyes fully opened at last by the fate to which they had led their followers, they stated that the movement in Germany was defeated, that Hitler was firmly in the saddle, that it would take a long period to rebuild the movement, and that only on an honest and realistic investigation into the causes of the defeat. Others in the International were saying the same. This for Stalin would have been a disaster. The plenum condemned them and called on "all sections of the Comintern to ruthlessly root out opportunism in all its forms, and, above all, right opportunism (Remmele, Neumann, the defeatists in other countries in their estimate of the prospects of the German revolution), for unless this is done the communist parties will not be able to lead the working masses up to the victorious struggles for the Soviet power." Social fascism remained and when it went it was not on account of the working-class movement but because Moscow's foreign policy had changed.

1937

4

The Philosophy of History and Necessity: A Few Words with Professor Hook

[*This essay was published in the July 1943 issue of* The New International *under the pseudonym "A.A.B." James says: "Hook had begun by writing sympathetically about the philosophical ideas of Hegel and Marx, and after that he gradually turned over and joined the establishment. Other people would call him reactionary, joining the bourgeoisie. We didn't go in for that: we dealt with him as a philosopher."*]

"It would certainly be very pleasant if a really scientific socialist journal were to be published. It would provide an opportunity for criticisms or counter-criticisms in which we could discuss theoretical points, expose the ignorance of professors and lecturers and at the same time enlighten the minds of the general public, working-class or bourgeois."

Marx to Engels, 18 July 1877.

The interpretation of history is a class question. When a worker joins the revolutionary movement he interprets history, acting instinctively on the basis of his class. When a professor joins the movement he often explains this on historical, sometimes on philosophical grounds. Usually, when he leaves, you discover that, except in the rarest instances, he has never really understood the fundamental method of marxism. The failure is due always to the same cause—the inability to realise that the understanding of marxist philosophy is a class question. Hook's recent book on history [*The Hero in History*], as was to be expected, shows not the slightest understanding of this basic fact. Instead he shows himself happy in the conviction that marxism is a form of religion. In the very second paragraph of this book, Hook lumps together "Providence, justice, reason, dialectic"—all are similar types of metaphysical abstraction. Hegel, Herbert Spencer and Marx were all bunglers in their philosophising about history. Hook pontificates: "It is easy to establish that orthodox marxism, particularly where it invokes the notions of dialectical necessity and historical inevitability, is shot through with metaphysical elements every whit as questionable as the views it criticised". Exactly how easy it is, we shall soon see. Of the appearance of great men in history, he says: "For Engels, social need is not only a necessary condition for the appearance of a great man but also sufficient. But how does he know that, even when a great and urgent social need is present, a great man *must* arise to cope with it? Who or what guarantees this blessed event? Not the Providence of Augustine and Bossuet, not the Cunning of Reason of Hegel, not the Unknowable of Spencer, but 'the dialectical contradiction between the forces of production and the relations of production.' This dynamic force works in a truly remarkable fashion.'' For Hook, Marx is a modern Moses, leading the proletariat out of capitalism into the inevitability of socialism on the same philosophical premises that Moses led the Israelites out of the house of bondage into the land of promise. Hook's point is that the great man does not appear of *necessity*. He comes from nobody knows where. The marxists have made valuable contributions to historical theory, but as can be shown by their treatment of great men, they believe in an economic *necessity* expressing a historical *purpose* which is no more than a form of religious mania. As Mr Joseph Ratner so eloquently described it in his essay on modern philosophy: ''The Marxian materialism goes along in ever more novel ways, developing itself and the universe (at the same time) in accordance with the magical antics of the Hegelian idealistic dialectic secreted in its vitals. Whatever one may think of the philosophical value of Idealistic Magic (even when covered up with materialistic sober sense). . . .'' Ratner is rough and tough. Hook prefers to snigger. But both of them, like the common run of American intellectuals, including most of the radicals, write and speak as if the question is not even worth discussing any more.

This religion of ''social determinism'', Hook treats of in one chapter on Hegel and Spencer, he devotes another chapter to the ''social determinism'' of Marx. These delusions being disposed of, Hook now faces the task of showing us his own conception of the movement of history. To do so he raises the question first posed by Meyer, the famous German historian of classical antiquity. What would have been the subsequent history of Europe if the Persians had conquered the Greeks? Says Hook: ''Meyer maintains with justification that the political history as well as the cultural values of Greek and European civilisation would have been profoundly different from the legacy that has come down to us.'' This is a miserable sentence, but its meaning can be divined. The political history as well as the cultural values of Greek civilisation would have been different. The legacy that would have come down to us would have been therefore different. The logic is impeccable. But to say that the political history and cultural values of Europe would have been ''profoundly different'', that, Mr Philosopher, is a ripe and rosy carbuncle which invites the marxist scalpel. After the ensuing operation, an easy one, and not worth doing for its own sake, we shall be nearer to marxism and Hook's more serious philosophical crimes.

It is to Hegel and Marx that are due the modern practice of dividing world history into a sequence which shows some historical inevitability or necessity, or on which according to the Hookites, that necessity is imposed. Marx, like Hegel, sought in history ''the pervading thread of development'' and he found it in the economic relations of the different social forms. Marx's divisions are therefore primitive communism, the classical slave society, feudalism, capitalism, and, tomorrow, communism. Marx saw each social system as flowing inevitably and of necessity from the other. Is this necessity "religious"? Let us see.

For a marxist, the determining feature of the classical world taken as a whole was slavery. The distinguishing political feature was the city-state. The empirical proof of its vitality is Rome, which from the beginning to the end of the Roman Empire remained a city-state. The economic basis of the early city-state was the free peasant who lived on the territory adjoining the city which was his administrative, military and cultural centre. By degrees more is produced and more consumed. As Rome expanded, the peasant economy declined and, aided by the great trade wars with Carthage, the inevitable concentration of production resulted in the creation of the wealthy landowners and financiers. This economic development enslaved the masses of the population and destroyed the old Roman Republic. What is the sense of attributing this or any part of it to the Greek legacy? The brothers Gracchi were educated by a Greek rhetorician and a Stoic philosopher. Does Hook really think that this made them lead one of the most famous agrarian and political revolutions in Roman history? Or that the wealthy Romans who murdered them did so because they had neglected to study Pericles on democracy?

The backward agricultural economy of Rome lacked the power to make economic connections with the outlying provinces. Hence Rome's relation with these was political. Rome was a city-state exploiting a continental hinterland. The plunder which is the reward of all empire-builders could be gained only by political means. Hence the intense political life of Rome. With the creation of the huge latifundia and the gigantic political bureaucracy in Rome, the Empire could go no further. It collapsed, and all the more easily because there was no unity in the production relations. What, pray, had the legacy of Greece to do with all this?

Now comes the question of inevitability in the change to feudalism. In 1859, discussing the barbarian invasions of the Empire, and the new distribution of property which resulted, Marx wrote: "Although the latter appears now as the prerequisite condition of the new period of production, it is itself but a product of production, not of production belonging to history in general, but of production relating to a definite historical period". Marx laid the emphasis on the mode of production brought by the Germans, although he recognised the reciprocal and receptive character of the latifundia. A dozen years later occurred one of the historical sensations of the nineteenth century.

Fustel de Coulanges was a Frenchman who in 1864 published a brilliant study of the ancient city-state, *La Cité Antique*. He was appointed to a post at Strasbourg, where Franco-German relations were very tense. (All this will teach Hook something about the role of the hero.) Fustel hated the German nationalistic historians and their boasting about German culture, and immediately after the Franco-German war he began the publication of his thesis that the invading German barbarians were Romanised Germans whose leaders simply took the place of the old ruling class while civilisation went on much as before. According to de Coulanges: "All the agricultural characteristics of the manor existed under the Empire and were plainly apparent in Merovingian times. . . . The Franks were not the authors of the change, but they aided it and gave it some traits that it would not have had." What these traits were can be argued even among marxists. We are stressing here the economic foundations. Invasions or no invasions, feudalism was the inevitable next stage rooted in the inner necessity of the Roman impasse. De Coulanges was no marxist. He had interpreted the city-state in terms of religion, and the contemporary monarchists in France have drawn much ammunition from his work on that subject.

We know today, and chiefly owing to Marx and Engels, that the Middle Ages were no age of darkness. Yet there was a period which is hard to reconcile as progressive in comparison with Rome of the decline.

During another Franco-German war, 1914–18, another professor of the Latin-German civilisation, this time a Belgian, wrote his views on the same period. Pirenne showed that there had been no destruction of the Roman civilisation of Europe by the barbarians. Civilisation continued to flourish on the basis of a wide exchange. Then in the seventh century the Moslem armies swept across North Africa, invaded Europe and remained in Spain for some seven hundred years. From the North the Norsemen did the same as far South as Sicily. Thus, directly and indirectly, these barbarians destroyed the internal economy and external trade of Europe. This was the cause of the darkest period in European civilisation. Protection became an important factor in European society and on this economic and social basis the politics and cultural values of medieval Europe were founded. St Thomas based his philosophy on Aristotle, but all the textbooks say that St Thomas's Aristotle was not the Aristotle of Greece but a medieval philosopher. The church of Rome, which had inherited the prestige of the Roman Empire, became an international landowner and the political and spiritual leader of society. Hence religion and not, as in classical times, politics, was the main sphere of medieval life.

From the hard conditions of the countryside the serfs ran away and settled themselves in the towns to protect themselves from the feudal lords. The word bourgeoisie comes from the Latin *burgensis*, meaning an inhabitant of a walled town. But whereas the city-state had been a protection for the peasants of the countryside and an administrative centre, the medieval city fought against the economic and political overlordship of the feudal barons. The two compromised in the national state, which was consolidated by the absolute monarchy. In the national state, agriculture and industry made a remarkable development, far surpassing the achievements of Rome or of the medieval manor. Ultimately the superior economy of the towns conquered the economy of agriculture and we have the modern economy, with its new values of bourgeois democracy and now, today, of socialism and the cultural values of the modern age.

The historical necessity is not a mathematical progression. Doubtless the Moslems threw Europe back. But it was their backward economy which was finally driven out of the continent by the national state of Spain. By degrees more is produced and more is consumed. But this necessity is geographically and otherwise conditioned. Marx pointed out that in the Oriental countries the geographical necessity of large irrigation works early gave the state an overwhelming authority which created a stagnation lasting for thousands of years. But just as the European economy conquered America and not *vice versa*, so we see the Orient adopting the economic forms of the developed capitalist civilisation, and India, for example, becoming a modern nation, fundamentally different from the loose association of semi-feudal states under Aurungzebe. And with this economic development come to India the modern values of nationalism, no taxation without representation, democracy, compulsory education and socialism. Hook thinks all this would have been different but for Plato and Aristotle.

In an article on Trotsky's place in history, J. R. Johnson writes as follows: "Rome fell . . . but when the Renaissance brought back the study of the classics, all the growing forces of liberalism in Europe nourished themselves on the vivid artistry and republican sentiments of Thucydides, Livy and Plutarch and cursed tyranny in the language of Tacitus. . . . The finer shades of European history are a closed book without an understanding of what the classics meant to all the educated classes" (*The New International*, September 1941, page 163). You can say more but not much more. Hook says that not only the values but the political history itself would have been "profoundly different" had it not been for the Greek legacy. But if the values and political history had been "profoundly different", the economic history would have been different too. We cannot imagine "profoundly different" politics and culture without "profoundly different" economics. So that in the end Boulder Dam, the Flying Fortress and the photo-electric cell are due not to the historical inevitability of marxist necessity but to the lucky

chance that the Persians were licked by the Greeks. Isn't it clear
that this philosopher has no philosophy of history, the moment
he deals with the concrete?

The foolishness of Hook does not prove the wisdom of Marx.
Still less does it prove the philosophical validity of Marx's doctrine of historical necessity. Yet the above sketch, inadequate as it
necessarily is, shows that the doctrine of stages developing inevitably from one another is one that can be empirically observed and
empirically established. We have seen where Hook lands in his
attempt to discredit the doctrine on purely historical grounds.
There still remains, however, the question of all this taking place
through some divine dialectic or otherwise phony purpose.

Dühring is Hook's grandfather, and Engels, exposing the
parent, used some words which are particularly applicable to the
"son". This nineteenth-century Hook, in his exposition of his
own philosophy, had introduced the idea of "purpose" in the
transition from inorganic to organic life. Says Engels: "Once
again, this is borrowed from Hegel, who in his *Logic—the
Science of the Idea*, makes the transition from chemistry to life
by means of teleology or the science of purpose. . . . It would
take us too long to examine here to what extent it is legitimate
and appropriate to apply the ideas of end and means to the
organic world. In any case the utilisation of the Hegelian 'inner
purpose'—i.e. a purpose which is *not* [our emphasis] imported
into Nature by some third party acting purposively, such as the
wisdom of Providence but lies in the necessity of the thing itself,
constantly leads with people who are not well versed in
philosophy, to the unthinking interpolation of conscious and
purposive activity." As W. C. Fields used to say: "How true!"

Note how carefully Engels differentiates the providential
purpose of St Augustine from the purpose of Hegel. Hook,
who, as a professor of philosophy, should be "well versed" in it,
jumbles them all together. But what about Engels's own idea of
purpose? While defending Hegel against the philosophical
barbarism of the Hook of his day, he himself shows what the
concept is and how it should be used. Says Engels: "The inner
purpose in the organism, according to Hegel operates through
impulse. Pas trop fort. [Go easy with that.] Impulse is supposed
to bring the single living being more or less into harmony with
the idea of it. From this it is seen how much the whole *inner
purpose* is itself an ideological determination. And yet Lamarck
is contained in this" (*Dialectics of Nature*). Maybe someone will
explain to us how to explain to Hook that an ideological
determination means a construction made by the mind. Note the
completely non-metaphysical "instrumental" manner in which
Marx and Engels dealt with such concepts as purpose and
necessity in nature, not to mention history. This procedure
Hook can attack if he likes. Then the debate would begin. But
this philosopher of history and professional philosopher prefers

to slander marxism by writing "the purposive idealism of Hegel and the dialectical materialists."

Let us continue with "purpose", for if we do not understand this, only faith and not reason can save us. If I see that all rivers run to the sea, then I say that the "necessity" of a river, when placed in its habitual earthly relations, compels it to run to the sea. Hence that is its "purpose". It acts that way because that is its nature, and my business as a scientist is to examine that, and not look for the hand of God or any outside agency. On this use of "purpose", both Hegel and Engels, as we see, had common ground. But both Marx and Hegel understood quite clearly that you could never finally prove this purpose or any necessity purely by empirical observation. No logic in the world can prove that the sun must of inevitable necessity rise tomorrow morning. Hegel refused to accept this, and all that a human being could do to make empirically observed necessity logically and philosophically watertight, Hegel did. That is why Engels writes of him in *Ludwig Feuerbach*: "With Hegel, philosophy comes to an end: on the one hand because in his system he comprehended its whole development in the most splendid fashion; and on the other hand, because, even if unconsciously, he showed us the way out of the labyrinth of 'systems' to real positive knowledge of the world."

What Hegel refused to accept, Marx and Engels accepted and made their basis. As Engels says: "The empiricism of observation alone can never adequately prove necessity. . . . But the proof of necessity lies in human activity, in experiment, in work." Could anything be simpler? Yet this is something which Hook with all his studies of Hegel and Marx has never understood. Marx did not seek a philosophy based on the traditional philosophical methods. "The philosophers," he said, "have *interpreted* the world in various ways; the point, however, is to *change* it." The emphasis is his own. This was a complete break with the old philosophy in the now stagnant waters of which Hook still puffs and blows.

Marx, an educated German of the fifth decade of the nineteenth century, read history and, looking at the events around him, came to certain conclusions, summed up forty years later by Engels, as follows: "The new tendency . . . recognised that the key to the understanding of the whole history of society lies in the historical development of labour." Having recognised this, the new tendency "addressed itself by preference to the working class and here found the response which it neither sought nor expected from officially recognised science." This was a conscious action, undertaken "by preference", deliberately linking thought to the past, present and future of the proletariat. Having made the fundamental break, Marx and Engels then turned back consciously to the classical philosophy to organise their own according to the laws of logical thought which had been worked out by philosophers from Aristotle down and had been brought to a high pitch of development by the German philosophers culminating in Hegel. Hence the next sentence: "The German working class is the inheritor of German classical philosophy." Though they illustrated, Marx and Engels never tried to prove the necessity of their system by the Hegelian or any other logical or philosophical method, *because they knew that couldn't be done*. And that is a thing Hook, Eastman & Co. will never understand to their dying day.

Marx used the Hegelian method to discover the "necessity" of historical movement and its "purpose". Then, seeing the forces which comprised the "necessity", he elaborated a philosophy which was a guide to action for the working class. Practice, action, activity, work, there could be no other proof. Hook thinks in all probability that the marxist insistence on activity is a bait to catch intellectuals and make them do political work. It is nothing of the kind. It is the deliberate, conscious repudiation of the traditional philosophy and its aims and methods in the way of proof. It is now one year short of a century since Marx first elaborated his philosophical position. The questions Hook should ask are as follows: has society travelled in the direction Marx said it would travel? Does the future of society rest with the emancipation of the proletariat? Has the philosophy of Marx proved a useful guide to the action of the proletariat? If, reasonably interpreted, the answer is yes, then *there* lies the Marxian proof of historic "necessity" and historic "purpose". There can be no other proof. As Marx said roughly: All other questions are scholastic questions.

But there is more to it, and here the question becomes one of practical political importance. The interpretation of history or philosophy being a class question, the persistence in raising scholastic questions is itself a class question, and much of the confusion about Marx's philosophy arises from the justifiable sternness with which he refused to tolerate any fooling with his basic premises. In 1844, when he was settling accounts with Hegel, he made this very clear.

To a hypothetical person who asked him: "Who has produced the first man and nature in general?" Marx replies: "I can only answer: Your question is the product of abstraction. Ask yourself how you arrive at this question. Ask yourself whether your question does not occur from a point of view which I cannot answer because it is an absurd one. Ask yourself whether that series exists as such for reasonable thought. Whenever you ask about the creation of nature and man, you abstract yourself from man and nature. You presuppose that you don't exist and yet you demand that I prove you exist. I now say to you: abandon your abstraction and you will give up your question. Or if you hold fast to your abstraction, accept the consequences.

Whenever you think of man and nature as non-existent, regard yourself as non-existent, since you are natural and human. Think not, ask me not, for as soon as you think and ask, your abstraction from the existence of nature and man makes no sense."

This philosophical approach is not for man in general. It is for a certain class of man, socialist man, the revolutionary proletariat. It is a philosophy of action for a class. Marx continues: "However, inasmuch as for the socialist man, the whole so-called history of the world is none other than the production of man through human labour, none other than the becoming of nature to men, he has the obvious irrefutable proof of its birth and genesis through himself. . . . [Socialism] begins from the theoretical and practical consciousness of men and nature as of the essence." In the same period he said in effect that the science of nature would become the science of man and the science of man the science of nature. Scientific investigation, yes. But he would have none of the attempts to solve these questions in the manner of Spinoza and Hegel.

Marx and Engels went to astonishing lengths in this attitude, and they could do this *only because they knew precisely what they were doing*. Thus in the *Dialectics of Nature* Engels writes: "We have the certainty that matter remains eternally the same in all its transformations, that none of its attributes can ever be lost, and therefore, also with the same iron necessity that it will exterminate on the earth its highest creation, the thinking mind, it must somewhere else and at another time again produce it." Pat and glib comes Hook's little snigger: "This is a certainty that dialectic (I had almost said religion) may give— science never" (*Marxist Quarterly*, April-June 1937). And yet it is precisely here that the non-religious earth-bound, class-based philosophy of Marx is being expressed. For Marx, life consisted of the relations between Nature (our particular Nature) and man. Nature created man and therefore that was Nature's "purpose" and that, *for the proletariat*, was philosophically sufficient. Nature's purpose might have been ten million things; it might have created a race of philosophical jackals whose successive generations would have spent their lives howling to the moon. Nature didn't. And the proletariat on whose shoulders fell the burden of changing society had no use for that purely scholastic philosophic doubt which perpetually wonders if after all something else could not have happened. To believe that Engels did not understand the philosophic implication and limitations of his phrase "iron necessity" would be a piece of impertinence on the part of Hook, if even the evidence did not exist that Engels was thoroughly aware of them. The same applies to history.

To conclude: marxists, neither in history nor philosophy, have any theological certainty of anything. Their method is scientific.

But it is a scientific method which knows what it wants to do, and, equally well, knows what it does not want to do. A revolutionary worker acts in accordance with these ideas because his material circumstances compel him to. When masses of workers take revolutionary action they act in accordance with historical "necessity" and fulfil a historic "purpose". Let Hook walk into any circle of those who rule the world today and make a short speech about Marx, ending with "Workers of the world, unite." He will get a very practical demonstration of how seriously the educated classes take the marxist doctrine of "dialectical necessity and historical inevitability".

1943

5

After Ten Years

[*This first appeared as an article in the October 1946 issue of* The New International, *under the pseudonym of "J. R. Johnson".* *The anniversary is that of Trotsky's book on the degeneration of the Russian revolution*, The Revolution Betrayed.]

No one will deny that *The Revolution Betrayed* contains all that Trotsky thought essential to an understanding of stalinist Russia as a new form of society. In reviewing this timely reprint I propose to re-examine Trotsky's basic analysis of stalinist production; the role of the working class in the labour process; the social functioning of the bureaucracy.

According to Trotsky, the distinguishing feature of the economy is the capacity to plan owing to the existence of state property. Apart from the general problem of backwardness, its main defect is the incompetence of the bureaucracy. The fundamental content of the activity of the Soviet government is the struggle to raise the productivity of labour. The bureaucracy claims that the Russian workers lack skill, but the Russian worker is "enterprising, ingenious and gifted". "The difficulty lies in the general organisation of labour." And the responsibility for this lies with the bureaucracy. "The Soviet administrative personnel is, as a general rule, far less equal to the new productive tasks than the worker." Productive organisation of piecework demands "a raising of the level of administration itself, from the shop foreman to the leaders in the Kremlin". "The bureaucracy tries fatally to leap over difficulties which it cannot surmount." Again: "Not knowing how, and not being objectively able, to put the régime of production in order in a short space of time. . . ." In conclusion: "the name of that social guild which holds back and paralyses all the guilds of the Soviet economy is the bureaucracy".

In regard to the workers Trotsky's main preoccupation is the relation between their wages and the wages of the bureaucracy. It is important to recognise the enormous emphasis and space which Trotsky gives to *consumption* in his analysis of "inequality" and "social antagonisms". What lies, he asks, at the bottom of the continuous repression? His reply is: "Lack of the means of subsistence resulting from the low productivity of labour". He returns to it again and again. "The justification for the existence of a Soviet state as an apparatus for compulsion lies in the fact that the present transitional structure is still full of social contradictions, which in the sphere of *consumption*— most close and sensibly felt by all—are extremely tense, and

forever threaten to break over into the sphere of production. . . . The basis of bureaucratic rule is the poverty of society
in objects of consumption with the resulting struggle of each
against all. . . .'' Trotsky, of course, is no anarchist. He
justifies a certain amount of inequality by the necessity for
bourgeois norms of distribution in a transitional régime. This
also justifies the state. The gravamen of his charge of betrayal of
the revolution is the monstrous *growth* of the state and the
monstrous *growth* of inequality.

He claims in more than one place that the economy is slowly
bettering the position of the toilers. But the future of Soviet
society depends upon the world revolution. Either the world
revolution enables the Russian proletariat to liquidate the
usurpations and incompetence of the bureaucracy, or the further
rule of the bureaucracy will lead to a complete liquidation of the
conquests of the revoltuion. Such in brief is Trotsky's economic
analysis. The problem of accumulation as such receives no direct
treatment and this is not accidental. After the most scrupulous
analysis of which he is capable, the present writer finds that
Trotsky operates on the principle that once private property is
abolished there is no *problem* of accumulation. If waste and
bureaucracy are kept down to a minimum, progressive accumulation is assured. *It is impossible to read this book and
learn from it what, if any, is the specific contribution of the proletariat to the building of the socialist society.*

Such a difference of view involves the very concepts of
Marxian thought. I propose, therefore, to state what in my view
is the Marxian conception of society, capitalist, socialist and
transitional to socialism, and then to show, in my opinion,
Trotsky's sharp and consistent departure from this conception.

Marx's theory of society is a theory of the activity of men, of
men as active in the process of production. The classical
economists, having discovered labour as the activity which
produces private property, *left it alone* and proceeded to deal
only with the material results of this activity. They did not
analyse the nature of the activity nor the relationship of the
results of the activity to the activity itself. Thus they viewed the
movement of society and the division of society according to the
division of the products of labour. Marx, on the contrary, based
his analysis on the division of labour itself. His philosophy was a
philosophy of the activity of men in the labour process. His
analysis of capitalist production was therefore the analysis of the
labour of man. In capitalism, labour was *alienated from its
true function*, the development of man. Thereby it was transformed into its opposite, man's increasing subjugation—
and rebelliousness. For Marx, therefore, the essence of private
property was the alienation of labour and not the fact that
property belonged to private individuals.

Marx states categorically that to see private property as the basis of alienated labour is to turn the truth upside down:

> We have, of course, achieved the concept of alienated labour (of alienated life) from political economy as the result of the movement of private property. But in analysing this concept, it is revealed that if private property appears as the basis as the cause of alienated labour, it is rather a consequence of it, as the gods are not originally the cause but the effect of human confusion of understanding. Later this relationship is turned upside down.

The handing over of his products to another, his alienation, is for Marx the result of his degraded labour, of the type of activity to which the proletarian is condemned. "How could the labourer be opposed to the product of his activity in an alien fashion if he were not estranged in the act of production itself? The product is only the résumé of activity, of production. . . . In the alienation of the object of labour is only crystallised the alienation, the renunciation in the activity of labour itself." Marx believed that this was his special contribution to the analysis of society. He says magnificently: "When one speaks of private property one thinks he is dealing with something outside of man. When one speaks of labour one has to do immediately with man himself. The new formulation of the question already involves its solution."

The result of this alienation of man from the product of his labour is that "his labour is therefore not free but forced, forced labour". That is to say, his labour is not his own free self-activity, the conscious exercise of all his powers, but merely a means to his existence. Secondly, an immediate consequence of this alienation of man from self-activity is the alienation of man from man. Capitalist society was the highest stage of alienation yet reached. As a result it carried to the highest possible stage the contradictions and hypocrisies of all previous class societies.

Alienation of labour corrupted society through and through. The greater the alienation, the greater the necessity of using all manifestations of society, science, art, politics, as a justification for the alienation. The solution is in what Marx calls the appropriation by the proletariat of the enormous possibilities for self-development existing in the objectified labour, the mass of accumulated capital. Man must become universal man, universal in the sense that the *individual* develops all his own *individual* powers in accordance with the stage of development of the species, that is to say, the potentialities embodied in the accumulated mass of productive forces.

The powers of man *as an individual* is the test. "Above all, one must avoid setting the society up again as an abstraction opposed to the individual. The individual *is* the social entity. The expression of his life . . . is therefore an expression and verification of the *life of society*."

The most vital expression of the life of the individual is his

activity in the labour process. For Marx, it is labour which
distinguishes man from the beast. Labour is the truest essence of
man. By that he lives and develops himself as a truly social
being. But in capitalist society his labour is an inhuman
degradation. We have the result that man, the labourer, "feels
himself as freely active more in his animal functions, eating
and drinking, procreating," whereas in labour, his specifically
human function, he functions more like an animal. "The animal
becomes the human and the human the animal."

Marx's philosophy is not one thing and his economics and
politics something else. His analysis of capitalist production, of
accumulation, of consumption, flow from this philosophical
concept of man in society with which he began. The quotations
above are from his early economic and philosophical manuscripts. *Capital* and the writings of his maturity are only the
embodiment and concretisation of these ideas. The difference between these conceptions and Trotsky's conceptions of
stalinist Russia can be seen immediately in the analysis of Russia
itself.

Where in modern society is there so perfect an example of
alienated labour and its consequences as in stalinist Russia?
Trotsky after page upon page about wages and consumption
suddenly states late in his volume the following: "The transfer
of the factories to the state changed the situation of the workers
only juridically." In other words, in the labour process he was
left just where he was. First, this is not true. And if it were, a
whole new world begins. But to continue: ". . . In order to
raise [the low] level [of technique and culture], the new state
resorted to the old methods of pressure upon the muscles and
nerves of the workers. There grew up a corps of slave drivers.
The management of industry became super-bureaucratic. The
workers lost all influence whatever upon the management of the
factory."

This is the situation of the proletariat today in production.
What is there new or socialist in this? How does the mode of
labour of the worker in stalinist Russia *differ* from the alienated
labour of the worker in capitalist production? Trotsky points
out similarities. The differences, if any, and their importance,
are outside of his consideration.

Failing to base himself upon the alienation of labour in the
process of production, Trotsky fails to see the consequence of
this *upon the bureaucracy itself*. Of what theoretical validity
is his constant emphasis upon the incompetence of the
bureaucracy? The Soviet bureaucracy is a reflection of the law
of motion of the Soviet economy. The bureaucracy has no free
will. It consumes more than the proletariat. But its social life
within itself is a form of jungle existence. No member of the
bureaucracy, except perhaps Stalin, knows whether tomorrow
his whole life may not be cut short and he himself and all his

family, friends and assistants disgraced, murdered or sent into exile. The various strata of the bureaucracy address each other in the same tone and manner as the bureaucracy as a whole addresses the proletariat. If the proletariat is imprisoned in the factories, the members of the ruling party are subjected to a regimentation, and unceasing surveillance and inquisition that make the coveted membership in the party a form of imprisonment. The stalinist official, from the highest to the lowest, excludes his wife and family from any participation not only in his public or political life but even in his thinking. It is a measure of protection so that when the arm of the NKVD falls upon him, they will be able to say with honesty that they knew nothing about his political ideas. That is their slender hope of salvation. Friendship is a permanent suspicion. The risk of betrayal by one chance word is too great. This catalogue of crime, fear, humiliation, degradation, the alienation from human existence of a whole class (or caste), is the fate of those who *benefit* by the alienation of labour. As for the proletariat, at least a third of the labour force is an industrial reserve army herded in concentration camps. That is the stalinist society, rulers and ruled. It is the ultimate, the most complete expression of *class* society, a society of alienated labour.

In socialist society *or* in a society transitional to socialism, politics, science, art, literature, education all become or are in process of becoming truly social. The *individual* is able to exercise his gifts to the highest capacity, to become truly universal, because of the essentially *collective* life of the society in which he lives. Look at stalinist society. No individual is more "political" than the individual in stalinist society. Nowhere are art, literature, education, science, so integrated with "society." That is the appearance. In reality, never before has there been such a prostitution of all these things for the corruption and suppression of the direct producer, with the resulting degradation of the producers and managers alike. From what aspects of Marxian theory is it possible to call this barbarism a part of the new society envisaged by Marx as emerging from the contradictions of capitalist society? But a false analysis of the social role of the proletariat in society is *always* either cause or effect of a false analysis of the proletariat in the process of accumulation.

Now let us see what role Trotsky gives to the proletariat. He says, for example, that for the regulation and application of plans, two levers are needed: "the political lever, in the form of a real participation in leadership of the interested masses themselves, a thing which is unthinkable without Soviet democracy; and a financial lever," a stable rouble. But when he concretises leadership of the interested masses, we find that he is referring to the interest of the masses in the quality of products in so far as it affects their consumption.

"The Soviet products are as though branded with the grey label of indifference. Under a nationalised economy *quality* demands a democracy of producers and consumers, freedom of criticism and initiative". This is no casual statement. It comes in the chapter "Whither the Soviet Union?" where he is summarising his position. On the previous page he had made it less sharp but more revealing. State planning, he writes, brings to the front "the problem of *quality*, bureaucratism destroys the creative initiative and the feeling of responsibility without which there is not, and cannot be, qualitative progress". Then comes what is, perhaps, the most astonishing statement in the book, from the point of view already enunciated: "The ulcers of bureaucratism are perhaps not so obvious in the big industries, but they are devouring, together with the co-operatives, the light and food producing industries, the collective farms, the small local industries—that is, all those branches of economy which stand nearest to the people". *So that Trotsky finds that there is more "bureaucratism" in light industry than in heavy.*

We want to leave no misunderstanding whatever in the minds of the reader as to our fundamental principled opposition to this analysis by Trotsky of bureaucracy and the relation to it of the proletariat and production. In *State and Revolution*, Lenin states: "Under capitalism democracy is restricted, cramped, curtailed, mutilated by all the conditions of wage-slavery, the poverty and misery of the masses. *This is why and the only reason why* (emphasis mine) the officials of our political and industrial organisations are corrupted—or, more precisely, tend to be corrupted—by the conditions of capitalism, why they betray a tendency to become transformed into bureaucrats, i.e. into privileged persons divorced from the masses and superior to the masses."

This is the *essence* of bureaucracy, and until the capitalists have been expropriated and the bourgeoisie overthrown, even proletarian officials will inevitably be "bureaucratised to some extent".

But even when the capitalists have been expropriated and the bourgeoisie overthrown, the *essence* of bureaucracy can remain or recur owing to the cramped, curtailed, mutilated life of the masses. But whence comes this cramping, this curtailment, this mutilation of the life of the masses? Is this a question of consumption and quality of goods? Or of light and heavy industry? Is it necessary to quote again Marx's famous summation of hundreds of pages on the worker in *heavy industry* and the general law of capitalist accumulation when he says that "be his payment high or low," the accumulation of capital leads on the part of the worker to accumulation of misery, agony of toil, slavery, ignorance, brutality, mental degradation? But production in stalinist Russia is not capitalist? Very well. Let the followers of Trotsky's theory demonstrate that accumulation of misery, agony of toil, etc., in the production mechanism of the workers' state, the state of planned economy, let them demonstrate that that is not "the reason and the only reason" why the officials of the political and industrial organisations of stalinist Russia become corrupted and transformed into privileged persons, divorced from the masses and superior to them. Trotsky's conception of the term "bureaucracy" is not ours.

Twenty-five years after he had written the early manuscripts, Marx stated in *Capital* that it was a matter of life and death for sociey to change the degraded producer of alienated labour into universal man. Presumably this was *only* philosophy. It would be interesting to have a symposium as to what interpretations a body of marxists would give to the following: "Modern industry, indeed, compels society, under penalty of death, to replace the detail-worker of today, crippled by lifelong repetition of one and the same trivial operation, and thus reduced to the mere fragment of a man, by the fully developed individual, fit for a variety of labours, ready to face any change of production, and to whom the different social functions he performs, are but so many modes of giving free scope to his own natural and acquired powers". Life and death for society! Marx did not use such words lightly. Here he uses them twice on a single page. To the extent that one accepts this passage, one is penetrating to the heart of the Marxian theory of society *and* the theory of accumulation. Marx was the last man in the world to base such a conception of universal man upon anything but the economic necessities of society.

It is to be understood that the degradation (and the revolt) is inherent in capitalist accumulation, or if you prefer, in the accumulation of modern industry *where labour is alienated*. In his analysis of machinery and modern industry, Marx points out that the "special skill of each individual insignificant factory operative vanishes as an infinitesimal quantity before the science, the gigantic physical forces, and the mass of labour that are embodied in the factory mechanism and, together with that mechanism, constitute the power of the 'master'". Let the 1946 theoreticians of the degenerated workers' state show that this gigantic bureaucratic mechanism in Russia confronts the individual worker with economic and political consequences other than those of capitalism.

The bureaucracy uses the old methods of pressure upon the worker. It is the greatest error of Trotsky that he nowhere in his book seems to find it necessary to answer (1) that the old methods of pressure are rooted in the relations of the expropriated pauperised proletarians to accumulated labour; (2) that this relation determines the economic movement. The present writer, as is known, believes that stalinist Russia is a form of state capitalism. He has no wish to hide that in this article, nor could he do so if he tried. But the fact remains that the desperate struggle for the productivity of labour, today at least, and for some years now, *compels* the bureaucracy to pay the individual proletarian at his value. From this follow certain economic consequences. The raising of the level of productivity, according to Trotsky the fundamental content of the Soviet government, can be accomplished in only one way, expansion of the mass of accumulated labour, decrease of the relative quantity of living labour. I submit that expansion of the degenerated workers' state is governed by the amount of surplus labour at its disposal after all the necessary expenses have been met. Now Marx's thesis, in the analysis of capitalist production, was that at a certain stage, the increased surplus labour which was necessary for the continued expansion and development of society on new foundations could be met only by entirely new perspectives of productivity. These could be opened up only by the proletariat, appropriating the mass of accumulated labour and using it to develop its own potentialities. Thereby it elevated the whole social system to a new level. But just so long as the proletariat continued in the stage of degradation, so the ruling class, bureaucracy or bourgeoisie, caste or class, would be compelled to raise productivity "by the old methods of pressure". Precisely because of this, the contradiction between the relatively decreasing labour force and the resultant increase in the *mass* but the fall in the *rate*, of surplus labour, becomes the theoretical premise of economic collapse. The greater the degeneration of the workers' state the more powerful the functioning of this law.

What, in Trotsky's analysis, is the relation between consumption and production in Russia? This is his *solitary* reference: "Superficial 'theoreticians' can comfort themselves, of course, that the distribution of wealth is a factor secondary to its production. The dialectic of interaction, however, retains here all its force." The dialectic of interaction! This fundamental problem he dismisses with a phrase. But he immediately goes on to make the tremendous statement: "The destiny of the state-appropriated means of production will be decided in the long run according as these means of personal existence evolve in one direction or another." The future of planned economy then depends on consumption. Then follows a characteristic analogy of a ship declared collective property but whose first-class passengers have "coffee and cigars" and the third-class passengers nothing. "Antagonisms growing out of this may well explode the unstable collective."

Equally unfortunate is his treatment of the thesis that Russia may be a form of state capitalism. He admits (and no educated marxist would dare to deny) the theoretical possibility of an economy in which the bourgeoisie as a whole constitutes itself into a stock company and by means of the state administers the whole national economy. "The economic laws of such a régime would present no mystery." Good. But then he proceeds to analyse the law of the average rate of profit which concerns the *distribution* of the surplus value among the capitalists. That is no problem. The relevant law is the law of the falling rate of profit. The problem is whether the national economy would be able to overcome the contradiction between the necessity of lessening and lowering the relative consumption of wage labour and at the same time accumulating sufficient surplus labour to continue the increase of expansion. Today, 1946, it is no longer a theoretical problem.

In a society of alienated labour, that is to say, in a society of such low productivity as compels the antagonisms of alienation, the idea of a planned economy is a fiction. The Soviet state undoubtedly was the first to distribute capital to those spheres of production which expansion especially required. In so doing it led the world. But today, 1946, isn't it perfectly obvious that no capitalist society distributes capital any longer according to the sphere of greater profit? Planning is merely a form of rationalisation. Monopoly capitalism was progressive in relation to individual capitalism. But it grew out of the contradictions of individual capitalism. It was a capitalistic method of attempting to solve those contradictions and merely sharpened them. In the same way planning today, without the emancipation of labour, arises out of the contradictions of monopoly capitalism and, like all rationalisation, is a more highly developed and refined form of exploitation, not lessening but increasing unbearably all antagonisms. How is it possible to plan socially when society is torn as it is by alienated labour and all the economic, political and social contradictions flowing from it? When Marx says that production by "freely associated men" will be "consciously regulated" by them in accordance with "a settled plan" he means literally and precisely that. The plan is the *result* of the freedom of individuals in society. No plan of bureaucrats, class or caste, can create anything else but chaos and crisis. As long as a section of society other than the proletariat controls the surplus labour, the plan can become the greatest calamity that can befall human society.

Trotsky once asked Shachtman, "Does Shachtman wish to say in relation to the USSR that the state ownership of the means of production has become a brake upon development and that the extension of this form of property to other countries constitutes economic reaction?" (*In Defence of Marxism*). This writer replies unhesitatingly "Yes." "*In relation to the USSR,*" in 1940 and in 1946, state ownership in the Soviet zone in Germany, in Poland, in Yugoslavia, and wherever else it is instituted, is reactionary in all aspects, economic and otherwise. There is no economic progressiveness in totalitarianism. The complete degradation of labour cannot be in any circumstances progressive. It cannot raise the productivity of labour, the fundamental criterion, except by the old method of pressure. And it is precisely because class society cannot do otherwise that all state ownership will end either in totalitarianism or social revolution.

This false conception of "plan" permeates the thought of Trotsky, but particularly in his later years. In 1938 he wrote "the disintegration of capitalism has reached extreme limits, likewise the disintegration of the old ruling class. The further existence of this system is impossible. The productive forces must be organized in accordance with a plan" (*In Defence of Marxism*). The formulation is characteristic and characteristically false. Once the question is posed that way, of necessity the second question then arises "Who will accomplish this task—the proletariat or a new ruling class of 'commissars.'" . . . But the problem is not to organise the productive forces "in accordance with a plan". The problem is to abolish the proletariat as proletariat and release the creative energies of hundreds of millions of men suppressed by capitalism. Released from capitalist degradation they can plan. The guiding party, the administration or superintendence, the state, must be the *expression* of the free producers. These cannot be the expression of the need for the productive forces to be organised in accordance with a plan. The proletariat is the most important part of the productive forces. To say that these must be organised in accordance with a plan merely makes the proletariat part of the plan. On the contrary, the plan is a part of the proletariat, but of the proletariat emancipated.

Trotsky understood as few men have ever done the creative power of the proletariat in revolution. But the full, the complete significance of the creative power of the proletariat in the construction of the socialist economy always eluded him. In the trade-union dispute, crucial for any understanding of Russian developments, Lenin told Trotsky: "Comrade Trotsky's fundamental mistake lies precisely in that he approaches . . . the very questions he himself raised, as an administrator." He told him again: "It is wrong to look only to the elect persons, only to the organisers, administrators, etc. These, after all, are only a minority of prominent people. We must look to the rank and file, to the masses" (*Selected Works,* vol. IX, pp. 3–80). Fifteen years after, the same error which Lenin attacked so fiercely and to which he referred in his testament, appears almost unchanged in *The Revolution Betrayed*. The approach is in essence administrative. For many years Trotsky led a profound and brilliant opposition to the stalinist bureaucracy despite his fundamentally false theoretical orientation. But a false theory always takes its toll in the end. It is taking toll of our movement today. Finally a word to those who think that this conception of the role of the proletariat belongs to some distant future after the god-bureaucrats have organised production "in accordance with a plan" and raised the level of the masses. It is necessary to refer these vulgar materialists and sceptics to Trotsky himself, who quotes and wholeheartedly approves Lenin's statement that the masses must *begin* to institute the new regime *on the day after the revolution*. That they will do, but they will need leaders and *the leaders must begin with the concepts of the new régime clearly in mind*.

1946

6

Dialectical Materialism and the Fate of Humanity

[*This was first published as a pamphlet in September 1947 under the pseudonym of "J. R. Johnson". James says of it, "This was the result of some years of study in the attempt to find out in what way we differed fundamentally from Trotsky's marxism. We felt originally that if we disagreed with Trotsky on whether the Soviet Union should be defended or not, it was not merely a question of defence; it was a question of the philosophy and the social ideas of marxism that would lead to such differences." It was to be followed in 1948 by the full-length study,* Notes on Dialectics.]

Mankind has obviously reached the end of something. The crisis is absolute. Bourgeois civilisation is falling apart, and even while it collapses, devotes its main energies to the preparation of further holocausts. Not remote states on the periphery but régimes contending for world power achieve the most advanced stages of barbarism known to history. What civilised states have ever approached nazi Germany and stalinist Russia in official lies, official murder and the systematic brutalisation and corruption of their populations? Only a shallow empiricism can fail to see that such monstrous societies are not the product of a national peculiarity (the German character) or a system of government ("communism") but are part and parcel of our civilisation. Everything that has appeared in these monstrous societies is endemic in every contemporary nation. Millions in the United States know that nazi Germany and stalinist Russia will have nothing to teach the American bourgeoisie when it finds itself threatened by the revolutionary American workers seeking the complete expression of democracy which is socialism. The dream of progress has become the fear of progress. Men shrink with terror at the hint of scientific discoveries. If it were known tomorrow that the crown of human technical achievement, the processes of manufacturing atomic energy, had been lost beyond recovery, this scientific disaster would be hailed as the greatest good fortune of decades.

But the seal of the bankruptcy of bourgeois civilisation is the bankruptcy of its thought. Its intellectuals run to and fro squealing like hens in a barnyard when a plane passes overhead. Not a single philosopher or publicist has any light to throw on a crisis in which the fate not of a civilisation but of civilisation itself is involved. The Keynesian theories are now part of the history of economics. The ridiculous "four freedoms" of the late President Roosevelt take their place with the Three Principles of Sun Yat-sen (the father-in-law of Chiang Kai-shek), the thousand years of Hitler's Reich and the "socialism in a single country" of Stalin. The chattering of Sidney Hook and Harold Laski is stunned into silence by the immensity of their own inadequacies. Thought has abdicated. The world is rudderless. All illusions have been destroyed. "Man is at last compelled to face with sober sense his real conditions of life, and his relations with his kind." And in face of this the bourgeoisie has nothing to say.

The method of thinking is rooted in society. Bourgeois thought has collapsed because bourgeois society has collapsed. We have learnt by hard necessity the truth of the following dictum of Trotsky: "Hegel in his *Logic* established a series of laws: change of quantity into quality, development through contradictions, conflict of content and form, interruption of continuity, change of possibility into inevitability, etc., which are just as important for theoretical thought as is the simple syllogism for more elementary tasks." [Trotsky, *In Defence of Marxism*.]

Hegel defines the principle of Contradiction as follows: "Contradiction is the root of all movement and life, and it is only in so far as it contains a contradiction that anything moves and has impulse and activity." [*Science of Logic*, translated by Johnson and Struthers, volume 2, page 67.] The first thing to note is that Hegel makes little attempt to prove this. A few lines later he says: "With regard to the assertion that contradiction does not exist, that it is non-existent, we may disregard this statement."

We here meet one of the most important principles of the dialectical logic, and one that has been consistently misunderstood, vilified or lied about. Dialectic for Hegel was a strictly scientific method. He might speak of inevitable laws, but he insists from the beginning that the proof of dialectic as scientific method is that the laws prove their correspondence with reality. Marx's dialectic is of the same character. Thus he excluded what later became *The Critique of Political Economy* from *Capital* because it took for granted what only the detailed argument and logical development of *Capital* itself could prove. Still more specifically, in his famous letter to Kugelmann on the theory of value, he ridiculed the idea of having to "prove" the labour theory of value. If the labour theory of value proved to be the means whereby the real relations of bourgeois society could be demonstrated in their movement, where they came from, what they were, and where they were going, that was the proof of the theory. Neither Hegel nor Marx understood any other scientific proof. To ask for some proof of the laws, as Burnham implied, or to prove them "wrong" as Sidney Hook tried to do, this is to misconceive dialectical logic entirely. Hegel complicated the question by his search for a completely closed system embracing all aspects of the universe; this no marxist ever did. The frantic shrieks that Marx's dialectic is some sort of religion or teleological construction, proving inevitably the victory of socialism, spring usually from men who are frantically defending the inevitability of bourgeois democracy against the proletarian revolution.

So convinced a marxist as Trotsky reminded the revolutionaries in 1939 that marxists were not fatalists. "If", said he, "the international proletariat, as a result of the experience of our entire epoch and the current new war, proves incapable of becoming the master of society, this would signify the foundering of all hope for a socialist revolution, for it is impossible to expect any other more favourable conditions for it." The Marxian expectation of socialism arising from the contradictions of capitalism would have proved itself to be utopia.

The law of contradiction is what for the moment we can call a "hypothesis" for the grouping of empirical facts. All men use hypotheses for the grouping of facts. That is what logic consists of. The bourgeois hypotheses are for the most part unconscious. They are the inevitability of bourgeois society, natural division of labour, more particularly of men into capitalists and workers, constantly expanding technical progress, constantly expanding production, constantly expanding democracy, constantly rising culture. But during the last thirty years, these have crumbled to dust in their hands. They have no hypotheses they can believe in and that is why they cannot think. Historical facts, large and small, continuously deliver shattering blows at the foundation of their logical system. Nothing remains for them but the logic of the machine gun, and the crude empiricism of police violence.

Quite different is the mode of thought of marxism. It understands its own logical laws. For marxists, the fundamental logical law is the contradictory nature of all phenomena and first of all human society. The dialectic teaches that in all forms of society we have known, the increasing development of material wealth brings with it the increasing degradation of the large mass of humanity. Capitalism, being the greatest wealth-producing system so far known, has carried his contradiction to a pitch never before known. Thus it is that the moment when the world system of capitalism has demonstrated the greatest productive powers in history is exactly the period when barbarism threatens to engulf the whole of society. The anti-dialecticians stand absolutely dumbfounded before the spectacle of the mastery of nature for human advancement and the degradation of human nature by this very mastery. The greater the means of transport, the less men are allowed to travel. The greater the means of communication, the less men freely interchange ideas. The greater the possibilities of living, the more men live in terror of mass annihilation. The bourgeoisie cannot admit this, for to admit it is themselves to sanction the end of the bourgeois civilisation. Hence the complete paralysis of bourgeois thought. Yet never was thought of a fundamental character so necessary to mankind. As our political tendency has recently written,

It is precisely the character of our age and the maturity of humanity that obliterates the opposition between theory and practice, between the intellectual preoccupations of the "educated" and of the masses. All the great philosophical concepts, from the nature of the physical universe (atomic energy) through the structure and function of productive systems (free enterprise, "socialism", or "communism"), the nature of government (the state versus the individual), to the destiny of man (can mankind survive?), these are no longer "theory", but are in the market-place, tied together so that they cannot be separated, matters on which the daily lives of millions upon millions depend. [*The Invading Socialist Society*]

Never were such universal questions asked by the whole of the civilised world. Never have such inadequate answers been given. All that the bourgeoisie can answer is the purely technical question of the manufacture of atomic energy, and it wishes that it could not.

Now it is precisely because this contradiction of society has reached its farthest point in stalinist Russia that the dialectical materialist analysis of Russia is the most important key to the perspectives of world civilisation.

The second law of dialectical materialism is the change of quantity into quality. At a certain stage a developing contradiction, so to speak, explodes, and both the elements of contradiction are thereby altered. In the history of society these explosions are known as revolution. All the economic, social and political tendencies of the age find a point of completion which becomes the starting-point of new tendencies. The Russian revolution is one such explosion. But the examination of the Russian revolution involves both the laws of development through contradictions and the change of quantity into quality.

Let us examine the Russian revolution in some of its most important features, such as would be agreed upon by most observers, excepting the diehard reactionaries.

The revolution was the greatest outburst of social energy and creativity that we have yet seen. Previously the French revolution had astonished mankind by the rapidity and grandeur of its achievements. So much so that to this day 14 July 1789 is the date in all probability most widely known among the great majority of mankind. But the Russian revolution exceeded the French. A combination of workers and peasants, the lowest classes of mankind, tore up an established government by the roots and accomplished the greatest social overturn in history. Starting from nothing, they created a new state, created an army of millions, defended the new régime against famine, blockade and wars of intervention on all fronts. They reorganised the economy. They made Russia a modern state. They passed and tried honestly to carry out a series of laws on popular education, equality of women, repudiation of religious superstition, sexual sanity, workers' control of production, all of which constituted the greatest potential democracy and enlightenment that the world had ever seen. They organised a world-wide Communist International devoted to the achievement of the same ideals in the entire world. The gradual decline and final failure are treated in the text. But the accomplishments are history, imperishable and of permanent significance for mankind. Taken in its entirety the heroic period of the Russian revolution is the most glorious episode in human history.

Lenin, the leader of the revolution, claimed always that one of the greatest achievements was the establishment of a new type of democracy, the Soviets of Workers', Soldiers' and Peasants' Deputies, which was able to unloose the creative energies of the great masses of the people. Their mere administration of the state in his opinion would make the further existence of capitalism impossible. This administration by the masses is "*not yet*" socialism, but it is no longer capitalism. "It is a tremendous *step* towards socialism, a step from which, if complete democracy is retained, no backward step towards capitalism would be possible without the most atrocious violence perpetrated upon the masses". [*The Threatening Catastrophe*]

Capital, in the form of state capital, once more rules in Russia. Democracy has not been retained. But this has been done only at the cost of the condition foreseen by Lenin. The most atrocious violence has been perpetrated upon the masses of the people. Thus, the Russian revolution, as it has developed and declined, shows us the two most violent extremes that we have known in history. It is only dialectical materialism that can unite these extremes in logical and intelligible connection. It is the creative power, the democratic desires, the expansion of human personality, the record of achievement that was the Russian revolution, it is these which have called forth the violence, the atrocities, the state organised as Murder Incorporated. Only such violence could have repressed such democracy.

One can see the glint in the eye of the enemy of the proletarian revolution. Without perspective, himself, intellectually helpless before the contemporary barbarism, indulging in nonsensical opposites like Yogis and Commissars, or searching diligently in his own writhing insides for the solution to the problems of the world, he hastens to use the *fact* of the Russian degeneration as an unanswerable argument against the ideas of Bolshevism. Patience, my friend, patience. "Bolshevism", says Trotsky, "is above all a philosophy of history and a political conception." Without the philosophy, the political conception falls to the ground. We have to get to the philosophy step by step. We have arrived at this much. The atrocious violence and crimes which now distinguish the state of Stalin are the necessary and inevitable response to the revolutionary fervour and democratic organisation and expression of the Russian people. Not the Russian people in general, however, but the Russian people as they had developed and expressed themselves in the socialist revolution of 1917. This is not merely a Russian phenomenon. The Russian revolution is a climax to a series of revolutions which have moved according to certain laws. Briefly: The British revolution in the seventeenth century embraced only small sections of the population—some revolutionary bourgeois, petty-bourgeois farmers and yeomen and a small number of artisans and others in the few and small towns. They could not create the new but they could destroy the old. The work of the revolution having been accomplished the counter-revolution, heir to the *new* social order, established itself by a mere invitation to Charles II to return. A handful of people only were punished. With the development of economy and its socialisation, i.e. the increasing inter-relation of all classes in production, the French revolution embraces the great mass of the nation. The revolution destroys feudalism and establishes the modern state. Its basic work accomplished, "order" must be restored to society by the counter-revolution, the heirs to the new régime, but this time there are millions of aroused people. It is the great body of the nation which is to be disciplined. No mild return of royalty, no forgiveness, no mutual amnesty. Only the military police-dictatorship of Napoleon can hold this country down. The contradiction between the revolution and the counter-revolution has sharpened.

Society established itself on new foundations. But the contradiction between the classes grows. If the revolution in Russia was the broadest and deepest development of the revolution of the seventeenth century, the stalinist régime is the similar development of the counter-revoltuion. The German revolution of 1918 did not overthrow bourgeois property. But the German proletariat, infinitely larger and more highly developed than the Russian, had a long history of democratic achievement and organisation behind it. After the revolution, its organisation continued and expanded. That is why the Nazi counter-revolution was as brutal as it was. But if the German proletariat in 1918 had established a Soviet state embracing workers, agricultural proletarians and semi-proletarians, the lower ranks of the petty-bourgeoisie and the sympathetic intelligentsia, then logically speaking, one of two things would have happened. Either the new democratic formation would have gone on from strength to strength awakening the deepest reserves of social power and aspirations of the already highly-developed German people and spreading throughout Europe; either this or something else. The atrocities and the violence which would have been needed to supress a successful German proletarian revolution and the response it would have awakened in the German and other European peoples would have exceeded the crimes of Hitler as much as Hitler exceeded the crimes of Napoleon.

The pervading barbarism of the stalinist régime, therefore, is not to be attributed to this or that weakness in the theory of "communism", or some partial aspect of the stalinist state. Stage by stage, we have seen the revolution and the counter-revolution develop in Europe over the centuries. At each new stage of development, both the revolution and the counter-revolution assume a new quality with the new quality of the social development. Precisely because the Russian revolution assumed a new quality in attempting to establish a universal democracy, the Russian counter-revolution assumes a new quality of universal barbarism in the sense that it embraces all aspects of the Russian state.

At this stage, to try to separate progressive aspects from so comprehensive and all-pervading an enemy of human development as is the stalinist state, is to strike down the dialectical method at the root. Hegel understood the limits within which one could designate a corruption as partial.

> The Reformation resulted from the *corruption of the Church*. That corruption was not an accidental phenomenon; it is not the mere *abuse* of power and dominion. A corrupt state of things is very frequently represented as an "abuse"; it is taken for granted that the foundation was good—the system, the institution itself faultless—but that the passion, the subjective interest, in short the arbitrary volition of men has made use of that which in itself was good to further its own selfish ends, and that all that is required to be done is to remove these adventitious elements. On this showing the institute in question escapes obloquy, and the evil that disfigures it appears something foreign to it. But when accidental abuse of a good thing really occurs, it is limited to particularity. A great and general corruption affecting a body of such large and comprehensive scope as a Church, is quite another thing.—The corruption of the Church was a native growth. [*Philosophy of History*]

The Russian revolution is the completion of a historical process, the development of class society. Its relation to past revolution can be illuminated by the laws of changes of quantity into quality. The British revolution, although it pointed the road for the rest of Europe, was only to a subordinate degree of international significance. The French revolution shook the whole of Europe to its foundations and established the logical lines along which revolution and counter-revolution would struggle in Europe for the suceeding century. It is in the very nature of modern society and the Russian revolution, that Russia today is symbolical of the whole fate of modern civilisation. There is no further stage. Either the revolution succeeds in encompassing the whole of the world or the whole of the world collapses in counter-revolution and barbarism. The whole path of Western civilisation for two thousand years has reached an ultimate stage in Russia. There is no by-pass. There is no third alternative.

Therefore, as dialectical materialists, we do not bewail nor do we underestimate or in any way attempt to minimise the monstrous character of the stalinist régime. We repudiate utterly any idea that what is there has any socialist character whatever. But we draw from it for Russia itself and for the whole world an ultimate, a universal conclusion. The barbarism is not to come. It is there.

In our previously quoted pamphlet, we have written:

> The unending murders, the destruction of peoples, the bestial passions, the sadism, the cruelties and the lusts, all the manifestations of barbarism of the last thirty years are unparalleled in history. But this barbarism exists only because nothing else can suppress the readiness for sacrifice, the democratic instincts and creative power of the great masses of the people.

Those are the two forces in conflict. The philosophy of history which is Bolshevism bases itself upon the destruction of the barbarism by the inevitable triumph of the socialist revolution. There are even revolutionaries who deny this. For them it is not scientific to believe in inevitability. Such a belief implies that dialectic is a religion or mysticism. For them the correct scientific attitude is to reserve judgement. Yet these very ones turn out to be the mystics and the practitioners of an ill-concealed religiosity. If they recognise the bankruptcy of bourgeois democracy, if they accept the need for universality in the masses, if they recognise that barbarism is the only force that can suppress this need, then to refuse to accept the inevitability of socialism leaves only one of two choices. Either the inevitability of barbarism, that is to say, the acceptance of the principle of inevitability which they have just rejected or the hope, the faith, the belief that history will offer some way out of the impasse. This is the denial of a philosophy of history, that is to say, the denial of a method of thought, for which the only name is irrationalism or mysticism.

The deniers of the inevitability of socialism can be routed both historically and logically.

Marx developed his philosophical doctrines in the years which preceded the 1848 revolutions. The revolution was obviously on the way. Yet society was dominated by the experience of the great French revolution which had achieved such miracles but had failed to achieve universality (liberty, equality and fraternity), and despite all its sacrifices and bloodshed, had ended in the triumph of the counter-revolution. The experience of 1830 had only multiplied both the fears and the hopes which had been engendered by the colossal experience of the French revolution. In this period, so similar to ours, philosophy came out of the study, particularly in Germany, and attempted to give some answers to the problems that were shaking society.

The utopian socialists of all stripes were distinguished precisely by this, that they argued interminably about the possibility as opposed to the inevitability of the socialist revolution. They were tortured by these doubts because, after the experience of the French revolution and its obvious failure to relieve the conditions of the great masses of the people, they themselves had lost faith in the inevitability of socialism. Which is only another way of saying the inevitability of the achievement by the people of complete self-expression, complete democracy, socialism. In so far as their beliefs were the result of theoretical speculation, they had, in the words of Marx lost the capacity to draw from the experience of man's past in order to establish perspectives for man's future.

The result was a complete chaos, disorder, confusion in their own thoughts with an absolute inability to meet the challenge of the approaching revolution. It was into this ulcer that Marx drove the knife of scientific socialism. Bolshevism is a philosophy of history. Marx first clarified himself philosophically. As he wrote to Ruge in 1843:

> Almost greater than the outer obstacles appear the inner difficulties. For although there is no doubt about the "whence", there prevails the more confusion about the "whither". Not only has a general anarchy broken out among the reformers; each of them also must himself confess that he has no exact conception of what ought to be. Precisely in this is the advantage of the new movement, that we do not anticipate the new world dogmatically but intend to find the new in the criticism of the old world. Up to now the philosophers have had the solution of all riddles lying in their desks and the dumb exoteric world had only to gape in order for the ready-baked pies of wisdom to fly into their mouths. Philosophy has become worldly, and the most decisive proof of this is that philosophic consciousness has been drawn into the anguish of the struggle not only superficially but thoroughly.
>
> If the construction of the future and the preparation for all time is not our affair, it is all the more certain what we have to complete at present, i.e. the most relentless criticism of all existing things, relentless both in the sense that the criticism fears no results and even less fears conflicts with the existing powers.

We face the same situation today in the radical and revolutionary movement. In 1947, however, not only is philosophy worldly. In the face of the universal character of the crisis, the world is driven to become philosophical. It is compelled to examine in their nature and in the totality of their relations (that is to say, philosophically), economics, politics, science and even the very nature of the universe and society. All agitation about the possibility of barbarism, third alternatives, the mysticism of the inevitability of socialism, these are no more than what they were in Marx's day, only infinitely more so: terror before the destructive contradictions of modern society, doubts of the capacity of the proletariat to resolve them. This amounts to no more than a defence of bourgeois society in so far as bourgeois society still can provide thinkers with freedom enough to substitute the analysis of their own thoughts for a positive intervention in the chaos of society.

So far historically. Logically, the inevitability of socialism is the absolute reverse of religion or mysticism. It is a consciously constructed necessity of thought. As we have quoted in the article on Historical Retrogression, Hegel recognised that without holding fast in thought to your ultimate goal, it is impossible to think properly.

> To hold fast the positive in its negative, and the content of the presupposition in the result, is the most important part of rational cognition: also only the simplest reflection is needed to furnish conviction of the absolute truth and necessity of this requirement, while with regard to the examples of proofs, the whole of Logic consists of these. [*Logic*, vol. II, p. 476]

Precisely because they held fast to the presupposition of the inevitability of bourgeois society, the bourgeois thinkers in the early days of capitalism made their tremendous contributions to the science of human thought. Even without philosophical perspective, the bourgeoisie at least has one reality, maintenance of power against the workers and rival bourgeoisies. But without presupposing the inevitability of socialism, that is to say, without thinking always in terms of the victory of the masses, thinking among those hostile to bourgeois society must become a form of scholasticism and gnosticism, self-agitation and caprice.

Over a hundred years ago, Hegel said that the simplest reflection will show the necessity of holding fast the positive in the negative, the presupposition in the result, the affirmation that is contained in every negation, the future that is in the present. It is one of the signs of the advanced stage of human development that this is no longer a mere philosophical but a concrete question. To anyone that does not accept bourgeois society, the simplest reflection shows that it is impossible not only to think but to take any kind of sustained positive action in the world today unless one postulates the complete victory of the great masses of the people. What is this but the exemplification in life of the logical theory, the inevitability of socialism?

The stalinist state, the Nazi state, and in their varying degrees all states today, based upon property and privilege, are the negation of the complete democracy of the people. It is this state which is to be destroyed, that is to say, it is this state which is to be negated by the proletarian revolution. Thus, the inevitability of socialism is the inevitability of the negation of the negation, the third and most important law of the dialectic.

I have said earlier that the laws of dialectic are "hypotheses". Any Deweyite pragmatist who is rubbing his hands with joy at this "reasonable" marxism is in for rude disillusionment. "Dialectics", said Lenin, "is the theory of knowledge of (Hegel and) marxism." So far I have been dealing with it as a theory of knowledge, as a mode of thought, examining more or less empirically contemporary society and the Russian revolution, and showing how by means of the dialectical approach, some order, some perspective, some understanding come out of them, showing equally why the bourgeoisie can make no sense of anything except to hold on to power.

But Marx's hypotheses were not hypotheses in general. They were not empirically arrived at, tentatively used, discarded if not satisfactory, experimental or instrumentalist. They were logical abstractions organised according to the *method* of Hegel and reflecting *the movement of human society*. This is no simple matter. But it has remained obscured and neglected too long.

The dialectic is a theory of knowledge, but precisely for that reason, it is a theory of the nature of man. Hegel and marxism did not first arrive at a theory of knowledge which they applied to nature and society. They arrived at a theory of knowledge from their examination of men in society. Their first question was: What is man? What is the *truth* about him? Where has he come from and where is he going? They answered that question first because they knew that without any answer to that general question, they could not think about particular questions.

Both Hegel and Marx in their different ways believed that man is destined for freedom and happiness. *They* did not wish this (or they did, that does not matter). They came to this conclusion by examining man's history as a totality. Man for Marx was not Christian man nor the man of the French revolution (nor Stalin's bloodstained secret police). The concept of man was a constantly developing idea which was headed for some sort of completeness. When Marx said that with the achievement of the socialist revolution the "real" history of humanity will begin, he was not being rhetorical or inspiring (or optimistic). He was being strictly and soberly scientific.

> The truth is the whole. The whole, however, is merely the essential nature reaching its completeness through the process of its own development. Of the Absolute it must be said that it is essentially a result, that only at the end is it what it is in very truth.

Thus Hegel in the *Phenomenology of Mind*; Marx worked on the same principles. The essential nature of man was becoming clear only as it approached its completeness in bourgeois society. It is in bourgeois society that we could see what man really is. And it is "only at the end" of bourgeois society that we can see what man is in very truth. Thus it is in the contemporary barbariem that can be seen most clearly what is the "real" nature of humanity. The need and desire for socialism, for complete democracy, for complete freedom, that is the "real" nature of man. It is this which explains his past. But it could be expressed within the concrete circumstances of past ages only to the degree that objective circumstances allowed. Did man, therefore, suffer through all those centuries to produce completed man? The defenders of bourgeois society are ready to defend and rage over all these unjustified sufferings of past mankind in their die-hard opposition to the proletarian revolution which will relieve present mankind. They will get nothing to comfort themselves with. "The truth is the whole." All the varous stages constitute the nature of man. Continues Hegel: "And just in that consists its nature, which is to be actual, subject or self-becoming, self-development." Man is the subject, that which is developing itself. The subject becomes more and more real, and therefore truth about man becomes deeper and wider, more universal, more complex, moe concrete. Complete universality, complete democracy in the sense that every man is able to do what every other man does, this is the ultimate stage. The Russian revolution was an imperfect, limited, handicapped but nevertheless decisive step in this direction. The nature of man, therefore, becomes the search for this completeness and the overcoming of the obstacles which stood and stand in its way. Past history therefore becomes intelligible and what is more important, the road to the solution of the overwhelming problems to the present day becomes open.

If today we say that now we know what is the "real" man, it is because we see him as a totality, as the result of his whole past. But from there we make another step. The terrible crisis of civilisation is the result of the fact that man is at last real, he has become himself, completely developed. But the old type of world which developed him cannot contain him. He must burst through it. That world was a world in which he was subjected to nature. It was in the subjection of nature that he fully realised himself, a continuous negation of the obstacles which impeded his development. That being accomplished, his real history will begin. He negates all that has previously impeded him, i.e. negated him, in the full realisation of his inherent nature. Socialism is the negation of all previous negations. It is obvious that these are large conceptions. But the death of a world civilisation is not a small thing.

The conception being stated, it is now necessary not to prove it (only life can do that) but to show where it came from.

Western civilisation, and therefore, the Hegelian dialectic

begins with Christianity.* It was Christianity which established
universality in its most abstract form, that very universality
which we are now seeing concretely striving for expression in the
proletariat all over the contemporary world. The very early or
"primitive" Christians attempted a universality that was extremely concrete, commonalty of goods and absolute equality.
But it soon collapsed. The abstract universality was established
by that historical Christianity which superseded the Roman
Empire. Christianity united all men, before birth, in the
universality of original sin, and after death, in the possibility of
universal redemption in heaven. Thus it carefully avoided a
concrete universality. It was the religion of the millions who had
been released from slavery by the collapse of the Roman Empire. The narrow straitened circumstances of their material lives
were compensated for by the subjective conception of an after-
life in which all their material needs would be satisfied or, better
still, there would be no need for material satisfactions at all.
But, extreme abstraction though it was, man is for the first time
established as universal man. Hegel expresses this idea in all its
fullness in the *Philosophy of History*:

> Man, finite when regarded *for himself*, is yet at the same time the
> Image of God and a fountain of infinity *in himself*. He is the object
> of his own existence—has in himself an infinite value, an external
> destiny. Consequently, he has his true home in a supersensuous
> world—an infinte subjectivity, gained only by a rupture with mere
> natural existence and violation, and by his labour to break their
> power from within. . . .
> These conditions are not yet a concrete order, but simply the first
> abstract principles, which are won by the instrumentality of the
> Christian religion for the secular state. First, under Christianity
> slavery is impossible; for man as man—in the abstract essence of his
> nature—is contemplated in God; each unit of mankind is an object
> of the grace of God and of the Divine purpose; "God will have *all*
> men to be saved." Utterly excluding all speciality, therefore, man,
> in and for himself—in his simple quality of man—has infinite value;

---

*Dialectic as a mode of thought had its origin among the Greek philosophers. In
fact, the more one penetrates into dialectics, the more one is astonished at the
colossal impudence and ignorance which passes for exposure of it. Lenin was
very conscious of its historic significance. As he wrote in 1915: "The division of
the one and the cognition of its contradictory parts (see the quotation from Philo
on Heraclitus at the beginning of Part III, 'Knowledge', in Lassalle's book on
Heraclitus) is the *essence* (one of the 'essentials', one of the principal, if not the
principal, characteristics or features) of dialectics. This is precisely how Hegel
also puts the matter (Aristotle in his *Metaphysics* continually grapples with it and
combats Heraclitus and Heraclitan ideas)." But although Hegel learnt more
about dialectic from Aristotle than from any other single philosopher, he himself
accepts Christianity as the starting-point of our civilisation.

and this infinite value abolishes, *ipso facto*, all particularity attaching to birth or country.

This is what Hegel calls an abstract universal. The history of humanity is no more than this abstract universal becoming concrete. International socialism is the concrete embodiment of the abstract principle of Christianity. And Christianity appeared and international socialism is now appearing because they are of the very nature of man. To call the recognition of this teleology and religion is a sign of the greatest ignorance, or, is not ignorance, a determination at all costs to defend bourgeois society against the philosophy of Bolshevism today so as not to have to defend it against the revolutionary masses tomorrow. To have been Christian and to be socialist is an expression of the need for concrete universality which is not so much *in* as *of* the very nature of man. And dialectic bases itself upon this precisely because it is not religious and not teleological. If this, scientifically speaking, is not the nature of man, then what do the opponents of dialetic offer instead? Either man has expressed these desires and these aims by accident, i.e. they have no significance whatever, for he might have expressed entirely different aims and had entirely different needs, and may do so tomorrow. Or these needs and aims are not the nature of man but came from some outside agency or God.

It is only in the sense described above that dialectic speaks of freedom and happiness being the purpose of man's existence. Purpose, not in the religious sense, but in the sense that if we examine man's history through the centuries he has sought these aims. It is difficult therefore to say what other purpose his existence has, and the anti-dialectician is left with the alternative that man's life has no purpose at all, which is only another way of accommodating one's self to the existing society, bourgeois society.

The logical principle of universality contains within it a logical contradiction, the contradiction of abstract and concrete. This logical contradiction is a direct reflection of the objective circumstances in which the men of early Christianity lived. Their physical and material circumstances were on the lowest possible level. And therefore, to make their existence a totality, they had to fill it out with this tremendous abstraction. Thus is established the basic logical contradiction in the universal between concrete and abstract, between objective and subjective, between real and ideal, between content and form. But both together form a whole and have no meaning apart from each other. They are opposites but interpenetrated. To Christian man, the conception of heaven was *real* and *necessary*, an integral part of his existence in the objective world. Those who accuse dialectics of being a religion understand neither dialectics nor religion.

The history of man is his effort to make the abstract universal concrete. He constantly seeks to destroy, to move aside, that is to say, to negate what impedes his movement towards freedom and happiness. Man is the subject of history "(The) subject, (man) is pure and simple negativity." This is a cardinal principle of the dialectical movement. The process is molecular, day by day, never resting, continuous. But at a certain stage, the continuity is interrupted. The molecular changes achieve a universality and explode into a new quality, a revolutionary change.

Previous to the revolutionary explosion, the aims of the struggle can be posed in partial terms, *possibility*. It is the impossibility of continuing to do this that interrupts the continuity.

The revolution, precisely because it is a revolution, demands all things for all men. It is an attempt to *leap* from the realm of objective necessity to the realm of objective freedom.

But in the limited objective circumstances to which the low level of productivity has confined society, what is demanded by, of and for all men, only some men can have. The concrete universality, therefore, becomes the property of some men, a class. They are therefore compelled to use objective violence against those excluded *and to substitute an abstract universality for the concrete universality of which the mass has been deprived*. But the absence of concrete universality from the whole also limits the universality of the few. Their own concrete universality therefore begins to be limited and its limitations substituted for by abstractions. This is the Hegelian process of "mediation". The new state established after the revolution, the ideology which accompanies it, are a form of mediation between abstract and concrete, ideal and real, etc.

The mediation usually assumes the form of the state power, and the specific ideological combinations of abstract and concrete to bind the new relations are developed by the philosophy of the age. A new equilibrium in the process of the development of man has been established. At a later stage, the same developing process will be repeated in the attempt to negate the actual stage of man previously established. There will be the mass revolution for undifferentiated universality, the class differentiation in its realisation, the splitting of the nation into opposing factors, and the attempt to realise in ideology the reconciliation of the opposing factors. Man is not only what he does but what he thinks and what he aims at. But this can only be judged by the concrete, what actually takes place. The truth is always concrete. But it is the concrete viewed in the light of the whole. In the decisive page of the preface to the *Phenomenology*, Hegel writes:

As subject it is pure and simple negativity, and just on that account a process of splitting up what is simple and undifferentiated, a process of duplicating and setting factors in opposition, which (process) in turn is the negation of this indifferent diversity and of the opposition of factors it entails . . . It is the process of its own becoming, the circle which presupposes its end as its purpose, and has its end for its beginning, it becomes concrete and actual only by being carried out, and by the end it involves.

Marx is expressing concretely just this concentrated Hegelian generalisation when he says:

For each new class which puts itself in the place of one ruling before it is compelled, merely in order to carry through its aim, to represent its interest as the common interest of all the members of society, put in an ideal form, it will give its ideas the form of universality and represent them as the only rational, universally valid ones. The class making a revolution appears from the very start, merely because it is opposed to a *class*, not as a class but as the representative of the whole society; it appears as the whole mass of society confronting the one ruling class. It can do this because, to start with, its interest really is more connected with the common interest of all other non-ruling classes, because under the pressure of conditions its interest has not yet been able to develop as the particular interest of a particular class. Its victory, therefore, benefits also many individuals of other classes which are not winning a dominant position, but only in so far as it now puts these individuals in a position to raise themselves into the ruling class. . . . Every new class, therefore, achieves its hegemony only on a broader basis than that of the class ruling previously, in return for which the opposition of the non ruling class against the new ruling class later develops all the more sharply and profoundly. Both these things determine the fact that the struggle to be waged against this new ruling class, in its turn, aims at a more decided and radical negation of the previous conditions of society than could all previous classes which sought to rule.

This organisation of historical development did not fall from the sky. It is the result of the concept of the dialectic worked out by Hegel and without the dialectic it could not be done at all. It is this Hegel that Burnham calls the "arch-muddler" of human thought. It is from the examination of this process, the developing conflicts between abstract and concrete, subjective and objective, the abstract universal assuming a certain content which becomes concentrated in a special form, the form gradually becoming infused with a new content until it can contain it no longer and explodes, it is from the examination of all this in society and nature but particularly in its ideological reflection in philosophy that Hegel works out the significance of categories and the movement of his *Logic*. Just as Marx's economic categories were in reality social categories, just in the same way the logical categories, contradictions, etc., of Hegel were a reflection of social categories and social movement. Hegel, and for very good reasons of his time, led his *Logic* into an impossible and fantastic idealism about world-spirit, etc. But the basis of his work was solidly materialistic. He himself explains that:

> The community of principle which *really* links together individuals of the same class and in virtue of which they are similarly related to other existences, assumes a *form* in human consciousness; and that form is the thought or idea which summarily comprehends the constituents of generic character. Every universal in thought has a corresponding generic principle in Reality, to which it gives intellectual expression or *form*. [*The Philosophy of History*]

Marx and Engels knew this. They could carry over the Hegelian dialectic into a materialistic form because it had been derived originally not from religion but from a study of the stages of man in nature and society and the reflection of these stages in human thought. The dialectic of negativity, the negation of the negation, the inevitability of socialism are a culmination in logical thought of social processes that have now culminated in contemporary society. You look in vain in writings of Hook, Professor of Philosophy at New York University and Burnham, a member of the same faculty, for the slightest understanding of this.

The beginning of this process for the modern world is Christianity and the beginning "presupposes its end as its purpose." For Hegel, these stages are the work of the universal spirit. Marx here is his diametrical opposite. Marx is a dialectical *materialist*. For him, and right from the very start, *these concrete revolutionary stages are the work of the great masses of the people forever seeking the concretion of universality as the development of the productive forces creates the objective circumstances and the subjective desires which move them*.

Hegel could see the abstract universal, the relation between abstract and concrete in historical Christianity and the developing relation in human history. Marx saw that, but because he was closer to the end, he could see more of the "real" man. Because he had seen the revolutionary *proletariat*, he was able to complete the dialectical analysis of previous stages by the recognition of the role of the revolutionary *masses*. These appear at the very beginning of history.

In his introduction to *Class Struggles in France*, Engels writes:

> This party of revolt, of those known by the name of Christian, was also strongly represented in the army; whole legions were Christian. When they were ordered to attend the sacrificial ceremonies of the pagan established church, in order to do the honours there, the rebel soldiers had the audacity to stick peculiar emblems—crosses on their helmets in protest. Even the wonted barrack cruelties of their

superior officers were fruitless. The Emperor Diocletian could no longer quietly look on while order, obedience and discipline in his army were being undermined. He intervened energetically, while there was still time. He passed an anti-Socialist, I should say anti-Christian, law. The meetings of the rebels were forbidden, their meeting halls were closed or even pulled down, the Christian badges, crosses, etc., were, like the red handkerchiefs in Saxony, prohibited. Christians were declared incapable of holding offices in the state, they were not to be allowed even to become corporals. Since there were not available at that time judges so well trained in "respect of persons" as Herr von Koller's anti-revolt bill assumes, the Christians were forbidden out of hand to seek justice before a court. This exceptional law was also without effect. The Christians tore it down from the walls with scorn; they are even supposed to have burnt the Emperor's palace in Nicomedia over his head. Then the latter revenged himself by the great persecution of Christians in the year 303, according to our chronology. It was the last of its kind. And it was so effective that seventeen years later the army consisted overwhelmingly of Christians, and the succeeding autocrat of the whole Roman Empire, Constantine, called the Great by the priests, proclaimed Christianity as the state religion.

The Christian revolutionaries, however, were not struggling to establish the medieval papacy. The medieval papacy was a mediation to which the ruling forces of society rallied in order to strangle the quest for universality of the Christian masses. In one sense the papacy merely continued the Roman Imperium, and, in Hobbes's phrase, was indeed "no other than the ghost of the deceased Roman Empire sitting crowned upon the grave thereof".

But it was much more than that. Primitive Christianity had begun as a mass revolt that had sought to establish the community of men upon earth. By the time of Gregory the Great, when the papacy began to take over the functions of the declined and fallen Roman Empire, the papacy was beginning its career as a combination of the Empire *and the tremendous impact of the mass revolution*. It was the ghost of the Roman Empire *and* living symbol of Christ on Earth. Heaven was too abstract to satisfy completely the masses of the people. The Church guaranteed them, in return for obedience, the happy future life. But it also took care of the life on earth, and performed the functions of teacher, protector and provider for the poor and sick and needy. It mediated between society and heaven and between the secular rulers of society and the masses. It succoured the poor and was a centre of learning and the improvement of agriculture. In the method by which it was established, in its mediation, of contending classes and its manipulation of concrete and abstract, the medieval papacy, as the culmination of the Christian revolution, contains in embryo all the development to the modern age.

The dialectical *materialist method*, the product of a stage nearer to the end, is infinitely superior to Hegel's dialectic. Constantly, contemporary events throw a penetrating light into tte past and thereby illuminate the future. It is, for example, the concrete history of the last thirty years of proletarian revolutions that for the first time makes it possible to grasp fully the meaning of Renaissance. But the dialectical materialist study of the Renaissance drives the last nail in the coffin of those who hesitate before the conceptions of the negation of the negation, the inevitability of socialism and the dictatorship of the proletariat.

The leading ideological characteristic of the early Renaissance can be usefully designated by the popular term "humanism". The medieval towns produced a brilliant civilisation. With the growth of wealth, chiefly a result of commercial capitalism, there arise classes of men for whom the early Christian contradiction between objective and subjective, abstract and concrete, is no longer tenable. It is not merely a question of objective wealth. The idea of universality becomes more concrete because of the "energetic position which man is sensible of occupying in his subjective power over outward and material things in the natural world, in which he feels himself free and so gains for himself an absolute right" [Hegel, *Philosophy of History*].

The papacy is itself mediated. It became humanised, i.e. more completely secular, and thus took the road to its own ruin. St Thomas Aquinas had already begun the rationalisation of faith, making it reasonable by a brilliant and profound misuse of the writings of Aristotle. Dante, whom Engels calls one of the first modern men, though profoundly religious, wished to substitute Emperor for Pope. The national monarchy begins to substitute for the papal authority.

So far so good. But, and here the marxist dialectic sharply departs from the Hegelian, the new universal was established and took its form by such violent revolutions of the European proletariat as Europe did not see again until the period which opened in 1917. It is only recently that bourgeois historians have begun to recognise these. The historians of the socialist society will in time make of this one of the great chapters of human history.

As always in critical periods, there were a series of peasant revolutions in Europe throughout the fourteenth century. They were of tremendous range and power, some of them semisocialistic. But they were not decisive. The decisive revolutions were revolutions of the workers and the petty bourgeoisie of the towns. If the phrase had not already been appropriated by marxists for the revolution of the socialist proletariat, it would be perfectly correct to say that within the various municipalities the workers aimed at, consciously, and in some few cases actually achieved, the dictatorship of the proletariat.

In the last half of the fourteenth century, these revolutions swept from one end of Europe to another. In Salonika, the sailors and the artisans ruled the rich, the landowners, the commercial magnates and the clergy for ten years. In Italy, the struggle between the "fat" and the "thin". In Bologna, in Genoa, in Sienna, the masses sought to obtain absolute mastery of municipal power. In Florence, under the leadership of Michel Lando, they organised the celebrated revolt of the Ciompi and established the dictatorship of the proletariat whom they called "God's people". Rome and other towns saw similar battles. But it was in the Lowlands, in towns of Ghent, Ypres, and Bruges that the workers made the most desperate efforts to establish their own dictatorship. Revolutionary history badly needs a study of the incidents which centre around the van Artevelde family. Over and over again during a period of decades, the workers rose. More than once they established their dictatorship, they proclaimed an equality of fortunes and the suppression of all authority except the authority of people who live by manual labour. They repeatedly defeated the flower of feudal chivalry. It is reported that in Ghent, the workers went so far as to plan the complete extermination of the bourgeoisie and the nobles with the exception of children of six years of age. In the German towns of Cologne, Strasbourg, Aix-la-Chapelle, Lubeck, Stettin and many others, in Barcelona, Valencia, and other towns of Spain, the same desperate battles took place. The working class and its allies closest to it fought for fifty years all over Europe to establish proletarian democracy. Why they failed to achieve substantial successes was due not only to the low level of production but the fact that they fought only as members of isolated municipalities. Some of them indeed aimed boldly at an international proletarian revolution. But their time was not yet.

Let Boissonade, a bourgeois historian, speak in the concluding paragraph of his *Life and Work in Medieval Europe*. The reader should read carefully and note particularly the words we have underlined.

> For the first time the masses, ceasing to be mere herds without rights or thoughts of their own, became associations of freemen, proud of their independence, conscious of the value and dignity of their labour, *fitted by their intelligent activity to* collaborate in all spheres, political, economic, and social, in the *tasks which the aristocrats believed themselves alone able to fulfil*. Not only was the *power of production multiplied a hundredfold by their efforts*, but society was regenerated by the incessant influx of new and vigorous blood. Social selection was henceforth better assured. It was thanks to *the devotion and spirit of these medieval masses that the nations became conscious of themselves, for it was they who brought about the triumph of national patriotism*, just as their local patriotism had

burned for town or village in the past. The martyrdom of a peasant girl from the marshes of Lorraine saved the first of the great nations, France, which had become the most brilliant home of civilisation in the Middle Ages. *They gave to the modern states their first armies,* which were superior to those of feudal chivalry. *Above all, it was they who prepared the advent of democracy and bequeathed to the labouring masses the instruments of their power, the principles of freedom and of association.* Labour, of old despised and depreciated, became a *power of incomparable force in the world*, and its social value became increasingly recognised. It is from the Middle Ages that this capital evolution takes its date, and it is this which makes this period, so often misunderstood, and so full of a confused but singularly powerful activity, the *most important in the universal history of labour before the great changes witnessed by the eighteenth and nineteenth centuries.*

This was the working class five hundred years ago. They were not proletarians in the modern sense. They were, for the most part, free workers in the guilds. They did not function within the socialised organisation of modern labour. But note, Messrs anti-dialecticians and anti-marxists, that these workers, five hundred years ago, all over Europe, believed that they were "fitted by their intelligent activity to collaborate in all spheres, political, economic and social in the tasks which the aristocrats believed themselves alone able to fulfil". That is what the millions of proletarians all over the world today believe. They will fight for it. We believe they will succeed. You believe what? Their ancestors of five hundred years ago were not as developed as are the workers of today. But they fought for complete equality, for complete democracy, for universality. They failed, but they established the foundations of what we know as liberalism. Some of you still live on it, thin fare though it has become. The bourgeoisie had the feudal lords, in terror of these workers, rallied behind the absolute monarchy and the national state. Both humanism and the national state of the absolute monarchy were mediations of the mass proletarian desire for universality no longer in heaven but on earth. Humanism was the substitution of a liberal culture for the rich in place of the complete self-expression desired by the workers; the national state, disciplining the church, supplemented the concrete objective protection of wealth by abstract subjective claims of being the arbiter of justice, the guardian of law and order, and the protector of all the people. The contradictions, the antagonisms in the quest for universality had grown sharper than ever.

So, Messrs doubters and sceptics and sneerers at dialectic, you will begin to see perhaps that what dialecticians believe in is not the result of religion. We have a certain conception of the nature of man based on history. When Marx and Engels wrote about the proletarian revolution in connection with the negation of the negation, when they wrote that in the present stage of society, man would either achieve this revolution or society would tear itself to pieces, they were being guided not by the dislocations of Marx's "psyche" as Edmund Wilson thinks or by any Hegelian triads or historical religiosity, as is the opinion of Burnham and Hook. It was a logical deduction from the experience of history. The struggle of the masses for universality did not begin yesterday. An intellectual like Dewey believes that men's quest is the quest for certainty. The intellectual believes that all men are intellectuals. That is wrong. Men seek not intellectual certainty. The quest is the mass quest for universality in action and in life. It is the motive force of history. And history has reached a climax because this quest has reached a climax.

Space compels rapid compression of the next great stages in the process of social development—the Protestant reformation and the French revolution. Rising capitalism expropriated the agricultural labourer and in the creation of wage-labour threw the masses further back from universality than they had ever been. Humanism had dragged universality from heaven down to earth and had by that made the contradiction between real and ideal an intolerable antagonism. The new proletariat could not play any great part in the struggles of the Protestant reformation, as the mature workers of the medieval towns had done. Hence the classes which took the lead were the bourgeoisie, the petty bourgeoisie and the peasants. Let us concentrate on one outstanding and familiar example, the English revolution.

The Puritans give us the key to the understanding of the whole period in the light of the struggle for democracy. The revolution of Luther had shattered for ever the claims of the Pope as mediator between God and man. It placed the responsibility for the individual's moral salvation squarely on the individual man. As Hegel put it: "This is the essence of the Reformation: Man is in his very nature destined to be free", and in his own peculiar but profound manner he sums up modern history. "Time, since that epoch, has had no other work to do than the formal imbuing of the world with this principle, in bringing the Reconciliation implicit (in Christianity) into objective and explicit realisation." If you stand it on its head, and say that the objective development of man in society has been the various stages through which various classes have sought to realise the freedom implicit in Christianity, a great truth will have been grasped.

But the mass of men do not think, and certainly do not act according to those terms. The Puritans of town and country, petty-bourgeois, and semi-proletarian, shut off from freedom by the state, attempted to establish democracy in religion. The sects each attempted to form a social community in which the individual would exercise the new freedom, unlimited except by the equal freedom of other men. James I of England did not misunderstand them one bit. He knew what their anti-Ecclesiasticism meant. To all their arguments for *religious* freedom he invariably croaked in reply, "No Bishop, no King." Their weakness was a social weakness, the lack of organisation which reflected the scattered character of their labour. But when the big bourgeoisie and some liberal aristocrats started the revolution, and the small farmers and small masters of the towns organised in the army, the Puritans showed what social passions were hidden behind their psalm-singing. In 1646, tired of the vacillations of their bourgeois and aristocratic leaders, they seized the person of the King and held him as a hostage. They then began negotiations with Cromwell and in the twin documents, the agreement of the People and the Heads of the Proposals, they put forward a programme for such a parliamentary democracy as was not even put forward in England until the Chartist movement two hundred years later. They put it forward to Cromwell; and in the discussion with Cromwell and his brother-in-law, Ireton, they raised the property question as a barrier to democracy in the most plain-spoken manner. These were not the Levellers, and the Diggers, who were the extreme left. These were the main body of the army. They were suppressed by a combination of fraud and force, but Cromwell, striking to the left, was compelled to strike at the right also. Charles I was executed and the monarchy was destroyed. In the familiar phrase, it was not monarchy but royalty which returned at the restoration. Monarchy in Britain was gone forever, destroyed by the religious democrats. They held power for eleven years, but as always, and particularly in this case, they were too few to represent the nation and the old process of mediation once more took place. They had cleared the way for capitalism, and nowhere was the antagonism sharper between developing capitalism and the masses of the nation than in England.

The history of the French revolution is familiar to all marxists and the conclusions for our main argument are therefore easy to draw.

The intervention of the masses, its range and power, the social desires, the capacity for achievement and sacrifice, revealed itself to an educated Europe which had not dreamt that the shabby exterior of workers and peasants and the common people hid such colossal energies and such social needs. The quest for universality was no longer a secret. Liberty, equality and fraternity were the slogans of the revolution. If the Reformation had sought to establish a "democratic" freedom of religion, the French revolution attempted to establish a social freedom of political democracy. If out of the individual's responsibility for his own salvation, there had leapt democracy, out of his political freedom, there leapt communism.

Robespierre's dictatorship was an attempt to establish the reign of virtue. But the French masses, not only Babeuf, saw and were ready for what was needed, drastic regulation and even confiscation of the property of the rich. The modern problem was posed. But it was the old problem in a new and more aggravated, a more contradictory form.

When the French revolution was over and men had time to think, it was seen that the revolution of reason and the mighty struggle for liberty, equality and fraternity had left men farther apart than ever before. Behind the formal equality before the law, capitalist production was accumulating wealth at one pole and misery, subordination and degradation at the other on a scale hitherto unknown. The universality of men, honour, loyalty, humanism, liberty, equality, fraternity, democracy, these were as abstract to the mass of men as the heaven of the early Popes. These ideals had a certain existence among the ruling classes, but thinking man could see that the needs and deprivations of the excluded mass reached with devastating effect upon the humanity of the rulers. The masses had tried to make the state a popular state. The result had been the creation of a monster such as had never been seen before and far surpassed in range and power of the state of absolute monarchy. It was in the throes of this contradiction which was shaking all Europe that Hegel, the culmination of the German classical philosophers, set himself to study the problem of human destiny and elaborated a theory of knoweldge. Hegel recognised what men were striving for and he recognised that the French revolution was a climax in this struggle.

Hegel understood Adam Smith and Ricardo. He understood the fragmentation and dehumanisation of man in the process of capitalist production. Many of Marx's most famous pages in *Capital* have as their direct origin some of Hegel's descriptions of the workers in capitalist industry. This was, for Hegel, the final insuperable barrier to any community of association among men. Hence universality for the mass of men was impossible. By means of his dialectical method he drew the necessary conclusions. We who live toward the end in the epoch of Hitler and Stalin can understand Hegel's conclusions better than most men of previous generations, with the exception of Marx.

Universality for the mass of men was impossible. Only the state, said Hegel, could embody universality for the community. But, in particular, the state was a defence against the revolutionary masses. Hegel had seen them and their activities in European history and now the French revolution had shown that nothing could ever come of it. So it had been and it would ever be. At each stage, a few chosen individuals represented the abstract spirit of mankind. Universality had to be restricted to these. This was the basis of Hegel's idealism. But with the clear insight of a great scholar of both past and contemporary history, and by his mastery of his method, he analysed and drew his analysis to its conclusion. The state would have to organise production. The chaos of capitalist production would have to be disciplined by organising the separate industries into corporations. The state would be the state of the corporations. Universality being impossible to all men, the state bureaucracy would embody universality and represent the community. Hegel did not know the modern proletariat. He operated therefore on the basis of the inevitability of proletarian subordination. But grant him that premise and his dialectical method shows that he made an astonishing anticipation in thought of the inevitable end of bourgeois society—the totalitarian state. Hegel must not be misjudged. He wrote and propounded in the name of freedom and Reason. But those who today sneer at him and his dialectic are not fit even to wipe the dust off his books. To this day, except for the writings of the great marxists, no single writer since the French revolution has so much to say that is indispensable to modern thought and particularly modern politics.

This is where Marx began. It was as impossible to go any farther along the road of Hegel as it is impossible to go farther than the totalitarian state of contemporary history. Beyond both lies only decay. Marx had to abandon the quest for universality or find a new basis for it.

A long line of European thinkers, Ricardo, Fourier, Saint-Simon, Feuerbach, and the classical economists, the ferment in Europe which preceded the revolutionary outburst of 1848, and, what Hegel had never seen, the emergence of the proletariat as an organised social force—these gave to Marx, already a master of Hegel's system, the impetus to the new system. Men had sought universality in heaven, in the freedom of religion, in the freedom of politics. Politics had failed. Neither Hegel nor Marx ever had any illusions about bourgeois democracy as a solution to the unquenchable desires and aspirations of men.

Nothing is more indicative of the philosophical character of marxism and its organic continuity of the tradition of the great philosophers of Europe than the method by which Marx dismissed democratic politics. For Marx bourgeois democratic politics was a fraud, but like all the great panaceas from Christianity on, it was an expression of the perennial need historically conditioned. The productive process of capitalism denied any real community to men. And democratic politics, like religion, was a form of mediation by which men gained the illusion that they were all members of one social community, an illusion of universality. How not to remember Hitler's insistence that his tyrannical régime represented the folk community. The more the Nazi régime deprived the masses of all human rights, the more imperative it was to substitute an abstraction of abstractions to create the totality of existence, a sense of universality, without which men cannot live.

Marx reversed Hegel at all points. It was not an intellectual construction. Men were doing it and had been doing it all around him for years.

Hegel saw objective history as the successive manifestation of a world spirit. Marx placed the objective movement in the process of production. Hegel had been driven to see the perpetual quest for universality as necessarily confined to the process of knowledge. Marx reversed this and rooted the quest for universality in the need for the free and full development of all the inherent and acquired characteristics of the individual in productive and intellectual labour. Hegel had made the motive force of history the work of a few gifted individuals in whom was concentrated the social movement. Marx propounded the view that it was only when the ideas seized hold of the masses that the process of history moved. Hegel dreaded the revolt of the modern mass. Marx made the modern proletarian revolution the motive force of modern history. Hegel placed the future guardianship of society in the hands of the bureaucracy. Marx saw future society as headed for ruin except under the rulership of the proletariat and the vanishing distinction between intellectual and manual labour.

That was the conflict. That is the conflict today. The proletariat, said Marx, is revolutionary or it is nothing. The proletariat, he said, will conquer or society will destroy itself. The bureaucracy as conceived by Hegel he subjected to a merciless analysis. Let the reader think of Hitlerite Germany and Stalinist Russia and see how profound, how realistic, how anticipatory of the absolute crisis was the battle between the last of the great bourgeois philosophers and the first philosopher of the proletarian revolution. The smug anti-dialecticians have not yet caught up with this conflict between the masters of dialectic over a hundred years ago.

Hegel's conception of history is nothing other than the speculative expression of the Christian-German dogma of the opposition of spirit and matter, God and the world. This opposition expresses itself within history, within the human world itself, as a few chosen individuals, active spirits, confronting the rest of humanity, the spiritless mass matter. Hegel's conception of history presupposes an abstract or absolute spirit which develops itself so that humanity is only a mass bearing this spirit unconsciously or consciously. Within the empirical exoteric history, he sees a speculative esoteric history. The history of mankind is transformed into the history of the abstract spirit of mankind, beyond actual men.

Parallel with this Hegelian doctrine, there was developed in France the theory of the doctrinaires proclaiming the sovereignty of reason in opposition to the sovereignty of the people, in order to exclude the masses and rule alone. The result is that if the activity of the actual masses is nothing more than the activity of a mass of human individuals, the abstract universality, reason, spirit, possesses abstract expression exhausted in a few individuals. It depends upon the position and the strength of imagination of each individual whether he will pass as representative of "spirit". [Marx, *The Holy Family*]

Hegel had observed the unconscious development of the process of mediation. The bureaucracy of his corporate state was a conscious final mediation. Marx, in the *Critique of Hegel's Philosophy of Right*, took up the challenge. The passage which follows might have been strange or difficult twenty years ago, not today. The reader must remember that both Hegel and Marx had common pre-suppositions—the recognition of the quest for universality, the recognition that the French revolution had brought the perpetual mediation of the growing contradictions to some final stage. The essence of the passage is that while Hegel believed that the bureaucracy can and must be a mediation for universality, Marx shows that the contradiction between objective and subjective, between ideal and real, concrete and abstract, has now reached such a stage, that the universality of the bureaucracy can have no reality. The quest for universality, embodied in the masses, constituting the great mass of the nation, forbids any mediation. The bureaucracy is compelled to become objectively the embodiment of the crassest materialism and subjectively, in its words, the embodiment of the crassest hypocrisy.

Here is the passage with certain words emphasised.

The "state formalism" which the bureaucracy is, is the "state as formalism" and as such formalism Hegel has described it. Since this "state formalism" is constituted as actual power and its own material content becomes itself, *it is self-understood that the "bureaucracy" is a network of practical illusions or the "illusion of the state". The bureaucratic spirit is a thoroughly Jesuitical theological spirit. The bureaucrats are the Jesuits and theologians of the state. The bureaucracy is the "république prêtre".*

Since the bureaucracy is essentially the "state as formalism", it is this also in its purpose. Thus the actual purpose of the state appears to the bureaucracy as a purpose against the state. The spirit of the bureaucracy is the "formal spirit of the state". *It makes therefore the "formal spirit of the state" or the actual emptiness of spirit of the state into a categorical imperative.* The bureaucracy thus is driven to the final end and purpose of the state. Since *the bureacracy makes its "formal" purpose into its content, it gets into conflicts everywhere with the "real" purposes. It is therefore necessary to substitute the form for the content, the content for the form. The purposes of the state are transformed into administrative ones or the administrative purpose into state purposes. The bureaucracy is a circle out of which no one can get.* Its hierarchy is a hierarchy of knowledge. The apex entrusts to the lower circles insight into particular things, and the lower circles entrust to the apex insights into the universal and thus they mutually interchange.

The bureaucracy is the imaginary state besides the real state, the spiritualism of the state. *Everything therefore has a double meaning, a real one and a bureaucratic one,* as knowledge is double, real knowledge and bureaucratic (also the will). The real essence is handled according to its bureaucratic essence, according to its other worldly spiritual essence. *The bureaucracy has* the essence of the state, the *spiritual essence of society in its possession, it is its private property.* The general spirit of the bureaucracy is the secret, the mystery, guarded internally through the hierarchy, externally as the closed corporation. The apparent spirit of the state, the opinion of the state, appear therefore to the bureaucracy as a treason to its mysteries. *Authority is therefore the principle of its knowledge, and deifying of authority is its principle. Within itself, however, spiritualism becomes a crass materialism, the materialism of passive obedience, of belief in authority, the mechanism of fixed formal behaviour, fixed principles, observations, traditions.* As for the individual bureaucrat, the purpose of the state becomes a private purpose, a hunt for higher posts, for careers. First, he regards real life as material, for the spirit of this life has its exclusive existence in the bureaucracy. The bureaucracy must therefore proceed to make living as material as possible. Secondly, it is material for itself, i.e. so far as it becomes an object of bureaucratic handling, for its spirit is prescribed to it, its purpose lies outside of it, its existence is the existence of administration. The state exists henceforth only as fixed spirits of various offices, whose connection is subordination and passive obedience. *Actual science appears as without content, actual life is as dead, for the imaginary knowing and imaginary living pass as the essence.* The bureaucrat must therefore believe Jesuitically with the actual state, be this Jesuitism now conscious, or unconscious. It is, however, necessary that as soon as his opposite is knowing, he also achieve self-consciousness and purposeful Jesuitism.

That is the political anatomy of the stalinist bureaucracy. In the review "After Ten Years", I could touch only briefly (such are the trials of political minorities) upon the dehumanisation of the Russian bureaucracy itself. The Russian bureaucracy, as the Nazi bureaucracy in its time, represents essentially the opposition to the universality of the people in every single sphere of life. As the same article says:

In socialist society or in a society transitional to socialism, politics, science, art, literature, education all become truly social. The *individual* is able to exercise his gifts to the highest capacity, to become truly universal, because of the essentially *collective* life of the society in which he lives. Look at stalinist society. No individual is more "political" than the individual in stalinist society. Nowhere are art, literature, education, science, so integrated with "society". This is the appearance. In reality, never before has there been such a prostitution of all these things for the corruption and suppression of the direct producer, with the resulting degradation of the producers and managers alike.

Hitler called his state the truest democracy, his community was the folk community of the whole nation. His régime was "socialism". The stalinist régime goes farther. The state possesses all the virtues. The internationalist conception of human welfare is maintained through the connection with the corrupt and depraved communist parties and the constant appeal to the masses of the world. The state guarantees a "*genuine*" democracy, a "genuine" freedom of speech. Science, art and literature, like production, exist only to serve all the people. The state only administers the property which is the possession of all the people. Liberty, equality (within reason) and fraternity, honour, loyalty, chivalry, geniality, are the possession of all the people (except the trotskyists). The leader is the leader because he possesses all these qualities to a superlative degree. Any oppositionist to the slightest of these claims becomes immediately an enemy devoid of all these virtues and fit only for extermination. The totality of the abstraction is to be explained only by the totality of the deprivation. Today this state is not only confined to Russia as an isolated phenomenon. It is spreading. Trotsky taught that the growth of the stalinist state was due to the struggle over consumption. We cannot accept this at all. The stalinist state is the completest expression of the class state—not the distorted beginning of something new but the culmination, the final form of the old. To believe that this state has roots only in consumption and not in the whole productive system is to saddle the concepts of Marxian socialism with a burden which they cannot indefinitely carry. The stalinist state is a class state, a culmination of the old, not in any shape or form the beginning, however distorted, of the new.

Of precisely the same genre are the abstractions of the bourgeois democracies, different not in quality but only in degree. Phrases like the "century of the common man" and the "four freedoms" are abstractions to satisfy the suppression of objective needs. The League of Nations of 1919 becomes the United Nations of 1947. The more concrete the negation of the need, the more abstract, empty and flamboyant becomes the subjective mediation.

There is a school of marxists today who preach the ridiculous doctrine that in Russia today politics governs production. In reality, production governs politics. In appearance, the state takes hold of capital. In reality, capital takes hold of the state, and upon the mediation of the antagonisms of social and political life is superimposed the antagonisms of capitalist production itself. In its most developed form, it is state capital.

It is this modern state, the negation of universality for so many millions, which is to be negated. The negation of this is the negation of the negation. The agent of this negation is the revolutionary proletariat. When the modern millions take hold of this state, they negate the root of their degradation, production itself, for to control the state of state capitalism is to control production itself. At this moment, the state begins to wither away.

I can sum up best by a quotation from an article I wrote in *New International* of June 1944:

> But the outstanding feature of the contemporary world is that the *principles* for which Christianity stood in its best days are now regarded as matters of life and death by the average worker. This is no accident at all though we can only state the facts here. European civilisation must become a unity? Hundreds of millions of European workers know that this must be achieved or the continent will perish. Equality of nations? That, too, the great masses of Europe passionately desire, not as an ideal but to be able to live in peace. A central government to represent the interests of all? As late as 1935, Lord Cecil could get eleven million votes in a plebiscite in Britain supporting the idea of a League of Nations. And when workers say a League of Nations and collective security they mean it. And that early attempt to succour the poor, to help the afflicted, to teach the ignorant? The great mass of the workers in European countries conceive of Labour Parties as doing just that, within the conditions of the modern world.

Our anti-dialecticians believe the negation of negation and the inevitability of socialism are religion. But when one attempts to penetrate into *their* philosophy of history, one increasingly meets a vacuum or the most arbitrary combinations of historical phenomena, tied together by bits of string, by subjective analysis and a crude determinism which even sometimes has the presumption to call itself marxism. For us there is no philosophy of history without marxism, and there can be no marxism without the dialectic. In the article quoted above, I continued:

> He who would exhibit the marxist method must grasp the full significance of that early uprising of the masses when Christianity proclaimed its message. We must watch not only the primitiveness and simplicity of its aims but their comprehensive scope. Then by slow degrees, through the centuries, we see one part of the aim becoming concrete for one section of the population, and then another part for another section. Ideas arise from concrete conditions to become partially embodied in social classes and give rise to further interrelations between the spiral of real and ideal, content and form. This is the dialectic to which Marx gave a firm

materialistic basis in the developing processes of production. As society develops, the possibilities for individual development of man become greater and greater, but the conflict of classes becomes sharper and sharper. We stand today at an extreme state of these interrelated phenomena of social development. When a modern worker demands the right of free speech, the right of free press, of free assembly, continuous employment, social insurance, the best medical attention, the best education, he demands in reality the "social republic". Spinoza and Kant would stand aghast at what the average worker takes for granted today. But he does not demand them as an individual or in the primitive manner the early Christian did. In America, for instance, there are some thirteen million workers organised for nothing else but the preservation and extension of these values. These are the values of modern civilisation. They are embodied in the very web and texture of the lives of the masses of the people. Never were such precious values so resolutely *held* as necessary to complete living by so substantial and so powerful a section of society. Socialism means simply the complete expansion and fulfilment of these values in the life of the individual. This can only be attained by the most merciless struggle of the whole class against its capitalist masters. The realisation of this necessity is the final prelude to full self-consciousness.

You still believe, gentlemen, that these ideas and conclusions are the result of a dialectical religion? Go your way. God be with you. Amen.

Bolshevism is above all a philosophy of life and a political conception. The political conception is the organised preparation for the proletarian revolution. Lenin was the originator of Bolshevism, the marxism of our time. The world was to be saved by reason, but reason lay not in the heads of philosophers and intellectuals but in the actions of the masses. The world as we know it, under the control of its present masters, is unreasonable, chaotic, lacking in energy and creative force, gangrenous, barbarism. For Lenin, reason, order, historical creativeness, lay precisely in the forces which would destroy the old world. This is how he saw the councils of the workers, the soviets, and the revolutionary actions of the masses in 1905:

The old power, as a dictatorship of the minority, could maintain itself only by the aid of police stratagems, only by preventing and diverting the masses from participating in the government, from controlling the government. The old power persistently distrusted the masses, feared the light, maintained itself by means of deception. The new power, as a dictatorship of the overwhelming majority, could and did maintain itself only by winning the confidence of the great masses, only by drawing, in the freest, broadest, and most energetic manner, all the masses into the work of government. Nothing hidden, nothing secret, no regulations, no formalities. You are a working man? You wish to fight to liberate Russia from a handful of police thugs? Then you are our comrade. Choose your delegate at once, immediately. Choose as you think best. We shall willingly and gladly accept him as a full member of our Soviet of Workers' Deputies, of our Peasants' Committee, of our Soviet of Soldiers' Deputies, etc., etc. It is a power that is open to all, that does everything in sight of the masses, that is accessible to the masses, that springs directly from the masses; it is the direct organ of the masses and their will. Such was the new power, or rather its embryo, for the victory of the old power very soon trampled upon the tender shoots of this new plant. [*Selected Works*, vol. VII, pp. 252-3]

There are innumerable people opposed to bourgeois society, as they think, but who fear the uprising of the proletarian masses from that passive obedience, which is precisely the basis of bourgeois society. They want socialism but want to be sure of order, system, reason. Lenin had a different conception of where order was to be sought:

When the history of humanity moves forward at the speed of a locomotive (the petty-bourgeois intellectual) calls it a "whirlwind", a "deluge", the "disappearance" of all "principles and ideas". When history moves at the speed of a horse and cart he calls it reason, system. Then the masses themselves, with all their virgin primitiveness, their simple, rough determination, begin to make history to apply "principles and theories" directly and immediately, the bourgeoisie takes fright and wails that "reason is thrust into the background". (Is not the very opposite the case, you philistine heroes? Is it not precisely in such moments of history that the reason of the masses is displayed rather than the reason of single individuals? Is it not precisely at such times that reason of the masses becomes a living, active force, and not an armchair force?) When direct action by the masses is crushed by shootings, executions, floggings, unemployment and famine, when the bugs of professorial science, subsidised by Dubasov, crawl out of the cracks and begin to speak on behalf of the people, *in the name of the masses*, and sell and betray the interests of the latter to a privileged few—the knights of philistinism imagine that an epoch of peace and calm progress has set in, that "the turn of sense and reason has now come again". [*Selected Works*, vol. VII, pp. 260-1]

The bourgeois world is rejected completely. Only what destroys it is reasonable. But the reason of the masses was not merely destructive. It was destructive of *the bourgeois world*. But it was itself a "mighty creative force".

The point is that it is precisely the revolutionary periods that are distinguished for their greater breadth, greater wealth, greater intelligence, greater and more systematic activity, greater audacity and vividness of historical creativeness compared with periods of philistine, Cadet, reformist progress. But Mr Blank and Co. picture it the other way about. They pass off poverty as historical-creative wealth. They regard the inactivity of the suppressed, downtrodden masses as the triumph of the systematic activity of the bureaucrats and the bourgeoisie. They shout about the disappearance of sense and reason, when the picking to pieces of parliamentary bills by all sorts of bureaucrats and liberal "penny-a-liners" gives way to a period of direct political activity by the "common people", who in their simple way directly and immediately destroy the organs of oppression of the people, seize power, appropriate for themselves what was considered to be the property of all sorts of plunderers of the people in a word, precisely when the sense and reason of millions of downtrodden people is awakening, not only for reading books, but for action, for living human action, for historical creativeness. [*Selected Works*, vol. VII, pp. 261–2]

This is creative reason during the revolution and this is creative reason after the revolution. Readers of the following articles in this pamphlet and of the documents of our tendency will know that for us *the economic planning of the new society* must be the result of the same creativeness and energy of the masses expressed through *their* soviets, *their* councils, *their* party or parties. As we have shown in our pamphlet this was Lenin's conception. For us therefore, once the masses in Russia were totally subordinated to the bureaucracy, then capital *as an economic force* resumed sway, and objective economic law reasserted itself. The proletarians of the fourteenth century failed, but the masses today begin from a society in which the socialisation of the labour process is the dominant feature of the economy. The education, the training, the discipline, the social awareness, the material and spiritual needs of the great millions have reached astonishing proportions. These are the new economic forces. They are worldwide. If the earlier revolutions were outstanding peaks in a world in which the periphery was large, backward and stagnant, it is not so today. Disparate as are the economic levels of the United States and China, the world is today one system and a social unit. The need for universality of the individual man is only part of the need for universality in the world at large; "only with this universal development of productive forces is a *universal* intercourse between men established which produces in all nations simultaneously the phenomenon of the "propertyless" mass (universal competition), makes each nation dependent on the revolutions of the others, and finally has put world—historical, empirically universal individuals in place of local ones." Thus Marx in *The German Ideology*, in 1846. Today we are at the end.

It would be a grave mistake not to attempt to show, however briefly, the theoretical link between these concepts and the practical activity of building a revolutionary organisation. The dialectician is often seriously thrown back by the fact that the great masses of the workers do not seem to think in a way that corresponds to these ideas. He should remember that the number who thought of socialist revolution in Russia in February 1917 was pitifully few. There was not one single republican in France on 14 July 1789. How many of the Founding Fathers advocated independence in 1776? The anticipations of these ideas accumulate and then under suitable conditions explode into a new quality.

But with the masses the matter goes even deeper. *They do not think as intellectuals do and this intellectuals must understand.* In one of his most remarkable pages Lenin confesses that at a critical moment of the Russian revolution he was performing the most critical of all tasks, evaluating the events of July in order to change the policy and organisation of the Bolshevik Party. He was living with a working-class family. The hostess placed bread on the table. "Look," says the host, "what fine bread. 'They' dare not give us bad bread now. And we had almost forgotten that good bread could be had in Petrograd."Let Lenin himself continue:

> I was amazed at this class evaluation of the July days. My mind had been revolving around the political significance of the event, weighing its importance in relation to the general course of events, analysing the situation that had given rise to this zigzag of history and the situation it would create. And debating how we must alter our slogans and party apparatus in order to adapt them to the changed situation. As for bread, I, who had never experienced want, never gave it a thought. Bread to me seemed a matter of course, a by-product, as it were of the work of a writer. Fundamentally, the mind approaches the class struggle for bread by a political analysis and an extraordinarily complicated and involved path.
>
> But this representative of the oppressed class, although one of the better paid and well-educated workers, took the bull by the horns with that astonishing simplicity and bluntness, with that firm resolution and amazingly clear insight, which is as remote from your intellectual as the stars in the sky. [*Selected Works*, vol. VI, pp. 280–81]

The key phrase in this passage is "although one of the better-paid and well-educated workers". Better paid and well-educated workers are very often corrupted by bourgeois education. It is the great millions, very often unorganised in unions but "disciplined, and united and organised by the very mechanism of capitalist production" itself that constitutes the most heroic, the most self-sacrificing battalions of the new social order. They do not approach great questions by a complicated and involved path "as intellectuals do. Their most effective method of expression is action, corresponding to the astonishing simplicity, bluntness . . . firm resolution and amazingly clear insight" of their speech when they do speak. For long years they appear entirely subordinated to bourgeois ideas and the place bourgeois society has reserved for them. But they have their own ideas and in the continuous crisis and catastrophic decline of society, they have in recent decades repeatedly entered upon the field of history with world-shaking effects. Since 1917, no lasting victory has been theirs but the future is with them or there is no future.

Revolutionary politics consists of a conscious relating of the needs of the objective situation to the state of development of the masses. But decisive always is the objective situation, the world of today, and a superficial conception of the stage of development of the masses can be a terrible trap for the unwary. The objective conditions of our world demand universal solutions. It is absolutely impossible to propose a proletarian programme to counter the imperialism of the "Marshall Plan" without counterposing an international plan of socialist economic construction. That is the world in which we live.

In Europe, adequate wages, stable prices, food, housing and heating are no longer partial questions. Any reasonable satisfaction of the needs of the people demands a total re-organisation of the economy, a plan for continental rehabilitation, and close association with the economic power of the United States. Peace is indivisible. The need for universality stretches out from the hearth to the whole world.

But the same need exists intensively. It is the crime of capitalism that it uses men only partially. Labour bureaucracies which call on men only for votes or sending telegrams, are only partially mobilising vast stores of creative energy which are crying for release. Bankrupt economies which cannot mobilise the universal contained in modern man are doomed to remain bankrupt. That and nothing else but that can rebuild the vast wreck which is the modern world. Objectively and subjectively the solution of the crisis demands a total mobilisation of all forces in society. Partial solutions only create further disorders in the economy; partial demands, as such, because they are abstractions from the reality, lead only to disappointment; partial demands by leaders on the workers fail to mobilise their energies and leave them with a sense of frustration and hopelessness. Thus not only the concept but the need for universality reigns throughout all phases of society.

This was the constant theme of Trotsky before he was murdered in 1940. In previous periods the socialists fought for partial demands and held before the masses the social revolution as a distant goal. Today those days are over. The revolutionaries hold always before the masses the concept of the proletarian revolution but do not neglect to snatch this and that partial demand to better the position of the toilers and mobilise them for the final struggle.

This only is reason. The modern intellectual, once he breaks with bourgeois conceptions, finds a vast new world of ideas open before him. But he can pursue and present these ideas in their inner essence only with the inevitable universality of the revolutionary proletariat in mind. Without this there is no dialectic, and without dialectic, thought soon bogs down in the chaotic disintegration of the modern world. Quite different is it with the dialectical materialist. In his boldest flights, he is conscious that he will not exceed the real history of humanity which is being prepared by the revolutionary masses.

1947

7

Two Young American Writers

[*This review of Norman Mailer's* The Naked and the Dead *and William Gardner Smith's* The Last of the Conquerors *was first published in the March 1950 issue of* Fourth International *under the pseudonym of "G. F. Eckstein".*]

With single books Norman Mailer (*The Naked and the Dead*) and William Gardner Smith (*The Last of the Conquerors*) have had, the one a brilliant, the other, a distinguished success. These young men, further, have shown that they are repelled by stalinism, without cultivating any illusions about bourgeois democracy. Here is the unmistakable sign of a new wave of radical intellectuals. Their appearance raises again the question of the relationship between young writers and the politics of our troubled times.

Mailer's book describes the course of a small task force on a Pacific Island during World War II. The misery of the men, the decadence and corruption of the fascistic officer caste, these emerge not from preaching but from the interplay of event and character, panoramic, yet built out of a rich detail. With tremendous courage, Mailer traces the civilian background of each of his numerous soldier characters; the crimes of American capitalism in the war appear as the intensive expression of the mean, cheated, degrading lives to which it condemns the majority of Americans in peace. In itself, and still more, as the work of a young man of twenty-five, this book is evidence of an amazing talent.

But it is more than that. In his strength as well as in his weaknesses (and he has grave weaknesses), this talented writer is a profound expression of American civilisation. His true analogue is not the host of war novelists of this or the last war with whom he is automatically included and compared. He is organically related to another American writer, a man of genius, who, ten years before the Civil War, produced perhaps the greatest of American novels—the *Moby Dick* of Herman Melville. So close is the continuity that to examine the two books together affords crucial insights into Mailer and provides a concentrated picture of a century of American development.

Whatever else Melville's book is, it is rooted in a meticulous study of a representative group of Americans, not soldiers this time but sailors, the common seamen, skilled harpooners, mates and captain of a whaling vessel. While Whitman sang paeans to great individuals, Melville in 1851 drew the individualism of American capitalism to the end. The maniacal captain, Ahab, leads society (the ship) to its destruction. So that there should be no possibility of misunderstanding, an "imperial" sky-hawk (the American eagle) is caught in the flag and affords the final view of the disappearing *Pecquod*. Melville is repelled but fascinated by Ahab, a man maniacal but heroic in his will to achieve his purpose.

Mailer's task-force is also representative of American society as a whole. And the central character of Mailer's book is Sergeant Croft, the man of will, effective and dominating. If the passion in Ahab seeks to overcome the white whale, Croft seeks to overcome the mountain. If to a far lesser degree, Croft, like Ahab, is torn by internal rages, Croft, a sadistic killer, is not the heroic character that Ahab is, but, like Melville, Mailer is fascinated by the will to achieve and the power to dominate of this evil man. Thus, with an interval of a century, American society in crisis projects out of itself imaginative symbols of its conflicting forces which create an almost identical pattern of central character and consequent relationships.

But 1947 is not 1851. If Melville visualised no embodiment of a force to oppose Ahab, it was because there was none at the time. Melville was no active politician and did not concern himself with the problem that the Civil War could solve. He penetrated so deeply below the surface of capitalist society that it took nearly seventy-five years before the crisis of world capitalism could make people begin to see what he was driving at. Hence the dynamic character of his imaginative vision. But Mailer? Imaginatively he has not moved an inch beyond Melville and that is because he does not in 1947 see the clash of contemporary forces as Melville saw them in 1851. Mailer's book, politically speaking, is suffused with a sense of the social crisis as actual. He is familiar with the ideas of marxism. But a writer creates from levels far deeper than his consciousness of political ideas. And in this book can be felt the whole retarded political development of the United States.

Revolutionary traditions have been overlaid by tremendous economic expansion. To this day America has no mass proletarian party. That the proletariat as a class is a candidate for the resolution of the antagonisms of capitalism, this concept, for most American intellectuals, is a European phenomenon from which America has been excepted. The CIO in 1936 was a visible sign that this was not true. But Mailer wrote in 1947. Less than a dozen years is a very brief time for so far-reaching a conception to become an integral part of the national consciousness and thus an unconscious heritage of the artist.

Precisely because he is unable to present artistically a counter to Croft, the book falls short of genuine dramatic power. The point is so important for Mailer's future as a writer that it demands illustration, particularly because the stalinists, taking advantage of the confusion of bourgeois thought, continue to make the most outrageous approximations between a writer's political beliefs and his artistic creation.

A stage of civilisation is coming to an end only when another is growing up within it, whence arise violent interlocked contradictions, dramatic conflict of representative personalities, or insoluble conflicts within the single personality.

The Orestes of Aeschylus is a man torn between the blood-feud morality of the aristocracy and the constitutional law of the new Athenian democracy. Dante, representative poet of religious medievalism, was so much aware of the new secular age, that Engels called him the first modern man. Shakespeare, politically an adherent of the radical aristocracy, was fascinated by the individualistic passion of the new bourgeois man.

To take a now familiar example of a pattern constantly repeated in the mature Shakespeare it is against the background of the typical feudal virtues of loyalty, honour, discipline, as expressed by Horatio that Hamlet engages in the dramatic but perilous search for inner conviction, freedom of choice, which distinguish bourgeois man in his progressive stage. Two centuries later Balzac, admiring the aristocracy, hating the new bourgeois and condemning socialism, yet was so stimulated by the clash of opposing forces that his gigantic creation is as fresh today as when it was written.

Most gifted writers are content to deal with only one aspect of a civilisation; in our day Joyce, Eliot and Proust described one side of bourgeois society, the decay of its values: at the opposite pole, Silone in *Fontamara*, Malaquais in *Men from Nowhere* do fine work by isolating clinically forces that directly or indirectly are in opposition to official society. But for the last half century, no imaginative writing has appeared comprehensive enough to convey the sense of active opposition of fundamental forces and fundamental values.

This is what Mailer has attempted. He is not a mere recorder of decay, nor is he a clinical student of some restricted section of the mass. He attempts to portray a whole. He shows us on the one side a fascistic counter-mobilisation in General Cummings, the plotter of fascism, and Croft, its living instrument. But on the other side there is, artistically, nothing, a mere mass of men. Near the end of the book, Red, the worker, has his chance to mobilise the men against Croft. He fails miserably. But he has failed long before that—in Mailer's imagination. Croft is a perfectly realised creation. Red is not. And in literature that is what counts. The book is therefore artistically imbalanced.

Melville constantly posed Ahab's struggle to prevent revolt among his men. He posed also the conflict of opposing forces within Ahab himself and with a truly cosmic grandeur, he makes the whole the symbol of man's eternal struggle in his attempt to master nature. Though his theme is ultimate destruction, he develops and integrates the various strands of his conception with the radiance and exuberance of conscious mastery. When he was finished, he wrote to Hawthorne that he had written a wicked book and felt as spotless as a lamb. But the situation today is too urgent for Mailer to envisage calmly the destruction of society. The problem which Melville imaginatively envisaged is now actually here.

Mailer is conscious of the violent contradiction between his political hopes and the reality he achieved in Croft. He therefore vents his rage on Hearn, the soul-sick intellectual. He humiliates him physically and intellectually before the fascist general. He places him in direct conflict with Croft and sends him to ignominious defeat and death. But in the book as conceived by Mailer, Hearn can offer no artistic balance to Croft and Cummings. In *Moby Dick* Melville treats his soul-sick intellectual, Ishmael, with genial contempt. Melville would not place upon any such person the main responsibility for checking Ahab.

Let us look at Croft again. This is a character that grows. At every crisis it is he who expands to meet it. But nowhere does Mailer ever seem to have visualised a collective, co-operative action arising from masses or groups of men, all to one degree or another burning with resentment. Hence the emphasis on Hearn's individual failure; hence too the unreal character of Red's failure: "If one man would move, they all would. But nothing happened. He kept telling himself to jump at Croft— and his legs wouldn't function." It all depended upon Red. And his legs shook. But even Oliver Twist was bold enough to ask for more.

A sense of the collective gives iron strength to many a leg which by itself would not only shake but crumble. Profoundly true and profoundly glorious is that moment in *Fontamara* when the peasant boy in prison, faced with torture and blows, suddenly realises that come what may, he must keep silent and not betray his companion of whom he knows little and understands less. It is the modern individual above all who can find himself only as part of a whole. Mailer who saw so much must certainly have seen revolts individual and collective. It was in that very Eastern theatre that at the end of the war the great GI revolts against being kept from home took place. But though he probably would have defended and supported them, they awakened no organising impulse in his imagination.

I sense here a type or rather, in this case, a stage of mind very familiar among American intellectuals, seeking an answer to social chaos or crisis in administrative efficiency, that stops short at the abstract analysis of economic forces and cannot make the leap to marxism which is the doctrine of the struggle of the proletariat to achieve the classless society. Mailer has the great virtue of sincerity. He refuses to have any part in the synthetic radicalism of the stalinists and their "proletarian" literature. There are depths in the dialectic of revolt and creation, of individual and mass, which Mailer has not plumbed. What is most hopeful is that he refuses to pretend.

The reality of revolt is precisely what Smith, the Negro writer, has. Smith in his book presents no collective conception of society. But for him as a Negro, the perspective of freedom, in relation to the Negro as he is, is a permanent part of his consciousness.

The novel describes the experiences of a Negro regiment in occupied Germany and the writer, as if relieved from the pervading blight of American race prejudice, expresses the lyricism of young people making love even in that unpropitious environment. Smith is a natural writer. In a few pages of flashback to his youth in Philadelphia, the easy style becomes hard and firm, and indicates what we can expect from him when, after this interlude, he returns to his native environment. American race prejudice puts a brutal end to the idyll. But before the book is finished, a Negro soldier, maddened by persecution, shoots an officer, and jumping into a truck seeks some sort of existence different from that which tortures him—the most convenient place is the Russian zone. The sense of universal social crisis so omnipresent in Mailer's book is absent from Smith's. Smith's book is in every way a much slighter work. Yet, for historical reasons, understanding of revolt comes easily to the Negro writer.

Revolt and violence are deep in American tradition. If it comes so easily to Smith, it is because of the special situation of the Negroes as Americans in American society. It should be noted that while *Uncle Tom's Cabin*, written in 1852, was sweeping the United States and the world, Melville in 1854 wrote *Benito Cereno*, where the revolt which did not take place in *Moby Dick* is the centre of the story and is a revolt of Negro slaves. The leader, Babo, is a heroic character to whom Melville (within the narrower range) gives the formidable qualities of Ahab without his conflicts. With a matchless irony, which to this day escapes his critics, and a perfection of realisation of his conception which was rare with him, Melville struck a blow at prevailing conceptions of the Negro which remains unsurpassed in modern literature. The revolt failed but at least it took place and Melville lavished all his forces upon it.

Mailer will yet have to find this, a social conception for the future of man in which his imagination and observation can take root and flourish, and project characters of the power of Croft in opposition to him. One such character in *The Naked and the Dead* would have made this novel one of the supreme masterpieces of the century. Find this road Mailer must. Because if he doesn't, his talents will not expand.

The miserable self-torturing and psychoanalytical preoccupation, the sense of isolation of contemporary writers is familiar enough and proof sufficient. Far more significant is the career of Melville after *Moby Dick*. Having sent society to its doom, Melville became immersed in incest, mother-fixation, hatred of the father, ending many years later in the morality for morality's sake of *Billy Budd*. The historical premonitory curve he traced in his decay is a tribute to Melville's essential greatness and his incorruptible integrity.

But those who today, 1950, are trying to claim Melville for their psychopathic preoccupations are as presumptuous as Schlesinger and his followers who are trying to claim him for their "new" liberalism. If Melville sent the *Pecquod* to the bottom of the sea in 1851 and then retired into himself, it was only because, as *Moby Dick* shows in many places he had sought desperately for potentially triumphant forces of revolt, and failed to find them. The man who drew Babo, Bulkington, Queequog, Daggoo and Tashtego, Steelkilt and the carpenter, would have understood the modern proletariat.

Yet today all opposites are balanced on a razor's edge. And many fine writers have sunk into the morass of self-analysis. What to do? We are here on the shore of an uncharted sea. However much his work is the expression of social forces, an artist's development is a very individual thing. Shakespeare in his thirties obviously went through some soul-shaking personal experiences. Gauguin went to the South Seas. Who can imagine what Dostoyevsky's imprisonment meant to him? It seems pretty certain that the study of Shakespeare, particularly King Lear, was one bridge by which Melville crossed over from the gay romancer to the philosophical insight and creative power of *Moby Dick*. It seems also that there was a version of *Moby Dick* written in 1850 before the reading of King Lear in which neither Ahab nor the white whale appear. It was obvious that social forces around Melville had not changed so violently within that period as to account for these profound changes in his artistic conception. All we can say is that Melville had changed, or he had absorbed new ideas, got rid of old ones. We have here only results, the ultimate sources and impulses are lost in the mysteries of personality. A writer must find his own way.

Yet a few remarks can be made. Artists do make violent leaps from one level of penetration to another, and have often struggled consciously to do so by ways suitable to the structure of their personality and their experiences. Today we can go even further. We live in an intensely political age and theory and historical experience show us that the condition of any artistic development is an uncompromising hostility to the values of stalinism and to those of American bourgeois society. Whoever capitulates to either of them is lost, and lost utterly is the creative writer whose imagination, like Mailer's, is active in social terms. Nor can resistance be merely passive or confined to a narrow political activity. There can be felt even in the pro-revolutionary writings of Malraux a tension of political activism which is characteristic of the impatient intellectual and foreshadows disillusionment and violent revulsions following upon defeats. The primary condition of strength and endurance is to see the enemy in all its amplitude. A babel of self-contradictory tongues, professional journalistic and unashamedly amateur, serve by their combined obfuscation no purpose except to protect the tottering foundations of a decayed bourgeois culture from serious examination. Against this heterogeneous body going everywhere except forward, the stalinists, armoured and equipped like a task-force, apply their "stand and deliver theory" of culture. Each side poses an "either-or" and seeks to encompass the whole field. Perhaps it is in the systematic and truly philosophical opposition to the decay and perversions of these two barbarisms that young writers, fortunate enough to begin where Mailer and Smith begin, can find their way to those deeper levels which will nourish and not dessicate their talents.

1950

8

Marxism and the Intellectuals

[*This two-part essay on Raymond Williams's* Culture and Society *and* The Long Revolution *was originally written in 1961 for the Detroit-based journal* Correspondence, *which James had helped to found in 1953 but which rejected its publication. It was eventually published under the pseudonym of "J. R. Johnson" by* Facing Reality *in May 1962.*]

The creative power of the working class

Honour to whom honour is due. There is a campaign on by the capitalist class in all the advanced countries to prove that capitalism is so affluent, that is to say, so prosperous, that workers everywhere are becoming middle class. The rulers of society want to imply that not only has capitalism solved what marxists say it cannot solve, its economic difficulties, but they want to throw water on the idea that socialism is an inherent need for working people. Where, as in England, there is a powerful Labour Party, they want to encourage voters to vote middle class, i.e. to abandon the idea that as workers they have their special political interests. By the same means they want to encourage voters everywhere to vote for reactionary parties. Raymond Williams, the English socialist writer, has given that bold example of capitalist lying propaganda a knockout blow which I gladly reproduce. This is what he says:

> Before World War II the condition of the working class in England was a world-wide scandal. Poverty, unemployment, social degradation in many "depressed areas" seemed permanent. Undoubtedly the Labour victory in 1945 improved working-class conditions of life. What is called "prosperity" is that the worst of the shocking conditions have been eliminated. The Conservatives accepted the change and promised, if they got back to power, not to go back to the old days. They have got back to power since 1951. They spend a vast amount of their resources and energy seeking to convince ordinary people that, owing to this new prosperity, labour must now desert the very idea of labour politics.

Mr Williams gives some figures. In 1924 the Labour vote was $5\frac{1}{2}$ million. In 1929 it was $8\frac{1}{2}$ million; in 1935 it was $8\frac{1}{2}$ million. To win the victory in 1945 Labour polled 12 million votes. But in 1950, the Labour poll was 13,235,610; in 1951, although Labour lost the election, it was 13,949,105. In 1955, when it lost again, in a poll which was generally low, the Labour vote was still high: 12,405,246. The Conservatives said the low poll was due, among other things, to bad weather. In 1959, after years of what the

Conservatives call prosperity, the weather was perfect. The general poll was still low. But Labour polled 12,216,166. Mr Williams sums up: in the days when capitalism was at its worst, the Labour vote was never more than 38 per cent of the total votes. Despite the yelling of the capitalists about the prosperity which is making workers into middle-class voters, the Labour vote during this prosperity has never been less than 43 per cent. "These facts," concludes Mr Williams, "reduce the usual analysis to nonsense." New houses and washing machines do not make the Labour voter a Conservative voter. It should be noted that not only the Conservatives make this nonsensical argument. Many labour leaders wish to remove socialism altogether from the Labour programme. This prosperity, they say, is making the workers middle class. Mr Williams sums up the essence of the argument well: it is whether a washing machine, and even at times a small car, destroys, alters or effectively changes the consciousness of the worker which is created in the labour process. That is exactly it. Mr Williams hints at but does not develop the facts about the poverty and low standard of living which still remain: even in a long book a writer cannot develop everything.

Now who is Raymond Williams and, apart from the facts, why is what he says of interest and concern to socialists everywhere? Mr Williams is the most remarkable writer that the socialist movement in England has produced for ten years or perhaps twenty. And that places him automatically at the head of all English writers on social subjects. He is also a man of character and will. In the tumultuous thirties, many British intellectuals went chasing after stalinism. The left socialists and even the marxist writers produced a crude theory of what they called class struggle which ended by leaving the ideas of the whole movement in discredit and disorder. Many dropped away because, soaked in stalinism during the pro-Russian years of the war, and then demoralised by the cold war and the Khrushchev repudiation of stalinism, they went back to the Labour Party. Socialist theory sank to the lowest stage for generations.

Ten years ago Mr Williams, of working-class origin but with a university education, made up his mind to correct this state of affairs. Now after ten years his work is recognised for what it has done and is doing. He has shown the origins of British socialism in the history of Britain itself. He has concentrated on the manner in which British writers and the British workers have created what exists in Britain today. He has developed the idea of culture from an exclusive possession of the educated and intellectuals and shown that the only meaning the word has for today is *a total way of life of the whole people*. He has exposed the pretences of capitalist society and its tricks. He is a genuine socialist in that he recognises that today the only way to a fully civilised society for all is the raising of the working class to a dominant position in society. For learning, hard labour, insight and devotion to the working class, his work and the support and controversy it has stimulated are the biggest events in British socialalist thought today. His work can be heartily recommended not only for the position it has won but for its own sake.

But precisely because of its virtues and the impression it is making, even while we bring the books to the attention of our readers (a thing we rarely do), marxists have to show large and grave gaps in Mr Williams' work, and in his thinking.

Not only is Mr Williams not a marxist. In the chapter he devotes to marxism, he does not seem to be aware of what marxism is. And too many devoted contemporary marxists either do not know or ignore Marx's preoccupation with historical research and with the labour process, with production. Without a grasp of Marx's use of history and the role of production, you will not understand the significance he attaches to those concepts so often used and so often abused—the concepts of class and of revolution.

Despite the title of his second book, Mr Williams ignores the idea of the revolution completely. In fact he obviously knows so little about it that I have to go into some detail about, not what Marx says, which Mr Williams has no doubt read, but what it means for us today, not for students but for everyone who is not a conscious anti-marxist. Marx believed that the revolution was inevitable and necessary above all from his historical studies. If even it was part of his adaptation of the Hegelian *Logic*, his approach was based on history. In his last years he reduced the whole to a simple formula. There had always been mass revolution against exploitation and the evils of a decaying society. Capitalist society could not escape this fate. The difference now was that the makers of the revolution were objectively prepared by capitalism itself to do what previous revolutions had been unable to do, establish a just and harmonious society.

Many honest socialists believe that the revolution is a wish, and an illusion or at best a regrettable necessity. That it is and has been an integral part of social development is so insignificant a part of Mr Williams's equipment that he does not even argue against it. The neglect of this in his thinking is the most lamentable and glaring defect in his work. He simply does not know what the working class really is and what are its potentialities. He talks a great deal about the workers, or the working class, but he has never seriously examined the concept of class, in history and in social development. Let me give a brief historical summary of where it stands today for me, a marxist.

In the English revolution, the petty-bourgeois farmers and the workers and petty bourgeois of the London area carried the revolution to a brilliant success. Without them Cromwell would have been nothing. Suddenly in 1646 Lilburne, his colleagues

and his followers in their struggle against Cromwell, hitherto
their leader, laid down imperishably the political premises of the
individualist revolt against semi-feudal society. It came like a
bolt from the blue. Why and how? The answer is crucial. Freed
from the mental domination of both the Royalist enemy and
their own Presbyterian leaders, they discovered their own ideas
of what political and religious freedom should consist of. They
discovered the political premises and perspectives of their own
class. Against their limitations is to be set the fact that it has
taken three centuries for society to approach, not to accomplish,
what they discovered. It is only within recent years that the
enduring splendour of their thought has been discovered and
made public.

The whole significance of revolution and the class are here
established. It was not only their fight against the King, but their
sudden discovery of the difference between them and Cromwell
that forced them to think for themselves, to draw the lessons of
their own independent class experience, fully and completely,
because they had to do it in opposition to all other classes. I am
convinced that they could do this only because the revolution
gave them the opportunity, forced them to think independently.

History and our use of history move. In the French revolution
we see a further stage. What for us today should be key
movements of the French revolution is not the work of Babeuf,
traditionally the first socialist. Babeuf is part of our tradition,
all of us begin with him. *For us today*, the key events of the
French revolution should be two. After the overthrow of the
King, power in Paris passed from the bourgeois National
Assembly to the petty-bourgeois Commune of Paris, backed by
the petty bourgeois and the neo-proletarians of Paris. After the
September massacre the Commune of Paris sent a circular letter
to the other cities of France asking them to join with the
Commune against the counter-revolution. They aimed at a
nationwide movement against the bourgeois National Assembly.
The other Communes did not accept the invitation. What would
have happened if they had I do not know. But this much is
certain, that for a time at least France would have been governed
by a combination of the petty-bourgeois and the masses of the
towns, supported by the peasantry. The socialist revolution on a
national scale was very near. They would have at least produced
profound conceptions of socialist beginnings.

The second incident was the revolt organised at Eveche by
the proletarians against the Assembly *and now against the
Commune.* Robespierre, in mortal terror that this extreme
revolutionarism of Paris would split France irrevocably into
two, managed to direct this revolutionary force into the
demonstrations of the days of May. Robespierre, if not right,
seems to have been justified in his fears, and much of the anti-
proletarian evil attributed to him (the psychologists have a

wonderful time here) springs from this justified concern.

But what we have to notice is that the class, forced back on its own resources, at once develops an audacity and profundity which is beyond empirical expectation. For brief periods it was able, was forced to think its own thoughts. Without them, the French revolution would have been defeated. Marx learned much from the French revolution, limited as was the material in his time. Today we have many more proved facts than even Lenin had.

Mr Williams is fascinated by the slow persistence and steadiness of the British working class. That has been wholly admirable, but that does not exhaust history. And it does not exhaust the history of the British working class. Production links it to all other workers.

In Russia in 1905 the Russian workers formed the Soviet and carried it to a triumphant climax in 1917. They rejected parliamentary democracy and created a new political form, they created a political democracy suited to themselves. They failed against stalinism for the same reason that Lilburne and the Levellers failed—they were too small a section of the population. It was the Hungarian revolution which carried the Russian experiment to its conclusion—the councils of workers in the factories formed the only government that there was for a few days. They carried the historical development of the working class further. While the Soviet was mainly a political body, the Hungarian workers' councils were both economic and political. I repeat. What happens in a revolution is that the class for the first time finds itself free to think its own thoughts and give some concrete form to its own experience accumulated over the generations. Whenever a revolutionary class moves, it establishes a stage for the international movement. I cannot believe that Mr Williams does not know this, or at least is not aware that this is marxism. When marxists talk about class they have in mind the history of the civilisation. The Soviet originated in the proletarian experience of production—a worldwide experience.

It is the absence of any conception of the spontaneous creativity of the working class (and all other progressive classes) that makes me view much of what Mr Williams projects into the future with scepticism and more. The British working class has not said its last word on socialism. From my point of view it has not said its first. Some intellectuals and union leaders speak for it and it adapts itself to these pronouncements chiefly as a means of struggle against capitalism knowing that capitalism is in command. The general history of the Labour Party is one of adaptation to capitalism and this is because the working class as a whole accepts the policy of adaptation and does its best within that policy. Revolutionary activity, revolutionary politics, creativity on a genuinely comprehensive and revolutionary scale, that occurs very rarely in the history of a class. (Often, as in the French revolution, the effect is immediately and powerfully felt in other countries.) That intellectuals and union leaders and political leaders have assisted the bourgeoisie in suppressing the independent activity and thought of the class is undoubtedly true. But fundamentally they have been able to do this because the class as a whole or a decisive section of it has not felt that the moment has come when at all costs they have to break out of the capitalist chains.

But Mr Williams can say with some justification: if the class has not made the decisive step, has not faced the necessity of thinking its own thoughts and working out its own actions, what do you expect me to do? Here we come face to face with another fundamental of marxism, the inevitability of socialism. It is possible that Mr Williams believes this to be marxist jargon, or a phrase to keep up the spirits of devoted fanatics. It is in reality the key to any serious marxist political analysis of socialism. Marx did not use it as an incitement. It can be said that philosophically he never accepted it as truth, as absolute truth. Over and over again he carefully said: socialism or barbarism. That is to say, either the working class establishes the socialist society or the contradictions of capitalism will lead society to barbarism. The precise meaning of barbarism is a matter for debate, for those who wish to. For my part, not only were fascism and stalinism barbarisms (literally), but the ultimate in human barbarism has been reached when the most powerful statesmen of today organise their societies with the physical destruction of total societies as their main object. This is due to the necessity of preserving what they very rightly call *their* way of life. Marx's inevitability of socialism was a philosophical, a theoretical postulate, a necessity of thought, based on his conviction that capitalism would inevitably end as it is ending. With this postulate you approach every political, every social, every economic problem or set of circumstances; you look for those forces, movements, objective or subjective, which advance the cause of socialism and hasten the destruction of capitalism. Unless this is the basis of your approach, marxism is nonsense. Or is what its opponents call it, an evil force of disorder and destruction based upon the stimulation and organisation of the worst elements in human nature and social life. Anything like this is completely foreign to Mr Williams.

Marx devoted the main effort of his working life to demonstrating in economic terms the inevitability of the degeneration of capitalism. That is what *Capital* is about. Today we know that Marx never placed the inevitability of its collapse upon the growth of the productive forces and the concomitant decline of the market, and it is extraordinary to contemplate the distinguished marxists who have poured forth their cataracts of ink on this barren soil. To put it briefly: all Marx's economics ended in ever-increasing proofs of the insoluble conflict capitalism inevitably developed between its mechanical and objective progress, the diminishing number of magnates who benefited by this progress; and the growing size, objective organisation, misery and revolt of the workers. Mr Williams prefers to see socialism, if any process of development can be discerned in his empiricism, he prefers to see socialist history as events that happened. They just happened. How, and more important, why, he does not seem to know, or even to be interested in. But this means that how or why future events may happen he does not, he cannot know. Things have reached where they are and observing things he thinks that socialism is the only answer. His basis seems to be the semi-religious "brotherhood of man". Marx understood the origin and importance of ideas. The great historical materialist also understood their limitations. And marxists today have seen ideas so degraded that one of their many concerns is to maintain them in their essential integrity. Lenin here is a model. No man has added so much that is new to marxism. None was always so vigilant in maintaining the integrity of Marx's basic ideas.

What then have we to be on guard against in reading Mr Williams? That, mainly, is the purpose of this article.

He examines and analyses with great insight and power where the British workers have reached today and where he estimates that they *are* going tomorrow. But he omits entirely the main lesson of history, the creative power of a class both in theory and action, when it is thrown on its own resources and is compelled to think and act for itself. I see no sign that he is at all aware of this. He is also unaware of the international significance of any great revolutionary working-class action, a significance due to the universality of production.

The historical origin of his method (or lack of method) is obvious. The British socialist workers have not created any great revolutionary actions that have become an integral part of British and world history, as the French and Russians have done. Because many, stalinists mainly, have attempted to base British revolutionism on a foreign, chiefly the Russian, example, Mr Williams has turned his back on that and based his devoted and profound work on the purely British experience. But he has fallen into another pit; he has based British socialism and its future purely on the British experience. Hence his great omissions of what the British working class has before it, being part, an integral part, of an international way of life.

There is here also, despite his undoubted devotion to the working class, the typical attitude of the non-marxist intellectual. Ideas and the development of ideas dominate him. I view this with more than caution. For history shows that when the revolutionary class expresses itself as it usually does, in action and with ideas based on action, the intellectuals who have been advocating the importance of the class, as a rule bitterly oppose this new and unexpected expression of the very class they have supported. That is the lesson of history. The intellectuals are unable to understand this sudden outburst of independent ideas and independent action. The only safe way out is the marxist preoccupation with theory, with history, and with socialism as an international movement. Writing about socialism in Britain, Mr Williams does not mention the Hungarian revolution once. But there is an even greater omission. He makes no reference to the American working class. I shall show next, that (with the possible exception of the Russian) it is from the American working class that we can as marxists expect the greatest advance in socialist action and socialist ideas. When exactly this will come I do not know and have only contempt for the time servers who want me to tell them the date. But I hope that here I shall demonstrate to Mr Williams the validity and indeed the necessity of marxism. I have to show, and I will, that marxism and its expectation of the independent and creative action of the working class is not mere wishing or speculation or psychology but a scientific process. Without this scientific process you either ignore the American workers or indulge in wild and essentially subjective speculations.

The American working class
First of all, before dealing with the American workers, I have to deal with what makes any human being into the social category we call a worker. What does so is work itself, the labour process. I said in my first article on the books of Raymond Williams that with the possible exception of the Russian, it is from the American working class that we must next expect big advances in socialist action and socialist theory about work.

In this article (and in the previous one) I speak often about "revolutionary" actions by workers. They are a commonplace of history. I believe that only the State Department could see in this analysis an incitement to what it calls subversive activity. *Correspondence*, I am glad to note, does not advocate "the revolution". As a rule, small papers which do that, usually make themselves ridiculous, and ineffective for what they can really do. No revolution in the world can be made or stimulated by a small newspaper. A small paper which advocates "the revolution" is usually viewed with scepticism if not amusement by workers. But any working class paper has not only the right but the duty to analyse marxism seriously.

First, what do I mean by an advance in socialist theory? I mean primarily the reorganisation of work, the reorganisation of the labour process. The Russian experience has proved that nationalisation of private property can result in greater slavery for the workers. How can workers reorganise their daily work in such a manner as to make it human, that is to say, a socialist procedure? That, today, 1961, is what socialism means. It plays a very small part in Mr Williams's two books. It plays so small a part in socialist theory as a whole that I have to spend some time on it.

Reorganisation of labour is the obvious next stage of socialist progress. I am so positive about this because the whole world today accepts the fact that the nationalisation of the essential means of production will follow automatically upon the overthrow or decisive defeat of capitalism. There are debates and necessary debates about the exact methods of planning. These will always be necessary. But it is today understood, even by the capitalists themselves, that the best way to develop the economy is to bring the whole under some central direction. To use a famous phrase of Marx, this belief has now gone far beyond the fixity of a popular prejudice. What every government had to do in World War II, as well as the Russian success, brought home this truth to general consciousness. The capitalists pay lip service to what they call private enterprise, by which they strive desperately to maintain their privileged position, but they too watch the economy as a whole and seek to fit their profits and privileges into some general plan. The leaders of any capitalist section of industry would not dream of carrying on without some sort of plan, only this plan is not for social welfare but for profits and to prevent losses. A genuine socialist government anywhere will not argue about the necessity of viewing the economy as a whole and planning it in the public interests. So, stage by stage, the socialist society establishes its premises in the consciousness of the world at large.

What is troubling the international working class is this. In that nationalisation, that so-called socialisation, where and how is the situation of the workers in the labour process organically improved? An assembly line in Moscow is an assembly line in Detroit. The Russian experience is a terrible barrier to progress. The Russians have nationalised, collectivised, and they plan. The result is the greatest tyranny known to history. But that is not the main obstacle in the development of socialist consciousness. Nowhere has the working class or its supporters worked out, in life or in theory, any procedure where the labour process can be altered in such a manner that the workers will feel that the old capitalist slavery has been left behind for something new, for socialism, a new society.

That is the problem. And though everybody knows it, few talk about it.

We have here to go back to what socialism is and what it is not. When Marx was laying the foundations of his theory over a hundred years ago, he and Engels did a profound analysis of work. His analysis has never been approached, far less surpassed or even developed. We know part of it popularly today as the alienation of labour. Marx's great point was that capitalist

production of its very nature destroyed the human capacities
and potentialities of the worker. One sharp basis of his conception of a new society was that work, the capacity to plan and
work to a plan, was what distinguished human beings from
animals. But under the domination of capital, man was made to
labour as an animal. The necessity and possible benefits of this
type of labour were the means of eating well and sleeping
comfortably with his wife. Thus, says Marx, capitalist
production made his specifically human qualities of being able
to think and plan his work into an animalistic quality, and
elevated to a special importance the characteristics he shared
with animals.

"Be his payment high or low" is one of the greatest phrases of
Marx about the degradation of he worker under capitalist
production. A socialist society does not have as its first aim
giving workers higher pay. It does not primarily aim at making
the working day six hours or four hours, or giving the worker six
weeks' paid holidays instead of two. The American worker has
the highest standard of living in the world. This has not made
him into a lover of capitalism. What marxism aims at is not
merely a decent living wage for all. It seeks above all to get rid of
the wearisome, dull, grinding labour day after day, year after
year, crushing the human personality, with no prospect of
developing the human interests, needs and capacities of man as a
human being with aspirations to live and develop a fully human
life.

The problem, and it is the last and final problem, is how to do
that. Marx's theory was based upon a very profound and
elevated conception (with its foundations in the history of
human society) of the development of man. He took the
necessity of this development for granted. Man's part of this
inevitable development was that he himself had to work out the
adaptation of his discoveries in science and engineering into
a truly human development of human personality at work.
History moves and man's conditions of work change. Marx
for the most part could concentrate only on the negative aspects inherent in capitalist production. Inasmuch as the change
would have to be the work of workers themselves, it is not
surprising that it is only the negative development of Marx's
analysis which has been briefly expanded, by intellectuals. Some
marxists say today that all this talk about leisure and the vast
sums and energy spent upon amusement is nothing more than a
part of the capitalist degradation. A worker today is so trained
and limited, wearied and stunted in his development by the
capitalist productive system that all he can think of when he
leaves work is amusement, relaxation by superficial and idiotic
newspapers; silly films; routine comic strips; books about the
most sensual love, i.e. the animal aspects of love; murder, either
plain or disguised as adventure; commonplace songs; by all of

which the capitalists not only make profit, but further deaden and reduce the worker's capacity for human life. Now and then a man of genius and a few men of talent can stamp this collection of nonsense with some artistic creativity, but the aim of it all is to maintain the consciousness of the great majority at the lowest possible level, corresponding to the stultification in the labour process. To such a pitch has this wholesale degradation of human life been carried that to fight consistently against it would demand an effort beyond the powers of the ordinary man. He simply accepts it and the capitalists either tell him that this is life (the more the better) or, when challenged, say that this is all the majority of men are fit for.

The families of capitalists, sections of the middle class, all those who can live a more human life, can produce for themselves or at least support a few high-class newspapers, special music, special literature and other ways of employing their leisure time and developing themselves. But an artist, a professional man like an architect or an engineer, is interested in his work as work; he often spends his leisure time on his work; he does not believe nor do others believe that his sole purpose in life is to do four hours work a day instead of six, or to get so much more per hour. If he has a really good job, he doesn't want to do as little of it as possible, for more money. That is the mentality that is carefully inculcated into the worker from his earliest school days (education), his whole life is shaped according to these principles, the amusement and relaxation the capitalists give him are aimed to strengthen this view of life.

Periodically, however, the workers break out. But only to fall back into it. For it will last as long as capitalism lasts. That is the nature of the beast.

Not that workers have not tried organisational ways out. In England at the end of the first war a section of the working class made a great attempt to establish workers' control of production. They failed, and the whole thing seems to be buried beneath later events. Today workers are more rebellious than ever but they seem limited to fighting the capitalists at the drop of a hat for all sorts of grievances. Sometimes it seems to the capitalist that they fight him for fighting's sake. Not only the capitalists themselves but labour leaders and sympathetic journalists are unable to find any reasons for this apparently purposeless and erratic behaviour. They are unable to understand that a ferocious struggle, for ten cents an hour, or against some grievance can only be understood as a periodical revolt against the very conditions of labour and expresses the sullen anger of workers at this degradation and their apparent helplessness before it. But until labour solves this problem, it cannot today think with hope, with confidence, about socialism as a new society. Workers know that nationalisation, collectivisation, planning, if these are done by their masters, can easily result in greater stultification for them.

Now that is how, as a marxist, I see capitalist society and the working class. Why do I think that it is in America that the working class will make the first breakthrough?

Lenin is a useful guide. He always worked on the following principle. In estimating and planning for the future revolutionary activities of a working class he taught that you should always begin, *begin*, with the highest point reached by the workers in their previous struggles.

What is the highest point of the American working class, where must we *begin*? There is no doubt about this among marxists. It was the movement, the type of struggles, which established the CIO in 1935–37. And it is evidence of the general backwardness of American social thought that this great movement is not firmly established as a part of American history and American consciousness.

The corresponding movement in England, the strike of the dock workers and match girls in 1889, though not anything near the range and power of the CIO movement, is an established part of the history of the British people, not only of the working class. But of all socialist-minded intellectuals (on whom development of the ideas of socialism mainly falls) the American intellectuals, for reasons which will appear, are the most backward.

On the surface the actions of 1935–37 merely established a new stage of unionism. The real truth is that we have no record of any working class which, apart from an actual revolution, took such grandiose steps to achieve its unionist aims. I can here mention only a few. First the American workers established the sit-in strikes: in other words they attacked capitalism at its root— the process of production itself. The fact, the actual fact, is that they seized capitalist property by force. Secondly, they opened their gates to Negroes, since the Civil War the biggest action on this running sore of American society. Thirdly, in general they acted in a manner that showed the revolutionary fervour that was moving in them. In dozens of thousands they did not wait to be told or urged. Many are the authentic episodes told of a worker rushing into one of the few groups of accepted organisers and saying, "We have shut down our plant. We have called a meeting to be organised. What do we do next?" The specific American readiness for action without theory is here seen at its best.

But perhaps the most significant and enduring memory of the formation of the CIO was the treasured possession of a worker in Flint many years after—he probably still has it. It was the first contract between the workers and capitalists of a big automobile plant. It consisted of only one typewritten page (full of creases from being constantly folded, opened and refolded). But by this contract, if the workers had a grievance, all workers in the department stopped work and went to discuss the matter with the superintendent. After discussion the decision was made on the spot.

This was not socialism or anything like socialism. Socialism is the organisation of production by people who work and are in charge of work. Socialism is not a continual fighting with the boss. But at any rate in those days the workers established their right and their wish to be something else besides a mere category of production like rubber or steel.

We must not lose sight of the vast changes in all aspects of social life which workers' mastery of production must inevitably bring. How far the workers' command of production could go was hinted at by Marx in *Capital*, volume I, and it should first be noted that Marx was very rough, on marxists even, who asked him what the workers should do "after the revolution". His answer was a warning to those learned idiots who read his books and then triumphantly announce, "Look. Things have not worked out as he said. Marx was wrong." History is constantly moving on, especially production. Marx was very conscious of this and to enquiries about what the workers would do "after the revolution", Marx replied: "They will do what they see it is necessary for them to do; do not ask me for any recipes for the cook shops of the future." Yet, tracing the lessons of history, and not indulging in psychological guesses about socialist workers, he hinted at what would happen to that great social organisation, the family, in the socialist future. The children would be educated in the labour process and the family would enter into a new stage of social development.

This is worth some space even in a necessarily brief survey as this. Most of the shallow profundities about the crisis in the modern family and about education are not worth even the time that it takes to read the titles. Nearly all of them accept capitalism as an eternal system. Hence the mess they are always in.

What Marx foresaw was that when workers were in full control of the labour process they would alter their family lives and their work to suit. If the labour process, work, were universally recognised as the first foundation of society and of man as a human being, then the education of children must begin in the labour process. This in principle is not as new and as revolutionary as it sounds. When, during the Middle Ages, the Catholic view of society and of man prevailed, everybody was educated in the fundamentals and practice of Catholicism from birth till death. In our day it is the labour process, work, the specific quality which distinguishes man from the animals, which will give to the world, not only to a nation, a common view of life and society. Dentists, artists, doctors, engineers, accountants, professors of languages, all will in time do their special studies. But all will begin with and share a common basis of thought. The special students of education, of psychology, will have a common basis for their researches into education. Not only will the family benefit by beginning life together. Side by side with the few specially planned and educative hours the children will do, our modern consciousness of a need to find useful work suitable to the aged will find its satisfaction. Workers will handle this automatically.

I have gone in some detail into the general outlines of this to make clear what socialism is and what workers are and what they are not. Workers do not write books on education, they do not read them. They will not as socialists become specialists on education. But the marxist bases his view of the future of society upon workers' independent action, because such action will alter the material circumstances of life and the family to such a degree that theories of education and of family life and the labour process itself will assume a new common purpose and possibly within which human thought will venture into new spheres and possibilities, working them out by trial and error as men have always done.

Now what is actually happening in America today in the labour process? Short-sighted and ignorant intellectuals babble about high wages, unemployment pay, pensions and greater and more diversified leisure and means of communication. A few even pontificate on work, but they cannot see that this is a problem which only workers themselves can settle. It is a practical problem for practical people, who are not given to writing books. Intellectuals either know nothing about it or are afraid of it. The plain truth is as all workers (and readers of *Correspondence*) know, the workers in Detroit for example are today worse off than they were in the years of 1935–37. The union leaders have year by year sold out the workers' hard-won privileges; after twenty-five years the workers know that they have lost the power even of fighting in the 1935–37 manner. They do not know what to do. It isn't the contract, now of many pages, that inhibits them. Workers can throw that aside in one day. It is that they have had an experience they all know or their parents know. American workers have the national impatience with what has been proved unworkable. They will not go through that same procedure again. This is not pure speculation. They have defied Reuther and his benefits by raising the question of "local grievances" on a national scale. They have got no place. They now know that this is a far bigger question than they thought. What to do? To a marxist the evidence is thick that they are today reviewing the whole problem. A marxist bases himself on the fact that they will be forced to do something, and, not being theoreticians, they will, when acting, start from the highest point where they had reached before and which had failed. This marxists base on the most thorough and continuing study of international labour that has ever been made.

This is the strictly economic view of the question. Mr Williams's analysis shows him to be totally unaware of this problem even in its strictly economic context. But despite the primacy that marxists give to economic analysis, we, above all, are aware that each working class is part of a distinctive nation, and that its economic actions are governed not only by the complexity and catastrophes of the historical present but by the historical past, not only of the working class but of the nation. American marxists seem singularly deficient in the historical appreciation of the American working class. When you compare the historical development of the American nation with that of the European nations—and you must compare with somebody—certain facts stand out. One certain fact. It is this: the American bourgeoisie has never been seriously challenged for the leadership of the nation. In the three great crises of American history, the War of Independence, the Civil War and the Depression, the bourgeoisie was able either to maintain unchallenged its official control of the state, or, in 1776, to form a state and an army to carry out its war. All the objective causes that can be given for this are subordinate to the fact itself. And one continuing cause and effect is that the American bourgeoisie has been able to establish itself abroad and at home, in the national consciousness, as the originator and guardian of individual liberty, freedom and equality. Marxists are inclined to forget that in social life and conduct these ideas are more firmly established in the United States than elsewhere. The American bourgeoisie did establish something new in the world. All this inhibits the working class in independent class action and independent class thinking.

But the hour approaches. That historical bourgeois domination of American society is running very thin. First there is the cold war. America is as busy risking the lives of Americans and of humanity as a whole as Russia is. The American bourgeoisie has accepted that the Negro question is a national scandal and a national weakness. It has promised the American people to solve it. But it is becoming clearer every day that the task is beyond it. Not unlike Russia, it openly sought to destroy the Cuban revolution. It played along with McCarthy until he was obviously unable to do the job that was wanted from him—discipline the working class. The supremacy America has held in the practical application of economic advances is now challenged and has received some decisive defeats. Most important of all, the whole society, not only the workers, is conscious that something is grievously wrong. There is a frantic struggle for a sense of national purpose. So powerful and all-pervading has been the bourgeois domination that, with all due respect paid to the lies copiously mixed with half-truth of the anti-Russian propaganda, the tradition of freedom is so strong that the American people genuinely turn with horror from

stalinism and its inheritance, only to see every day the American
bourgeoisie striking blow after blow at liberty.

Large sections of the American population are horrified and
revolted at the rapid degeneration of American society. The
sense of crisis is national, and has attained such a scope that one
cannot see how the American bourgeoisie will be able to handle
it. Whatever form a solution or the beginning of an attempt at
solution will take, it seems fairly obvious that for the first time
the American working class will have to assume, will be forced
to assume national responsibility, think its own independent
thoughts, carry out its own independent actions.

Thus, although the working class has its own special
problems, the state of the nation is pushing it towards some
action. Any action that it may take involves at once the national
solution of the national and international problems. But history
warns us that a class, forced into independent action, will think
its own thoughts and act to solve its own problems. It is to me
certain that if the American working class should find itself, not
necessarily at the very start, but rapidly enough, forced to in-
tervene independently in the task of national regeneration, then
one of the first things it will do is to reorganise the process of
production. If it will act at all—and either it will act or the
degeneration of American society (and world society) will
continue—its main, perhaps its first action will be to reorganise
its daily life, that is to say the labour process. This, I have to
repeat, is not merely nationalisation or more wages in less hours.
It cannot mean another mobilisation for continuous fighting
with the capitalist class or with a class of bureaucrats or
managers (capitalist bosses under a new name). It must mean a
total reorganisation of the labour process, with the working
class in complete charge of production and its energies and
experience devoted to making production a fully human occupation. America is the country of production, and more
than any other will be able to understand and accept such a
transformation. American workers, more than all others,
accept production as a way of life. They know that it is production which has made the American nation what it is. They
have the experience of production being boldly changed to suit
the necessities of production. They will not fail to change
production for the necessity of human existence and national
regeneration. No one else but they themselves can do it.

But there will be bitter opposition. And it is regrettable that
those intellectuals and labour leaders who have been talking
most loudly about the new society will be the most dangerous
opposition. Most dangerous because from their previous interest
in and sympathy with the working class, they are likely to gain
positions and voices of leadership. The dyed-in-the-wool
capitalist reaction will recognise that for the time being they will
have to accept other leadership and they will rally behind them,

waiting for the time and the opportunity when these fail, as they are bound to fail, once more to take control.

This is the perspective. Without it you may do good work, but you weaken the first condition of success—the belief of the workers in themselves. The marxist organisation and above all the marxist propaganda knows this. He knows that his great task is to work side by side with the workers on day-to-day problems, welcoming and in fact encouraging all possible allies. As a marxist he is on guard always himself to avoid and to be in militant opposition to whoever and whatever will lessen the confidence of the working class in itself and in its own independent action. How exactly to do this is a difficult and at times apparently impossible problem. That is our daily burden, even if solved today, appearing in new forms tomorrow. But unless you know the problem and daily strengthen yourself in it, you will not only go wrong, but your best intentioned actions will do great harm to the very cause for which you are working.

Let me end with a historic weakness. As the crisis deepens numbers of the middle class and stray intellectuals become deeply perturbed and in their usual intemperate manner wish "to do something". They may even attempt some independent actions. In America their record of recognising the power of the working class is very bad. Small marxist organisations, hitherto confined to propaganda, may catch the fever, forget the special responsibilities which they have as marxists and even find or indicate the solution of the ills of the day in the ideas and temper of these groups. Particularly they are inclined to do this if, as often happens, the working class is watching and weighing the situation, knowing the gravity of its problems and its own heavy responsibility. Here Lenin can be, as always, a model of policy. In 1905 when Russian capitalism received a dreadful blow from its defeat by the Japanese, Lenin warned that even reactionary classes might be moved to fight against Tsarism and the disasters it had brought upon the nation. He advocated support of these. But in 1905 as in 1917 friends observed that when the party was deep in action and excitement over the revolutionary upheavals, Lenin (though leading the concrete struggle) used every spare moment to reread the classics of Marx. The great marxist, although the leader of a mass party, was holding tight to the fundamental principles. He knew how easy it was to slip away from them.

The working class did not disappoint him. In 1905 it initiated the first general strike in history. It created the Soviet. It was in his mastery of marxism that Lenin was able to expect and recognise these creative achievements for what they were. These two articles are a study of theory, stimulated by the theoretical work of a gifted and devoted theorist of socialism. May I, without offence, say that Mr Williams can add enormously to

his equipment and possibilities by mastering marxism in its basic
theories and the practice of its greatest exponents.

1961

9

The West Indian Middle Classes

[Party Politics in the West Indies, *from which this is a chapter, was written and first published in Port of Spain in 1961, as James's epitaph on the failure of the West Indies Federation.*]

The middle classes in the West Indies, coloured peoples, constitute one of the most peculiar classes in the world, peculiar in the sense of their unusual historical development and the awkward and difficult situation they occupy in what constitutes the West Indian nation, or, nowadays, some section of it.

Let me get one thing out of the way. They are not a defective set of people. In intellectual capacity, i.e. ability to learn, to familiarise themselves with the general scholastic requirements of Western civilisation, they are and for some time have been unequalled in the colonial world. If you take percentages of scholastic achievement in relation to population among the underdeveloped, formerly colonial, coloured countries, West Indians would probably be at the head and, I believe, not by a small margin either. What they lack, and they lack plenty, is not due to any inherent West Indian deficiency. If that were so we would be in a bad way indeed. I set out to show that the blunders and deficiencies of which they are guilty are historically caused and therefore can be historically corrected. Otherwise we are left with the demoralising result: "That is the way West Indians are," and closely allied to this: "The man or men who have brought us into this mess are bad men. Let us search for some good men." As long as you remain on that level, you understand nothing and your apparently "good" men turn rapidly into men who are no good. That is why I shall keep as far away from individuals as I can and stick to the class. I am not fighting to win an election.

For something like twenty years we have been establishing the premises of a modern democratic society: parliamentary government, democratic rights, party politics, etc. The mere existence of these is totally inadequate—the smash-up of the Federation has proved that. We now have to move on to a more advanced stage. To think that what I say is the last word in political wisdom is to make me into just another West Indian politician. I am posing certain profound, certain fundamental questions. Their urgency lies in the fact that our political pundits and those who circulate around them, consistently ignore them, try to pretend that they do not exist.

Who and what are our middle classes? What passes my comprehension is that their situation is never analysed in writing, or even mentioned in public discussion. That type of ignorance, abstinence, shame or fear, simply does not take place in a country like Britain. There must be some reason for this stolid silence about themselves, some deep, underlying compulsion. We shall see.

Our West Indian middle classes are for the most part coloured people of some education in a formerly slave society. That means that for racial and historical reasons they are today excluded from those circles which are in control of big industry, commerce and finance. They are almost as much excluded from large-scale agriculture, sugar for example. That is point number one. Thus they as a class of people have no knowledge or experience of the productive forces of the country. That stands out painfully in everything they do and everything they do not do. Mr Nehru talks about India's new steel mills, President Nasser talked about his dam which caused a war, President Nkrumah talked and preached about his Volta Dam for ten years before he got it. A West Indian politician talks about how much money he will get from the British government or from the United States. It is because the class from which he comes had and has no experience whatever in matters of production. It is the same in agriculture. They have never had anything to do with the big sugar estates. Banking is out of their hands and always has been. There is no prospect that by social intermixing, intermarriage, etc., they will ever get into those circles. They have been out, are out and from all appearances will remain out. That is a dreadful position from which to have to govern a country. In Britain, France, Australia, you have capitalist parties, men who represent and are closely associated with big capital, big agriculture, finance. You have also labour parties. In Britain a hundred members in the House of Commons are placed there by the union movement. The Labour Party members are the heads or connected with the heads of the union movement, of the Labour Party, of the co-operative movement; thus, apart from Parliament, they have a social base. In the West Indies some of the politicians have or have had posts in the labour or union movement. But as a class they have no base anywhere. They are professional men, clerical assistants, here and there a small business man, and of late years administrators, civil servants and professional politicians and, as usual, a few adventurers. Most of the political types who come from this class live by politics. All personal distinction and even in some cases the actual means of life and the means of improving the material circumstances of life, spring from participation, direct or indirect, in the government, or circles sympathetic to or willing to play ball with the government. Thus the politicians carry into politics all the weaknesses of the class from which they come.

They have no trace of political tradition. Until twenty years ago they had no experience of political parties or of government.

Their last foray in that sphere was a hundred and thirty years ago, when they threatened the planters with rebellion of themselves *and the slaves* if they were not permitted to exercise the rights of citizens. Since then they have been quiet as mice. On rare occasions they would make a protest and, the ultimate pitch of rebellion, go to the Colonial Office. They did not do any more because all they aimed at was being admitted to the ruling circle of expatriates and local whites. More than that they did not aspire to. It is most significant that the father of the anti-imperialist democratic movement is a white man, A. A. Cipriani, and the biggest names are Alexander Bustamante who spent a lot of his life in Spain, Cuba and the United States, and Uriah Butler, a working man: not one of them is a member of the ordinary middle class. Sir Grantley Adams may appear to be one. He most certainly is not. After being educated abroad, he came back to Barbados, which alone of the West Indian islands had an elected House of Representatives. He neglected what would have been a brilliant and lucrative profession at the bar to plunge himself into politics. Middle-class West Indians do not do that.

Knowledge of production, of political struggles, of the democratic tradition, they have had none. Their ignorance and disregard of economic development is profound and deeply rooted in their past and present situation. They do not even seem to be aware of it. For several generations they have been confined to getting salaries or fees, money for services rendered. That is still their outlook.

For generations their sole aim in life was to be admitted to the positions to which their talents and education entitled them, and from which they were unjustly excluded. On rare occasions an unexpected and difficult situation opened a way for an exceptional individual, but for the most part they developed political skill only in crawling or worming their way into recognition by government or big business. When they did get into the charmed government circles or government itself, they either did their best to show that they could be as good servants of the Colonial Office as any, or when they rose to become elected members in the legislature, some of them maintained a loud (but safe) attack on the government. They actually did little. They were not responsible for anything, so they achieved a cheap popularity without any danger to themselves.

Thus the class has been and is excluded from the centres of economic life, they have no actual political experience, they have no political tradition. The democracy and West Indianisation was won by mass revolt. Even this revolt was led by men who were not typically middle class. When, after 1937–38, the democratic movement started, it was a labour movement. Gradually, however, the British government, felt itself compelled to make the Civil Service West Indian, i.e. middle-class.

By degrees the middle class took over the political parties. The Colonial Office carefully, what it called, educated them to govern, with the result that the Federation is broken up and every territory is in a political mess.

Let us stick to the class, the class from which most of our politicians come, and from which they get most of their views on life and society.

All this politicians' excitement about independence is not to be trusted. In recent years the middle classes have not been concerned about independence. They were quite satisfied with the lives they lived. I never saw or heard one of them around the politicians who was actively for independence. Their political representation faithfully reproduced this attitude. I can say and dare not be challenged that in 1959 one man and one only was for independence, Dr Williams. I do not know one single West Indian politician who supported him except with some non-committal phrases. You cannot speak with too much certainty of a class unless you have made or have at your disposal a careful examination. But of the politicians I am absolutely certain. Independence was not an integral part of their politics. The evidence for this is overwhelming and at the slightest provocation I shall make it public. The drive for independence now is to cover up the failure of the Federation.

If you watch the social connections of the politicians and the life they live, you will see why their politics is what it is. I do not know any social class which lives so completely without ideas of any kind. They live entirely on the material plane. In a published address Sir Robert Kirkwood quotes Vidia Naipaul who has said of them that they seem to aim at nothing more than being second-rate American citizens. It is much more than that. They aim at nothing. Government jobs and the opportunities which association with the government gives, allows them the possibility of accumulating material goods. That is all.

Read their speeches about the society in which they live. They have nothing to say. Not one of them. They promise more jobs and tell the population that everybody will have a chance to get a better job. They could not say what federation meant. They are unable to say what independence means. Apart from the constitution and the fact that now they will govern without Colonial Office intervention, they have nothing to say. They are dying to find some communists against whom they can thunder and so make an easier road to American pockets. What kind of society they hope to build they do not say because they do not know.

Their own struggle for posts and pay, their ceaseless promising of jobs, their sole idea of a national development as one where everybody can aim at getting something more, the gross and vulgar materialism, the absence of any ideas or elementary originality of thought; the tiresome repetition of commonplaces aimed chiefly at impressing the British, this is the outstanding characteristic of the West Indian middle class. The politicians they produce only reproduce politically the thin substance of the class.

Let us stay here for a while. These people have to know what they are. Nobody except our novelists is telling them.

We live in a world in the throes of a vast reorganisation of itself. The religious question is back on the order of discussion. Two world wars and a third in the offing, Nazism, Stalinism, have made people ask: where is humanity going? Some say that we are now reaching the climax of that preoccupation with science and democracy which well over a hundred and fifty years ago substituted itself for religion as the guiding principle of mankind. Some believe we have to go back to religion. Others that mankind has never made genuine democracy the guiding light for society. Freud and Jung have opened depths of uncertainty and doubt of the rationality of human intelligence. Where the West Indian middle class (with all its degrees) stand on this, who is for, who is against, who even thinks of such matters, nobody knows. They think they can live and avoid such questions. You can live, but in 1962 you cannot govern that way.

Are they capitalists, i.e. do they believe in capitalism, socialism, communism, anarchism, anything? Nobody knows. They keep as far as they can from committing themselves to anything. This is a vitally practical matter. Are you going to plan your economy? To what degree is that possible, and compatible with democracy? To West Indian politicians a development programme is the last word in economic development. They never discuss the plan, what it means, what it can be. If they feel any pressure they forthwith baptise their development programme as "planning".

Where does personality, literature, art, the drama stand today in relation to a national development? What is the relation between the claims of individuality and the claims of the state? What does education aim at? To make citizens capable of raising the productivity of labour, or to give them a conception of life? West Indian intellectuals who are interested in or move around politics avoid these questions as if they were the plague.

Some readers may remember seeing the movie of the night of the independence of Ghana, and hearing Nkrumah choose at that time to talk about the African personality. This was to be the aim of the Ghanaian people with independence. Is there a West Indian personality? Is there a West Indian nation? What is it? What does it lack? What must it have? The West Indian middle classes keep far from these questions. The job, the car, the fridge, the trip abroad, preferably under government auspices and at government expense, these seem to be the beginning and end of their preoccupations. What foreign forces, social classes, ideas, do they feel themselves allied with or attached to? Nothing. What in their own history do they look back to as a beginning of which they are the continuation? I listen to them, I read their speeches and their writings. "Massa day done" seems to be the extreme limit of their imaginative concepts of West Indian nationalism. Today nationalism is under fire and every people has to consider to what extent its nationalism has to be mitigated by international considerations. Of this as of so much else the West Indian middle class is innocent. What happens after independence? For all you can hear from them, independence is a dead end. Apart from the extended opportunities of jobs with government, independence is as great an abstraction as was federation. We achieve independence and they continue to govern.

It has been pointed out to me, in a solid and very brilliant manuscript, that the accommodation of the middle class to what is in reality an impossible position is primarily due to the fact that, contrary to the general belief, it is in essence a position they have been in for many years. They or their most distinguished representatives have always been in the situation where the first necessity of advance or new status was to curry favour with the British authorities. The easiest way to continued acceptance was to train yourself to be able to make an impact as British and as submissive as possible. Now they have political power their attitude is the same only more so. Where formerly they had to accommodate themselves to the Governor and all such small fry, today they deal directly with the British Colonial Secretary and British cabinet ministers, with foreign business interests themselves instead of only their representatives abroad. The strenuous need and desire to accommodate, the acceptance of a British code of manners, morals and economic and political procedures, that is what they have always done, especially the upper civil servants. They have had to live that way because it was the only way they could live. That new combination of a West Indianised Civil Service and a West Indianised political grouping are a little further along the road, but it is the same road on which they have always travelled. The man who has worked out something usually finds the aptest illustration of it. In conversation with me the author of this really superb piece of insight and analysis has said: "If they had had to deal with, for instance, Japanese or even German businessmen they would act differently. They would have been conscious of a sharp change. With the British they are not conscious of any break with the past. Accustomed for generations to hang around the British and search diligently for ways and means to gain an advantage, they now do of their own free will what they formerly had to do."

Having lived, as a class, by receiving money for services rendered, they transfer their age-old habits to government. But as this recent analysis shows, the very objective circumstances of their new political positions in office have merely fortified their experiences out of office.

It is such a class of people which has the government of the West Indies in its hands. In all essential matters they are, as far as the public is concerned, devoid of any ideas whatever. This enormous statement I can make with the greatest confidence, for no one can show any speech, any document, any report on which any of these matters—and the list is long—are treated with any serious application to the West Indian situation. These are the people from whom come the political leaders of the West Indies. The politicians are what they are not by chance.

What is the cause of this? A list of causes will be pure empiricism allowing for an infinite amount of "on the one hand" and "on the other hand". The cause is not in any individual and not in any inherent national weakness. The cause is in their half-and-half position between the economic masters of the country and the black masses. They are not an ordinary middle class with strong personal ties with the upper class and mobility to rise among them and form social ties with them. From that they are cut off completely. And (this is hard for the outsiders to grasp, but it is a commonplace in the West Indies) for centuries they have had it as an unshakeable principle that they are in status, education, morals and manners, separate and distinct from the masses of the people. The role of education in the West Indies has had a powerful influence here. The children of an aristocracy or of a big bourgeoisie take education in their stride. Their status is not derived from it. But where your grandfather or even your father had some uncertain job or was even an agricultural labourer, a good education is a form of social differentiation. It puts you in a different class. Twenty years is too short a time to overcome the colonial structure which they inherit, the still powerful influence of the local whites, still backed by the Colonial Office. The Civil Service open to them fortifies this sentiment. It is not that no progress has been made. Writing in 1932 and analysing the political representatives of the coloured people, I had this to say:

> Despising black men, these intermediates, in the Legislative Council and out of it, are forever climbing up the climbing wave, governed by one dominating motive—acceptance by white society. It would be unseemly to lower the tone of this book by detailing with whom, when and how Colonial Secretaries and Attorneys-General distribute the nod distant, the bow cordial, the shake-hand friendly, or the cut direct as may seem fitting to their exalted highnesses; the transports of joy into which men, rich, powerful and able, are thrown by a few words from the Colonial Secretary's wife or a smile from the Chief Justice's daughter. These are legitimate game, yet suit a lighter hand and less strenuous atmosphere than this. But political independence and social aspirations cannot run between

the same shafts; sycophancy soon learns to call itself moderation; and invitations to dinner or visions of a knighthood form the strongest barriers to the wishes of the people.

All this is and has been common knowledge in Trinidad for many years. The situation shows little signs of changing. The constitution is calculated to encourage rather than to suppress the tendency.

That has been overcome. A black man of ability and influence can make his way. In personal relations, in strictly personal relations, the political types meet the white economic masters with a confidence and certainty far removed from the strange quirks of thirty years ago. But their ancestry (as described above) is bad. They are political *nouveaux-riches*. And all such lack assurance (or are very rude in unimportant matters). This middle class with political power minus any economic power are still politically paralysed before their former masters, who are still masters. The only way of changing the structure of the economy and setting it on to new paths is by mobilising the mass against all who will stand in the way. Not one of them, even the professed communist Jagan, dares to take any such step. They tinker with the economy, they wear themselves out seeking grants, loans and foreign investments which they encourage by granting fabulous advantages dignified by the name of pioneer status. (It is impossible to conceive any people more unlike the pioneers who extended the American nation than these investors of little money with large possibilities.) Here is the hurdle against which the Federation broke its back. Sitting uneasily on the fence between these two classes, so changed now from their former status, the middle classes and the middle class politicians they produce saw federation as everything else but a definitive change in the economic life and the social relations which rested upon it. The economy lives for the most part on a sugar quota granted by the British government. In a society where new political relations are clamped upon old economic relations, the acceptance of the quota system appears to give an impregnable position to the old sugar plantation owners. This reinforces the age-old position of the classes and fortifies the timidity of the middle classes. They therefore are frantic in building more roads, more schools, a hospital; except where, as in Jamaica, it cannot be hidden, they turn a blind eye to the spectres of unemployment and underemployment, in fact do everything to maintain things essentially as they were. It is no wonder, therefore, that they discuss nothing, express no opinions (except to the Americans that they are anti-communist), keep themselves removed from all the problems of the day, take no steps to see that the population is made aware of the real problems which face it, and indeed show energy and determination only to keep away or discredit any attempts to have the population informed on any of the great problems which are now disturbing mankind. They know very well what they are doing. Any such discussion can upset the precarious balance which they maintain. Any topic which may enlarge the conception of democracy is particularly dangerous because it may affect the attitude of the mass of the population. How deeply ingrained is this sentiment is proved by the fact that nowhere in the islands has the middle class found it necessary to establish a daily paper devoted to the national interest. In fact in Trinidad when it became obvious that this was not only possible but everyone expected it, the political leadership was indifferent when it was not actively hostile. After twenty years nowhere have they felt it necessary to have a daily paper of their own. The obvious reason for that is that they have nothing to say. They want to win the election and touch nothing fundamental.

It is obvious to all observers that this situation cannot continue indefinitely. The populations of the islands are daily growing more restless and dissatisfied. The middle classes point to parliamentary democracy, trade unions, party politics and all the elements of democracy. But these are not things in themselves. They must serve a social purpose and here the middle classes are near the end of their tether. Some of them are preparing for troubles, trouble with the masses. Come what may, they are going to keep them in order. Some are hoping for help from the Americans, from the Organisation of American States.

Without a firm social base, they are not a stable grouping. Some are playing with the idea of dictatorship, a benevolent dictatorship. But different groupings are appearing among them. Those educated abroad are the most reactionary, convinced as they are of their own superiority. The lower middle class locally educated are to a large degree ready for political advances—they are socially very close to the mass. There are also groupings according to age. Those over fifty have grown up with an innate respect for British ideals. They welcome in the new régime positions of status from which they were formerly excluded, but they accommodate themselves easily to authority. But the younger generation has grown up with no respect for any authority whatever; even some from abroad who have gone into good government jobs bring with them from Europe and the New World the scepticism prevailing there of any particular doctrine or social morality. Independence will compel the posing of some definite social discipline. The old order is gone. No new order has appeared. The middle classes have their work cut out for them. Their brief period of merely enjoying new privileges after three hundred years of being excluded is about over.

The West Indian middle classes have a high standard of formal education. They are uneducated and will have to educate themselves in the stern realities of West Indian economic and social life. Independence will place them face to face with the immense messes the imperialists are leaving behind. The economic mess is the greatest mess of all, and the other messes draw sustenance from it. It is not insoluble. Far from it. Economic development on the grand scale is first of all people, and history has endowed us with the potentially most powerful and receptive masses in all the underdeveloped countries. The effects of slavery and colonialism are like a miasma all around choking us. One hundred and fifty years ago, when the Non-conformists told the slave-owners, "You cannot continue to keep human beings in this condition," all the slave-owners could reply was, "You will ruin the economy, and further what can you expect from people like these?" When you try to tell the middle classes of today, "Why not place responsibility for the economy on the people?" their reply is the same as that of the old slave-owners: "You will ruin the economy, and further what can you expect from people like these?" The ordinary people of the West Indies who have borne the burden for centuries are very tired of it. They do not want to substitute new masters for old. They want no masters at all. Unfortunately they do not know much. Under imperialism they had had little opportunity to learn anything. History will take its course, only too often a bloody one.

1962

10

"Othello" and "The Merchant of Venice"

[These two short talks were written in 1963 and given on the Caribbean Service of the BBC in the following year. James has written of Shakespeare: "Thought and feeling were always experienced in terms of nature, the physical responses of human beings and the elemental categories of life and labour. This is the basis of his incomparable vividness and facility of expression and the source of his universality."]

"Othello"

Othello is a play entirely different from *Hamlet*, *Macbeth* and *King Lear*. Government as a problem is not raised at all. There is an excellent government at Venice and Shakespeare shows it to us in all its majesty. A senate discussing political and personal problems freely; the Duke, its president, dignified, competent and very human; the Venetian public full of respect for its senate. When Othello, having murdered Desdemona, has to be arrested, the Commission already sent by the senate to recall him from his post conducts itself in a manner which is firm but a model for any age. This is not background. It is an integral part of the play. Our audience must see this government, beautifully robed, with much majesty and formal dignity. It is from this august and impressive body that Othello is excluded. Not by his colour, not by his race, I say with the fullest confidence, that you could strike out every single reference to his black skin and the play would be essentially the same. Othello's trouble is that he is an outsider. He is not a Venetian. He is a military bureaucrat, a technician, hired to fight for Venice, a foreign country. The senate has no consciousness whatever of his colour. That is a startling fact but true. They haven't to make allowances for it. It simply has no place in their minds. When Desdemona confirms that she married him because she loved him, the Duke tells her father, "Well, I suggest you reconcile yourself to what seems settled." I agree that this is a somewhat unusual view. But let us stick to the play and listen to Othello himself at the moment when he decides that come what may he must kill Desdemona.

> Had it pleas'd heaven
> To try me with affliction; had he rain'd
> All kind of sores and shames on my bare head,
> Steep'd me in poverty to the very lips,
> Given to captivity me and my hopes,
> I should have found in some part of my soul

A drop of patience; but, alas, to make me
A fixed figure for the time of scorn
To point his slow unmoving fingers at!—O, O!
Yet could I bear that too; well, very well;
But there, where I have garner'd up my heart,
Where either I must live or bear no life,
The fountain from the which my current runs,
Or keep it as a cistern for foul toads,
To knot and gender in! Turn they complexion there,
Patience, thy young and rose-lipp'd cherubin—
I, here, look grim as hell.

That is the key to the whole drama. There is not a word about
his race. Othello could have faced up to anything, grave ill-
fortune or personal disaster. But for him Desdemona was his
life—"Where either I must live or bear no life". We must take
these words as literally as we can. For Othello was not a member
of that splendid court. We should see that not only in his
words—Shakespeare takes care of that—but in his manner, even
in his dress. As he tells us in that superb story of his life, from
his earliest days he had been a soldier, fighting in far and strange
places. The arts and graces and community of civilised life he
did not know and had never known. He commanded troops and
risked his life in battle. That was all he knew. And now in middle
age this beautiful, gracious and highly civilised young Venetian
woman had brought to him a vision, personal experience of a
life he had never known, had never dared to hope for. *She* had
made the marriage. As he tells us:

Yet she wish'd
That heaven had made her such a man. She thank'd me;
And bade me, if I had a friend that lov'd her,
I should but teach him how to tell my story,
And that would woo her. Upon this hint I spake.

A life which he had looked at from outside as beyond him had
suddenly opened up for him. Race has nothing to do with it.
Othello is a magnificent person, but let us beware of trying to
make his race tolerable to our race-ridden consciousness by
insisting on the nobility of his character. I think that what
Shakespeare insists upon all through, is not Othello's inflated
"magnificence", but his limitations. He is a soldier and sees
everything and everybody in military terms—duty first, and
when duty fails, it must be paid for in military terms, that is to
say, by death. He is asked to go to war on the very day of his
marriage. He agrees at once—if they think that he is being affected by his personal wishes he will pay with his life. He loves
his lieutenant, Cassio, but Cassio fails in his military duty and he
is instantly dismissed.

All through there is this iron sense of military discipline and

stern military punishment. That is the man who must kill
Desdemona, for otherwise "she will betray more men". You
see: the soldier who fails in his duty thereby betrays other
soldiers. The only cure is death and he sees the death of
Desdemona in terms of the only code of life he knows. The man
playing Othello must register Othello as a soldier and a man who
thinks in military terms: discipline or death. Then we will be able
to feel the change, the softening, that the slightest conversation
with Desdemona, a mere sight of her, causes in him. And we will
be all the more prepared for the violent return to his sternest
military self when he thinks that she has betrayed him. Hear him
on Desdemona and on war.

> I had been happy if the general camp,
> Pioners and all, had tasted her sweet body,
> So I had nothing known: O now for ever
> Farewell the tranquil mind, farewell content:
> Farewell the plumed troop and the big wars
> That make ambition virtue: O farewell,
> Farewell the neighing steed and the shrill trump
> The spirit-stirring drum, the ear-piercing fife;
> The royal banner, and all quality,
> Pride, pomp and circumstance of glorious war!
> And, O ye mortal engines whose wide threats
> Th' immortal Jove's great clamour counterfeit
> Farewell! Othello's occupation's gone.

Desdemona has destroyed even his love of war. This too, I
suggest, will make more credible that perplexing character Iago.
Of him Coleridge has used a phrase that has lasted and I think
will last: motiveless malignity. It is magnificent, but it is not
Shakespeare. As he usually does with an important character,
Shakespeare right at the start makes Iago tell us the reason for
his hatred. He should have been appointed second-in-command
to Othello. (Note that he doesn't complain about not being
made Commander—like all the others he accepts Othello's
military superiority.) This is the first thing Iago says:

> One Michael Cassio, a Florentine
> A fellow almost damn'd in a fair wife,
> That never set a squadron in the field
> Nor the division of a battle knows
> More than a spinster; unless the bookish theoric,
> Wherein the toged consuls can propose
> As masterly as he—mere prattle without practice
> Is all his soldiership. But he, sir, had the election
> And I of whom his eyes had seen the proof
> At Rhodes, at Cyprus and on other grounds
> Christian and heathen, must be be lee'd and calm'd
> By debitor and creditors counter caster:

He in good time must his Lieutenant be
And I, God bless the mark, his worship's ancient.

In the old days, says Iago, the man who was second was appointed when the senior post was vacant. But now all that is gone. Here too we must be on guard against being misled by race. Iago is in the position of a man in an underdeveloped country who sees himself passed over for strangers with modern qualifications and modern ideas: I personally know the type well. And Iago's easy success in deceiving Othello (which so annoys Mr Leavis) is due to the fact that Iago, subtle Venetian, knows that Othello is dominated by the conception of military discipline. If that is not made clear Othello will not fail to give the impression of being a somewhat stupid man, and Iago a monster of irresistible malignity. Shakespeare took care to tell us exactly what type of malignity moved in Iago. And today with the violent social changes in many countries, we ought to know it well.

Let the last word be with Othello. You remember his speech before committing suicide? It begins by saying he had done the state some service. That tells us that he felt himself an outsider. And what does he end with? Once in Aleppo a turbanned Turk, a Moslem, insulted Christian Venice, and Othello killed him on the spot. That is the note on which he dies—telling them that, outsider though he was, he had been faithful to the state and civilisation of Venice. Such acute consciousness of loyalty to Venice, not mere military loyalty, can only come from one who was very conscious that he was not a Venetian. Desdemona had opened that door for him, but when it seemed to him that she had not really accepted him, there was no more in life for him. His black skin accentuated his problem, but the problem posed was more fundamental than the colour of his skin. This is how Othello ends:

> Soft you; a word or two before you go.
> I have done the state some service, and they know't.
> No more of that. I pray you, in your letters,
> When you shall these unlucky deeds relate
> Speak of me as I am; nothing extenuate,
> Nor set down aught in malice. Then must you speak
> Of one that lov'd not wisely, but too well:
> Of one not easily jealous, but being wrought
> Perplexed in the extreme; of one whose hand
> Like the base Indian threw a pearl away
> Richer than all his tribe; of one whose subdued eyes
> Albeit unused to the melting mood
> Drops tears as fast as the Arabian trees
> Their med'cinable gum. Set you down this:
> And say besides that in Aleppo once
> Where a malignant and a turban'd Turk
> Beat a Venetian and traduc'd the state

> I took by the throat the circumcised dog
> And smote him—thus.

Then he stabs himself. Othello, we may say was the first of the great Romantics—love mattered so much to him because he was not an integral part of the society in which he lived. But we can go into these fascinating investigations only upon the solid basis of the play as played on the stage. If we do not stick to that we may well find ourselves among people quite as strange as those among whom the youthful Othello fought his battles:

> The Cannibals that each other eat
> The Anthropophagi and men whose heads
> Do grow beneath their shoulders

Neither Othello nor Iago were such men. They were people, as St Paul said, moved by like passions as ourselves. If they were not, Shakespeare would not have lasted so long.

"The Merchant of Venice"

Our preoccupation with semitism and anti-semitism distorts our view of the play that Shakespeare wrote entitled *The Merchant of Venice*. Shakespeare had no trouble whatever with Shylock. He saw the possibility of a dramatic crisis in public prejudice and he used it to the full. In addition he made matters perfectly unqualified by giving Shylock a lovely and charming daughter, Jessica. Yet in this play, Shakespeare is in real trouble with three of his main characters: Antonio, the Merchant of Venice; Portia, one of his most attractive and charming women; and Bassanio, the male character whose function it is to match the powerful attractiveness of Portia.

Shakespeare never wastes time, and in the very first line of the play Antonio himself tells us:

> In sooth, I know not why I am so sad.

Next Bassanio is introduced as follows:

> Good signiors both, when shall we laugh? Say, when?

Then Portia, to whom Bassanio would be a successful suitor, introduces herself:

> By my troth, Nerissa, my little body is aweary of this great world.

Shakespeare is in trouble with them from the start. To the idea that love may be the cause of his sadness Antonio gives a sharp "Fie, fie."

As soon as Bassanio and Antonio have some privacy, Antonio asks him directly:

> . . . ., what lady is the same
> To whom you swore a secret pilgrimage
> That you today promised to tell me of?

Shakespeare now begins a task of which he never tires: rubbing
Bassanio's nose in the dust. To this direct and reasonable
question, Bassanio rambles about the money he owes Antonio
and gives a philosophical illustration of why he should be lent
some more. All this to the extent of nearly thirty lines. Antonio
loses his patience and asks him to speak up. Whereupon
Bassanio ruins himself forever in this play by his genuine
response to Antonio's impatience.

> In Belmont is a lady richly left;

Shakespeare has no superior in placing his material before his
audience. "In Belmont is a lady richly left" coming where it
does shows that Bassanio is primarily concerned with Portia's
wealth. In fact he goes on to say so. He wants to borrow more
money from Antonio in order to make himself an appreciable
suitor.

Portia is not only extremely wealthy and a world-famous
beauty, she is heiress to her father's wealth and is manager of a
great medieval household. She treats her suitors with grace but
firmness and is not without wit and irony at their personal
weaknesses. Antonio has borrowed the requisite sum from
Shylock (to show goodwill Shylock inserts in the bond that if the
money is not paid, all that he will ask in return is a pound of
Antonio's flesh). Thus equipped Bassanio turns up at Belmont
where the lady is "richly left". Meanwhile he has neither improved his character nor personality. This bankrupt hires a
servant and includes the servant's father as part of his bounty.
One of his friends asks him for a favour and Bassanio grants it
to him at once without knowing what it is. But we get a glimpse
of the origin of Bassanio's status in the account of his departure
from Antonio.

Bassanio says that he will hasten to return. Antonio asks him
not to do that but to spend as much time as he needs on his
projected courtship.

> *Salerio*:   And even there, his eye big with tears,
>   Turning his face, he put his hand behind him,
>   And with affection wondrous sensible
>   He wrung Bassanio's hand; and so they parted.
> *Solanio*:   I think he only loves the world for him.

Bassanio wins the complicated selection from caskets which
makes him the successful suitor. And here we come to the first
real crisis Shakespeare has to face: how to make this Bassanio a
suitable mate for Portia. So far Portia has been a dominant
character, Bassanio nothing. Only the utmost audacity can drive
this relation forward. Shakespeare is audacity itself. Portia
declares her love for the successful Bassanio in one of the most
remarkable declarations of love in Shakespeare. A striking
personality, a beautiful woman, extremely wealthy, she says that

she wants to be trebled twenty times herself, one thousand times more fair, ten thousand times more rich to be worthy of Bassanio. She confesses herself to be an unlessoned girl, unschooled, unpractised, happy that she is not too old to learn, happier that she is not bred so dumb that she can't learn, happiest that she has committed herself to Bassanio to be directed by him as from "her lord, her governor, her king".

But Portia, while making Bassanio and the staff of her great household see Bassanio as the man who is her lord, is quite aware of what the real facts involved are and she concludes:

> Myself and what is mine to you and yours
> Is now converted. But now I was the lord
> Of this fair mansion, master of my servants,
> Queen o'er myself; and even now, but now,
> This house, these servants, and this same myself
> are yours, my lord . . .

No wonder Bassanio standing in his borrowed plumes begins by saying:

> Madam, you have bereft me of all words.

At this moment comes the news that Antonio's ships have all been wrecked, the loan is due, Antonio cannot pay it and Shylock is demanding his pound of flesh. At this critical moment Portia is at her best and bravest; Bassanio at his worst. All he seems able to think about is the money that has been borrowed for him and the fact that Antonio is thereby in danger. It is Portia who by her questioning drags from him his single notable exposition of Antonio's superior personality. Antonio has sent a beautiful letter which ends:

> all debts are cleared between you and I if I might but see you at my death. Notwithstanding, use your pleasure: if your love do not persuade you to come, let not my letter.

Portia is overwhelmed and the projected wedding is indefinitely postponed.

> O love, dispatch all business and be gone!

It is common knowledge that Portia gives Bassanio enough money, twenty times over, to pay the debt. And disguising herself and Nerissa as lawyers, she goes to Venice where the trial is to be held. We now come to the court scene, one of the greatest Shakespeare ever did, and one which is most often grievously misunderstood.

First of all it is a scene that should be played with every emphasis on official scope, order, legislation and government. One has to be constantly aware of what Shylock is up against. His injustice must not only be done but must be seen to be done. Secondly the conflict as written so far and for which we have been prepared is not only between Shylock and Portia but Shakespeare has taken care to bring a new relation into the play; the relation between Portia and the man who is far more suited to her than Bassanio, the Merchant of Venice himself. He says what a good actor and stage manager would have made obvious from the first line of the play: Antonio is a homosexual. He says so himself:

> I am a tainted wether of the flock,
> Meetest for death. The weakest kind of fruit
> Drops earliest to the ground, . . .

This confession, however, he makes before Portia enters, as is proper in any play and in a play by Shakespeare. There must be the utmost concentration not only on what the performers say but on what they do, how and when they move, where their eyes glance, from where their eyes retreat, etc.

Let us really look at Portia. She comes into the court. It is obvious that Portia's main concern is to see the man who is Antonio. Not only does she want to see him, it is obvious that as she comes into the court she casts her eyes around and fastens them instinctively on him. Therefore when she asks which is the Merchant and which the Jew, an acute actress makes it an obviously rhetorical question. Every word now can matter. The Duke says:

> Antonio and old Shylock, both stand forward.

That word "old" can make it clear that Antonio is not an old man. Note now how Portia continues. Portia asks:

> Is your name Shylock?

Who else could it be? There can be no serious confusion between Antonio and Shylock. Portia continues to speak *to Shylock.*

> Of a strange nature is the suit you follow;
> Yet in such rule that the Venetian law
> Cannot impugn you as you do proceed.

The legal recognition of Shylock's case gives her the opportunity to see what kind of a man this friend of Bassanio is. Only then does she turn to Antonio and ask:

> You stand within his danger, do you not?

Antonio is casual in his reply.

> Ay, so he says.

Portia will not have it.

"Do you confess the bond?" she asks him sharply. Antonio is more respectful: "I do." He begins to take notice of her.

Portia makes the great speech on the quality of mercy. At the time it must sound as if she is appealing to the humanity of

Shylock because she does not have the law behind her. Shylock thinks so and merely insists on the penalty and forfeit of his bond. Portia asks if there is not money enough to pay Shylock. Bassanio, to whom she has given a lot of money, says:

Yes, here I tender it for him in the court, . . .

He then asks the Duke to ignore the law, to do a great right, to do a little wrong. Portia says no:

there is no power in Venice
Can alter a decree established.

She then asks to let her look upon the bond. She reads it through and tells the court that the Jew may lawfully claim a pound of flesh nearest the Merchant's heart. She begs Shylock to be merciful. Shylock says no. Portia then says to Antonio directly:

Therefore lay bare your bosom.

Antonio does so. Determined to make some contact, Portia asks Antonio if he has anything to say, whereupon the whole scene leaps forward. Antonio replies:

But little. I am armed and well prepared.
Give me your hand, Bassanio. Fare you well!
Grieve not that I am fall'n to this for you;

After a few more words he brings Portia directly into the scene.

Commend me to your honorable wife; . . .

And now he turns directly to Portia:

Tell her the process of Antonio's end;
Say how I loved you, speak me fair in death;
And when the tale is told, bid her be judge
Whether Bassanio had not once a love.

These words should be said directly to Portia. Bassanio is so moved that he says:

Antonio, I am married to a wife
Which is as dear to me as life itself,
But life itself, my wife, and all the world
Are not with me esteemed above thy life.
I would lose all, ay, sacrifice them all
Here to this devil, to deliver you.

Portia here intervenes:

Your wife would give you little thanks for that
If she were by to hear you make the offer.

Formerly this scene was played as if it were a comic interlude. Today it has been played upon the London stage with deadly seriousness.

There is no need to continue in greater detail except to show once more that Shakespeare misses no opportunity to show that Bassanio is a lesser man than Antonio. The case being won, Bassanio goes up to Portia and gives her the three thousand ducats due unto the Jew.

We freely cope your courteous pains withal.

Money, always money, and that is made terribly obvious when Antonio adds:

And stand indebted, over and above,
In love and service to you evermore.

In conclusion, who can explain the following lines from Portia when alone with Nerissa? She has returned to the garden of her house at Belmont.

Portia:	That light we see is burning in my hall.
	How far that little candle throws his beams!
	So shines a good deed in a naughty world.
Nerissa:	When the moon shone, we did not see the candle.
Portia:	So doth the greater glory dim the less.
	A substitute shines brightly as a king
	Until a king be by, and then his state
	Empties itself, as doth an inland brook
	Into the main of waters. Music! hark!
Nerissa:	It is your music, madam, of the house.
Portia:	Nothing is good, I see, without respect.
	Methinks it sounds much sweeter than by day.
Nerissa:	Silence bestows that virtue on it, madam.
Portia:	The crow doth sing as sweetly as the lark
	When neither is attended; and I think
	The nightingale, if she should sing by day
	When every goose is cackling, would be thought
	No better a musician than the wren.
	How many things by season seasoned are
	To their right praise and true perfection!
	Peace—ho! The moon sleeps with Endymion,
	And would not be awaked.

Except in terms of her secret comparison between Bassanio and Antonio the above lines are inexplicable. Shakespeare saw the problem, dramatised it but could find no solution. Neither have we, after three centuries. That is why we continue to find in the character of Shylock difficulties which Shakespeare has solved in ease and style.

1963

11

Parties, Politics and Economics
in the Caribbean

[*This essay first appeared in the Summer 1964 issue of*
Freedomways. *It was later issued as a separate pamphlet under
the title "Towards a Caribbean Nation".*]

To think correctly and fruitfully of parties and politics in the
West Indies demands that the politics and the parties be seen
within the context of an affinity which exists and must be borne
in mind in every estimate of their future.

Any survey of the kind must take warning from the example
of two great sons of the Caribbean, Marcus Garvey and George
Padmore, and one American thinker, W. E. B. Du Bois.
Twenty-five years ago, different, even antagonistic, as their
individual opinions and activities might have been, they saw and
therefore worked for an Africa that was far closer to the reality
than the Africa that was being administered by authoritative
officials and analysed by learned pundits and travellers of the
day. The Africa of today did not fall from the sky. Below the
superficial surface, Garvey, Padmore and Du Bois saw the
African reality. To see realistically (and charitably) the politics
and parties of the West Indies requires an awareness of the
underlying reality, a reality which is not too far below the
surface.

There is an apparently bewildering variety of West Indian, or
more strictly speaking, Caribbean politics and parties and
governments. There is the vigorous and revolutionary government of Cuba, a focus of the world conflict which dominates
our age, a focus also of the struggle of an underdeveloped
country to achieve the concrete independence which it considers
an indispensable requirement for its full development. There is
only one party in Cuba and its political constitution and personalities and procedures are of a type familiar to all who have
the most casual acquaintance with political parties striving to
project a country from one stage into another. Just next door is
the Puerto Rican government constitutionally dominated for
many years by the political party headed by Muñoz Marín.
Underlying its consistent adherence to democratic procedures
and forms is an ambiguous relation with the government of the
United States. Is it to become the fifty-first state or is it to
continue as some sort of as yet undefined territory enjoying the
double privileges of independence and the benevolent patronage
of the United States? Muñoz Marín continues to exercise
dominance while holding this vital question in abeyance for the
simple reason that for the people of Puerto Rico the decision

calls for an agonising reappraisal which they are not ready to make. The basic reason is not far to seek and can be visualised in quite different territories. Jamaica, and Trinidad and Tobago, two former British colonies in the Caribbean, have been granted independence and the Prime Minister of Trinidad, Dr Eric Williams, has clarified the dilemma which is a ball and chain at the feet of all West Indian political parties and politicians. Feeling the strains hidden behind the freedom of a national flag and a national anthem, and in face of the Medusa-like visage of the British government which says, "OK. You are independent. Be independent, especially of my economic resources," the Prime Minister declared that Trinidad and Tobago found a closer affinity with Yugoslavia and Egypt than with the Britain which had ruled and guided it for 150 years. What has a Caribbean territory in common with Egypt of the Pyramids or of the Nile, with its native language, a religion and way of life thousands of years old? Yet this statement expressed an urgent reality, the abiding reality of all West Indian politics and parties.

What are they? Who are they? Where are they going? They do not know, and their position is therefore a constant series of spurts, now to right and now to left, unpredictable by anyone because they themselves do not know (or will not see) where they are, and therefore cannot take two firm steps either forward or backward. The drift, however, is clear, towards reaction internally and a neo-colonialist relation with a great power, preferably the United States.

The political problem which faces Muñoz Marín was stated with his customary disregard for conventional opinion by General de Gaulle. Martinique and Guadeloupe are no longer French colonies. They have been made into departments of France and a few months ago were paid an official visit by the General. It certainly was not by accident that the General stated most brutally his response to the perennial West Indian problem. Africa, he said, could be decolonised because Africa had a native civilisation and an African way of life. "But you West Indians," continued the General, "have nothing of the kind. You are French;" and warming to his theme, he continued, "look at yourselves on the map, you are no more than dust."

Thus thrown back on their small and insignificant selves, not only by history but in their own consciousness, West Indian politics waver between the democracy of Muñoz Marín, Trinidad and Tobago, and Jamaica, seeking a national identity; and the ferocity amounting not infrequently to savagery of the regimes of Duvalier in Haiti and the bandit Trujillo and his successors in the Dominican Republic.

It may seem strange and even extreme to encompass politics and parties so different as the politics of Fidel Castro, Juan Bosch (the successor of Trujillo, recently expelled from the

Dominican Republic after winning an unquestioned majority in a democratic election), the apparently stable government of Muñoz Marín and the routine of constitutional elections that seem established in Jamaica and Trinidad. Yet the underlying identity is deeply rooted in the social and economic relations of centuries. Whatever the form of government, or the coloration of political parties, the permanent features of Caribbean society, dominating their politics, are three, three in one and one in three.

The whole population is expatriate. Slaves, freed slaves, former non-slaves, emigrants from India, economic masters, none is native in any admissible sense of that word. The languages, the pattern of life are European. Even where, as in British Guiana and Trinidad, there is a large East Indian population, they do not seek to return to their land of origin, they strive with notable success to master the Western language.

This potentially explosive population lives enclosed within what is accurately entitled: the old colonial system. Banks, agricultural estates, industries, newspapers, radio (now television), import and export forms, are 90 per cent in the hands of foreign firms or what are in essence their local representatives. In this respect 1964 is no different from 1664. Twice this iron framework had been broken through: in 1792–1804 Toussaint L'Ouverture and the slaves of French San Domingo got out of it by smashing the system completely. In 1958 Fidel Castro did the same. The crisis with which he struggles shows the tremendous break with the past, the whole past, which is involved. The degeneration of Haiti is an example not of Negro backwardness but of the consequences of a partial break out from the old colonial system.

The third constituent of the Caribbean trinity is the sugar plantation. That is and always has been the social basis of the Caribbean system.

That environment, a population of expatriates, trained and daily educated in the existentialia of Western democracy and way of life; the total ownership and control of the nerve-centres of economic and social life by foreign economic and financial powers; the discipline into acceptance of the régime by the large mass of the population on sugar plantations, with here and there thousands of small peasants who eke out a precarious existence between their small plots of land and in crop-time going to work on the plantations.

To this day the West Indian Negro must be seen as a historically different social being from his brothers of the United States. In his seminal work, *The Masters and the Slaves*, Gilberto Freyre writes:

The Brazilian Negro appears to us, throughout the whole of our colonial life and the first phase of our independent life as a nation, as a being deformed by slavery, by slavery and by the one-crop system, of which he was the instrument, the firm point of support, unlike the Indian, who was always on the move.

That is the general key to the history of the Negro people in the Americas. The particular West Indian variety is that the sugar plantation was the most striking example of the one-crop system and, slavery or no slavery, continues to this day.

A new and apparently indigestible element has been added to the centuries-old pattern. Companies, again foreign, have introduced the production of oil, bauxite and mine industries. The workers organised in these, freed from the demoralising discipline of the sugar plantation, express the national resentment by continued strikes for higher wages, fringe benefits, the ill-manners of a superior, anything. It therefore becomes a function of government to reduce to colonial subordination this intrusion from a new age. All that the old colonial system can conceive is to fit modern labour into the old system—a very hard task.

This new system of independence is only the old colonial system writ large. Contemporary Caribbean politics consists essentially of the capacity to administer the old colonial system either by means of the brutality of a Trujillo or the democratic forms of Trinidad or Jamaica, or the skilful balancing on the fence of Muñoz Marín.

The Caribbean territories have a universal significance far beyond their size and social weight. They seem to be a slice of Western civilisation put under a microscope for the scientific investigation of the fundamental predicates and perspectives of that civilisation itself. Owing to the expatriate character of the whole Caribbean all the old problems seem posed anew in terms which are easily grasped, new in that they are not dominated as in the older countries by long established growths and accretions; urgent in that the Caribbean problems demand some settlement if not solution; comprehensive and very modern in that politics, economics and sociology are one indivisible unit. Here are some startling and far-reaching examples.

1. Take the racial problem. The world is pained and even horrified by what is believed to be the indestructible racial antagonism between Negroes and East Indians in British Guiana, led on the one hand by the East Indian Dr Jagan and on the other by the Negro Burnham. The truth of these apparently suicidal politics is that in 1952 Jagan and Burnham were joined together in one party—and were virtual masters of British Guiana, the races closer together than they were ever before, and showing every sign that they were eager for further integration. It seems to me that the racial antagonism in British Guiana is an effect, not a cause, the effect of the unwillingness or inability of some leaders there to challenge the old colonial system.

2. Mr Manley of Jamaica, defeated by Sir Alexander Bustamante over federation and in the struggle for power, had recently made the public announcement that the similarity (hostile critics say identity) of the two rival parties in Jamaica is the condition of democracy and order. If the two parties, he declared, had fundamentally different ideas as to the kind of society they envisaged or aimed at, the democratic regime would be impossible. Mr Manley is quite correct. Both parties intend not to interfere with the old colonial system. Whence a growing discontent, even anger, in all West Indian territories. In territory after territory it is the same. In political policy the opposition parties are indistinguishable from the government party. Recently Dr Williams, Prime Minister of Trinidad and Tobago, declared that 90 per cent of the economy is in the hands of two or three foreign firms. The leader of the opposition, we may be sure, is thinking about it no less and no more than Dr Williams.

3. After the assassination of Trujillo in the Dominican Republic Senor Juan Bosch was elected by a large majority. But he made no attempt to touch the old colonial system. He therefore aroused no popular enthusiasm and was easily ejected by the old gang.

4. Federation is on the order of the day and this is how the British West Indian Federation collapsed. The old colonial system consisted of insular economies, each with its financial and economic capital in London. A federation meant that the economic line of direction should no longer be from island to London, but from island to island. But that involved the break-up of the old colonial system. The West Indian politicians preferred the break-up of the Federation.

5. The French Caribbean territories find that becoming departments of France has doubly and trebly strengthened the old colonial system. It is the finished pattern of the French community in Africa and the Dutch community in South America.

6. Contrary to general belief, the West Indies are not sunk in irremediable poverty. There is room for only two proofs, each of such diverse origin that together they are irrefutable. The first is the American government. In *The New York Times* of 8 October 1962 appeared a report of Mr Chester Bowles, appointed special adviser to President Kennedy on underdeveloped areas. Mr Bowles divided recipients of American aid into three categories. In the first category Mr Bowles places nations with a per capita gross national product of more than $350. Their current problems, the report stated, would be sufficiently acute to require aid, but their difficulties would result primarily from the "misuse and maldistribution of their wealth". In this category along with Greece, Venezuela and others we find Jamaica and Trinidad. He added that these countries should be able "to put their financial houses in order". In addition to

corrective measures which the United States should suggest, they would be advised to introduce tax and land reforms.

That mishandling and maldistribution of resources is the direct continuation of the old colonial system.

The other critical view of the West Indian economy and West Indian society is that of Professor Arthur Lewis. When he was Principal of the University of the West Indies in Jamaica, Professor Lewis, former head of the faculty of economics at Manchester University and at the time of writing a member of the faculty at Princeton, tried to remove some cobwebs from the eyes of his fellow West Indians:

> This opinion that the West Indies can raise all the capital it needs from its own resources is bound to shock many people, because West Indians like to feel that ours is a poor community. But the fact of the matter is that at least half of the people in the world are poorer than we are. The standard of living in the West Indies is higher than the standard of living in India, or China, in most of the countries of Asia, and in most of the countries of Africa. The West Indies is not a poor community; it is in the upper bracket of world income. It is capable of producing the extra five or six per cent of resources which is required for this job, just as Ceylon and Ghana are finding the money they need for development by taxing themselves. It is not necessary for us to send our statesmen around the world begging for help. If help is given to us let us accept it, but let us not sit down and say nothing can be done until the rest of the world out of its goodness of heart is willing to grant us charity.

In other words the economic problem is soluble but as in far larger countries soluble only by political means. The question is: who will bell the cat?

The problem does not imperatively or inescapably demand revolutionary measures, e.g. violence such as took place in French San Domingo in 1791 or in Cuba in 1958. Many elements both at home and abroad recognise the explosive character of the Caribbean scene. The West Indian white is not a foreigner. He is a West Indian and many of them recognise that something must be done and can be done. That, however, is another story and involves the ways and means to a federation of the whole Caribbean area. That may sound utopian, as utopian as Garvey, Padmore and Du Bois must have sounded when they talked of an independent Africa.

1964

12

On Wilson Harris

[*"Wilson Harris and the Existentialist Doctrine"* is the text of a lecture delivered at the University of the West Indies in Trinidad in 1965, an occasion for which James was temporarily paroled from the house arrest to which he had been subjected by the Williams government. The introduction to Wilson Harris's essay *"Tradition and the West Indian Novel"* was published in May 1965 by the London West Indian Students' Union.]

Wilson Harris and the Existentialist Doctrine

I would be very much surprised if, except in a private home, there was a copy of Heidegger's *Being and Time* in the West Indies. Therefore you will understand why I will speak at greater length than usual on certain philosophical aspects of Harris's work. I should warn you in advance that, as far as I am concerned, strict philosophy is as difficult and technical a business as marine engineering, or medicine. It is not a thing in which amateurs can fool around. Nevertheless, I make a certain response to Harris which is not unconnected with philosophy. May I say that everybody has a philosophical view of the world and of politics and of literature and everything else. He may not know it, he may militantly deny that he has, but he has one. Whether he knows it or not everybody has a certain philosophical view and those people I have found who very vigorously deny that they have any are precisely those who have one, but they have an uneasy feeling that it is not a very presentable one so they say, "I haven't any, leave me out of that altogether." (I don't leave them out, I try to put them further in.)

So here is what I am going to do. I shall begin by giving you an idea of one of Harris's novels *Palace of the Peacock*, the first one that he wrote. I shall then move straight into some aspects of the philosophy which I think has to be understood or appreciated in some degree or other in order really to understand what Harris is doing. Then I will go back to another novel of Harris. Finally I will take up with you some writing that Harris has been doing for the students in the West Indian hostel in London and which we have recently published. So that you can follow me easily, let me repeat: first of all, one of Harris's novels, the first one, usually said to be the most difficult, *Palace of the Peacock*. Secondly, some philosophical ideas connected with Harris's work in the way that I see it. I recommend to you to go into it; you can reject them, do whatever you like, but at least make yourself familiar and get some sort of view. Thirdly, once more, a novel of Harris's. And finally a publication (of which I have here some proofs) that will be brought out very soon and may even now be already in circulation in Britain, something Harris has written recently—a lecture published in a small pamphlet which undoubtedly will be available here shortly.

The novel I am going to begin with is *Palace of the Peacock*. Harris wrote it about 1960 and you will have to pay very close attention to it in order to be able to get some idea of what he is doing. In *Palace of the Peacock* Harris begins on the first page by saying that somebody has seen a horseman, his elder brother. The horseman is dead. Now you have not gone very long before you find out that the man who is writing the novel is himself dead. Harris is taking you along a journey, made along a river of British Guiana where the rivers have a peculiar habit of going down suddenly—waterfalls or rapids. These men are engaged on this difficult journey, about six or eight of them, and they are all dead. The novel is a mystical reconstruction of the lives of each of them—Harris takes the reader carefully into the preliminary lives of each, how this one was living in Georgetown and how this one was a surveyor and that one was an engineer and that one a common boatman, etc., and takes each life up to the moment of death. Thus he gives you the preliminary life and then at the moment of death, at the moment when the man falls out of the raft or the canoe that they are travelling in, or the moment when somebody in the canoe stabs somebody else, this man who is dying has some conception of what he is trying to be and has a vision of where he is reaching and what he expects is going to happen to him. Harris does that with those six or eight characters. Their previous lives in ordinary existence, what is happening to them at the moment they are travelling in the canoe, their ideals and visions, which are quite individual to them, the moment of death, and at the moment of death, what they are looking for. There are one or two of them who are nearly dead, or really dead, I am not sure, but they see some kind of vision of the life they are going to live afterwards. All that within about 120 pages.

Now there is one thing you recognise at once. This is a very original, a very audacious novel, and, believe me, after some experience of the novel, I find that original and audacious novels are very rare. That is *Palace of the Peacock*. The Palace they are seeking is the Palace where they are going to achieve their life's ambition. But each has his own conception of happiness based on his past life, based on his racial associations, based on his vision of the world, based on the work that he is doing in getting the canoe down the river, and based on his relations with the people who are with him.

Now, I have frightened you sufficiently. I can fortify that discomfort by telling you that there are many people who say that Harris is very difficult, including myself, some time ago. But the other day I met a young woman who told me: "You are always talking about Wilson Harris. I went to the library and got a book called *Palace of the Peacock*, but I read it through from start to finish without trouble. You had given me the impression he was difficult." Well, that shows I was wrong. I shouldn't have done it, but nevertheless, you are a university audience and any difficulties you can easily surmount, I am quite sure.

So that is *Palace of the Peacock*, that is Harris's novel. It has been compared by reviewers (and I am ashamed to say that I am going to have to use British reviewers about Harris in order to fortify the case I am making, but I will not do that during the talk, that will be done during question time and you will have to ask me for it)—it has been compared by British reviewers to *The Drunken Boat* by Rimbaud, which is one of the peaks of imaginative creation of a visionary world. That is what Harris does.

So now let us get down to it. Let me put on my glasses, so as to be able to see the looks of consternation on your faces. I believe Harris is to be seen as a writer of the postwar period who is in the full philosophical tradition and has carried to an extraordinary pitch the work of two German philosophers. There are others but we need only two—they are hard enough by themselves. One of them is Heidegger and the other is Jaspers, and I very much regret you have not got a Professor of Philosophy and Literature to pester as soon as you leave here, to tell you all about Heidegger, what he knows of Heidegger and Jaspers. I am glad to say I have found in this university somebody with whom I have had a conversation about Heidegger. He has not only a great knowledge of and interest in him but has had some personal connection with him. I tell you that because you ought to make it your business that he should speak to you and tell you what he knows. I am sure he will. People who are interested in Heidegger rejoice when they know that somebody wants to hear something about him.

Harris is not easy. That is why I want to speak of Heidegger, Jaspers (and Jean-Paul Sartre) and show you that it is in some consideration of those remarkable philosophers who have attracted so much philosophical attention after World War II, that Harris will be seen as being in the same stream.

Now Heidegger. I have read various translations of Heidegger, but the great book that matters is *Being and Time* and I say again that philosophy in a real sense is as difficult as marine engineering or medicine. That I know: but I read philosophical books, I have read them for many years, I am absolutely fascinated by Heidegger. And in my opinion *Being and Time* is one of the greatest philosophical works that I have ever read. Now all through Heidegger's great book (he published it in 1927) he is concerned about the everyday life, the life that is lived by you and me and Heidegger himself. It is the life of "everydayness". He is a great man for making up words: "everydayness". He says that the lives which people live they live according to a certain "average", they do not know *exactly* this, or *exactly* that, but they have an everyday or average view.

He notes that most people read the same newspapers, they read the same books, they eat the same food, they listen to the same politicians, they live more or less a certain type of life. They may seem to communicate with one another but Heidegger says they don't. They use a special mode of communication, "idle talk". He says, about science, there are people who study anthropology and write anthropological books. He says they get a lot of facts and put them together but there is nothing to it. I accept that. I do not know anything about anthropology but he says the same about history. They put a lot of facts together— that is all, and Heidegger is not the only person saying so. Specialists in these various departments are today quite plain in their condemnation of the lack of some serious grasp of a subject, chiefly I would mention the sociologists. They are constantly asking, what is sociology? They do not know. Psychology. What is psychology? They do not know. All those books about Freud and Jung, etc. etc., Heidegger says that all the scientists do is to gather up a lot of facts, they go to the moon or they cross the Atlantic in one hour, but he says it is all just an accumulation of facts and of things that are happening. That is the general view of the world in which we live and everybody lives in that world.

Now, there is one word which I want you to remember about Heidegger and which you will have to grapple with. He says in that way I have sketched we live an "inauthentic" existence, but he says, there is another type of life which he calls *"dasein"*. That is the only word you have to remember about Heidegger. *Dasein*; if you remember that, you remember everything. *Dasein*: that is the German word meaning "being there", and when the *dasein* begins to function, when a man is "being there" in the world of everydayness, of average behaviour, of idle talk, he begins to live an authentic existence. Before that his existence was inauthentic. With *dasein*, you begin to lead an authentic existence. Now, what are the distinctive forms of this authentic existence? I will mention a few words, a few terms, leave you with them and then go to Jaspers first and then go back to Wilson Harris.

One of the terms is "truth". Heidegger says that although Plato and Aristotle knew better, they set us on a path which has made us completely lose sight of what truth is. He says truth is in nobody's mind. You have to find out truth by being there, by living an authentic existence in this inauthentic world. Truth is covered over and the finding out of truth means you uncover what is there, but it can be uncovered not by philosophy, not by knowledge of any kind, but by the fact of *dasein*. You are living there and seeking what you need for your life, for an authentic life, and so you uncover the truth. Otherwise truth remains covered over. He says the modern world has followed the Greeks and thus have seen truth as something in the mind. Aristotle's logic has resulted in modern science which as he says, is a wonderful example of the discovery of a multitude of individual, separate *beings*: this and that and that, Newton and all these scientific discoveries. But Being, the nature of existence as a whole, *that* they have ignored and that they have to get back to, and that is what he is concerned with: the nature of Being. And the *dasein*, the "being there", is an uncovering of the truth of Being that exists. Not beings but Being itself. Further he says mountains are, horses are, books are, but only man *exists* and the source of man's existence is not only the *dasein*. The means he uses to find what he is finding out, to live an authentic existence, is language, and I have seen that nowhere stated as sharply as Harris states it. Language. Language is not a tool; politics is a tool, painting is a tool, scientific procedures are tools of mankind, but language is not. In Heidegger's view man lives a human life because of language. Without that he would be, I do not know what he would be, but he would not be a human being, and critics say that Heidegger's analysis of language is profoundly important for the study and practice of language.

Heidegger goes on to give his conception of history; some translators (these translators have a wonderful time with Heidegger) say that what he says about history should be translated as historicity. Others say it should be called historicality. I say, "Gentlemen, go right ahead, I know what he means," but I accept historicality. I like the long words, they are more important and imposing. Historicality and Temporality. Both of them I take together. Now I want to explain Heidegger's view of that because that is exactly what Harris is doing in *Palace of the Peacock* and what he is doing all through his fiction. Heidegger says, you say, now, today, you say what is happening today? Ordinary time tells you that on 25 March James came here to lecture to you, or speak to you on Wilson Harris, and yesterday James was doing something and tomorrow he will be doing something else. Heidegger says that is ordinary time, an ordinary event, in ordinary time. He says man does not live that way. He says he has a time of his own which Heidegger calls temporality. Each man has his own conception of time. He says what is the now? All these philosophers of the now, and now, and now, history writers speak of this and then this and then this. He says: that is not how it goes at all. He says at any moment the now is the result of all that has happened before and your conception of it. He says also you are considering something which he calls the futural. He says you are aware that you are going to be dead. He says that is the only thing nobody can do for you, you have to die for yourself. He says, we live between birth and death—a man at a certain stage is looking at a certain totality and he is aware that he is there and he has lived up to that time, and he knows this and that and the other but he is aware that he will ultimately be dead and sometime or other what he is doing is going to arrive at a certain conclusion. He isn't sure what it is, but an actual moment is always a sort of approximation between the antiquarian, the historical point of view and the futural point of view. There is no actual time or actual part of history which is to be taken away from the fact that man is living there in the stream of actual existence. Now I have found that profound and illuminating. At question time you may ask me about personal experience. A great deal of what I have seen in Heidegger is due to my own personal experience.

Heidegger also uses the concept of "dread". He says, man lives with the concept of care, is very concerned with what is likely to happen, but he has the basic concept of dread. Man is not afraid of anything in particular or of any person in particular, not at all. He says the mere fact that you are living, you are going to be dead and you do not know exactly what is going to happen to you, he says that makes in your existence the necessity of some kind of dread as to what is going to happen to you in the future. You don't know. He insists that you are not afraid of this or that or the other, or of this person, or that earthquake, or that subversive law or anything. He says you are just afraid, you have this concept of dread. Now, the authentic existence, this way of being there, these problems that you deal with, the finding out of truth as something hidden, the concept of dread and care, he says all these things are there and you can live an inauthentic existence but there can take place a transcendescence from these ordinary things, a transcendescence arising above them. He says everything that really matters to you in an authentic existence is a transcendescence, and with your kind permission (and I hope your lively curiosity) there I leave you with Heidegger.

I have given you some conception of what I got out of him and apart from technical questions of philosophy, I repeat that I find it one of the most fascinating and illuminating books that I have ever read. I can't talk very much about it unless I have it here, you see, but I am very much aware of *dasein*, that I am in the world: when I am reading Heidegger, and after I have read him, and being there, and the things present to hand, and all those technical matters. There is somebody on the campus who would be able to tell you about that, it is up to you whether you want it or not.

Now, the other man I want to speak about is Jaspers. Both these old men are still alive and very lively. Jaspers also wrote his first book before World War II began. (All this to me is the result of what happened to mankind in World War I. People became aware of the inauthentic nature of their existence, were aware of the permanent feeling of dread, of the uncertainty, of truth, and these philosophers wrote. It is my firm belief that a philosopher writes because he feels a special impact of the particular age in which he lives.)

Heidegger is, by the way, very careful and strong about that. He says, you study philosophy, you read Plato, you read Leibniz, you get a degree, you write a doctorate on philosophy, you understand Plato, you understand Aristotle, you understand the pre-Socratic Greeks etc., *only when you are yourself taking part in philosophy*. He says, otherwise, unless you are philosophising, fighting out an authentic way of philosophy, you are not only doing nothing but you cannot even understand the men you have been reading. He says you must philosophise i.e. take part philosophically in the problems of the day, otherwise you cannot even understand the great philosophers of the past. I believe he has in mind a certain famous professor, but what amuses me is a devastating paragraph he has about Ernest Cassirer (Cassirer is a very learned man who died the other day) and his American supporter Suzanne Langer. They say man is a maker of symbols (you know, some say man is a tool-making animal, others say God made him, other people say Darwin discovered the origin of species; they, at least Cassirer, discovered that man makes symbols). Heidegger says it is a lot of nonsense and for a long time I have thought the same. You can find out for yourself.

Now we must go over to Jaspers. Heidegger published in 1927; go to your Library and insist on their having *Being and Time*.

I can deal with Jaspers in two or three minutes. Jaspers, as far back as 1931, wrote one of his early philosophical books where he said that mankind found out what he was when he was living in a limit situation, in an extreme boundary situation. He says previously you live an ordinary life—it was not too different from the everyday existence that Heidegger talks about. He says that when you are in an extreme case, then you find out what man is, what he can do, what he is likely to do. The extreme boundary limit situation is the philosophy of Jaspers. Now Jaspers has been accused of being Christian, and that does not worry me at all. He can be what he likes. But he has made clear that man today is living in an extreme situation and it is when he is living in that extreme limit boundary situation that you find out what man really is and what he is likely to become.

Most of Harris's work, a great deal of it, is divided between these very topics. Man lives the everyday life in Georgetown, everydayness, and then lives in an extreme situation in the hinterland of British Guiana, in which he has to deal with rivers, floods, wild animals, with difficulties of food, and the realities

of human life are stark and clear. So that for Harris, in British
Guiana you have the everydayness and average life in
Georgetown and small towns and villages (we ought to know
that here in Trinidad); and also you have this life of the extreme
boundary limit situation in which the harsh realities of existence
tell men what they really are, which is what Jaspers has been
saying all the time. An important note. Heidegger says the
transcendental is the way in which the man who is living the life
of *dasein*, works his way to something out of everyday existence.
Jaspers is here different. Jaspers says the transcendental is
mystical and he wavers around about Christianity and even
God, I think—I am not so sure. But that, as a thinker of the
boundary situation, is his particular sphere. I have read his
philosophy with interest, parts of it with a certain scepticism,
but I recognised that he is watching something, aware of certain
aspects of life, still untouched.

Now these were philosophers whom nobody would have
bothered with particularly except German philosophers, German students and specialists. But France went through the
period of being occupied by the Germans and tortured by the
Gestapo, and produced undoubtedly the greatest writer of the
present day, Jean-Paul Sartre. Sartre wrote philosophy of his
own, a huge book called *Being and Nothingness*. In it he introduced a great deal of Heidegger, he introduced some of
Jaspers (he also introduced both Descartes and Hegel), and it is
a philosophical work that is fit to take its place with the
traditional masterpieces of philosophy. Now he was close to
Heidegger in that he says you have to make a choice, the choice
depends on you, on your being there—Sartre somewhat
vulgarises this question of choice. He rather insists that you have
to make a political choice between the inauthentic existence and
the authentic. But there is a lot of Jaspers in Sartre. Sartre went
through the occupation in France, the French citizen had to
decide what he would do when tortured by the Gestapo, whether
he would betray or not. Nobody would ever know what you had
decided. And he has a peculiar sentence where he says, "We
were never so happy as under the German occupation," because
you see they had to choose and they knew what was right and
what was wrong. In those days the limit was very plain, you were
in an extreme situation and that is what Jaspers had taught for
years and was still teaching. Sartre has made Heidegger and
Jaspers popular. Everybody talks about them now, not only in
philosophical circles, but in most intellectual circles. Heidegger
and Jaspers who wrote between the wars are now very widely
known because Jean-Paul Sartre has introduced these questions
into philosophy.

Now let us go rapidly back to Wilson Harris. What is
noticeable about Sartre is this—he writes his philosophical
books, *Being and Nothingness*, etc., you have to wrestle with

Heidegger, you have to wade through Kant's theories; but although Sartre writes that kind of book, he also writes novels and plays, and his existentialist philosophy he seeks to portray in novels and plays. I have never known a philosophy so closely reported in fiction or drama.

But Harris has done more than that. Within the covers of one small book of ninety or one hundred pages Harris gives you a big slab of actual everyday existence, the inauthentic life we all lead, and then, within that same novel, he takes you to an extreme situation right away in the interior of British Guiana with men pulling a canoe or raft up some waterfall or descending it with all sorts of dangers around them. And then he does what Sartre does not do, within the covers of the same volume he proceeds to give you pages of philosophical exploration. There is no other novelist that I know of doing the same thing today. There is a woman in England called Ivy Compton Burnett. There is another woman called Iris Murdoch, you should see the reviews they get. I find it hard to take them seriously. There is a bunch of them in Paris, Claude Simon, a woman called Natalie Sarraute. They write "anti-novels": I agree completely, the novel as I have known it—what they write is anti that. There are some novelists in America, I read one or two of them, the only one that matters to me is James Baldwin. To all of them I prefer—I put it that way—Lamming and Naipaul. Now to them is added Harris. Harris is a remarkable novelist whether he writes about everydayness, or of the life that the men and women living in the boundary situation out in the wilds of British Guiana. The contrast is between their lives in the everyday situation and their lives in a boundary situation; and then he proceeds to write philosophical views of the world in general. I think it is most remarkable that this West Indian, uneducated in German, uneducated in European universities, should have found out these things practically for himself and should be writing the kind of book that he does.

I have read Harris's latest novel—it hasn't been published yet—it is called *The Eye of the Scarecrow*. But I will not deal with this. I will deal with a novel called *The Secret Ladder*. Now I hope you will remember what I have been saying about Heidegger and Jaspers. Fenwick is a young man who has been living an inauthentic existence in Georgetown. He is a land surveyor and has gone into the interior to survey a piece of land on which live some African Negroes, descendants of the former escaped slaves. The head of this group of Negroes is a man called Poseidon, a name with Greek and very widespread connotations which you will find out for yourself. Poseidon is a hundred years old and it is clear that he and his people distrust Fenwick and his party. They feel they have come there to do a scientific job which will improve the situation. Poseidon and company do not accept this at all. They consider that Fenwick and the people who have come there to carry out all these experiments, putting gauges and measuring temperature and measuring depth of rainfall and so on, they are a menace, they have come to do something harmful to these African descendants of slaves who have been living there for over a hundred years. Now that is an extreme situation for Poseidon and his followers. It also becomes a very extreme situation for Fenwick. Fenwick has a talk with Poseidon and he notices that the way that Poseidon's lips move is contrary to the things that Poseidon is supposed to be saying. In other words the physical appearance of Poseidon is one thing but the things that he is saying come from a different age and a different generation. Fenwick writes to his mother and he tells her: "I didn't understand him but I have a peculiar feeling that unless I understand what he is saying, this generation to which I belong is doomed." Harris you can see is a very bold writer. So Fenwick sends this letter to his mother and he again meets Poseidon this time in the company of a young Negro called Bryant. Poseidon talks again and Fenwick is very much aware that Poseidon thinks that the best thing that could happen is that Fenwick and all his crew and all their instruments should get out of there. Fenwick gets very angry. He tells Poseidon or he tells Bryant rather: "You seem sympathetic to him. You think that we are going to cut short his freedom. What is this freedom, what kind of freedom does Poseidon have, he and his ex-slaves? Can't you see that in bringing science here and surveying the place and seeing what is to be done we are bringing some real freedom?" To his astonishment Bryant says: "I do not think so." Bryant says: "I think Poseidon is freer than you or me." Fenwick says: "What kind of nonsense is that? You are forgetting yourself." Bryant says: "Well, that is what I think. I think he is freer than you or me"; and then Bryant says something which I recommend for your careful consideration. This young West Indian of the present day, having got into touch with Poseidon who is fighting for freedom, he tells Fenwick: "When Poseidon dies he is going to go back to Africa." Now Bryant did not learn that in school or in university, what he learnt in school was that such an idea was the illusion under which African slaves committed suicide. But, you see, under the pressure of the extreme situation and siding with Poseidon he recovers the historical ideas of the slaves. He tells Fenwick that Poseidon was his grandfather: "At least I feel that way towards him." Fenwick is deeply disturbed, first of all at Poseidon and at what Poseidon is doing to Bryant. They bring news to Fenwick that some of Poseidon's men have broken down the gauges that he has put up to measure rainfall and waterfall and so on. And two of Fenwick's assistants, they are foremen in charge, tell him: "Now look at what these savages did. We should deal with them." But Fenwick begins to experience the *dasein*. He says, "I do not think that what they did was in opposition to us." Fenwick adds: "Yes, they may have broken the gauges, but I think they were seeking to establish some sort of freedom which they think we threaten." The foremen are eager to punish Poseidon's men. Fenwick says, "No, leave them alone. I think I will be able to work it out with them." Fenwick, in other words, is experiencing the *dasein*. He is "living there", and the previous existence whereby he came from the government with the instruments and a group to measure the land and to do things which he thought of benefit to them, he has lost that completely, it was inauthentic. He is quite sympathetic now to the fact that they are breaking down his gauges and saying that they do not want him. He says he thinks he understands what they are doing.

Now there is only one more point I wish to make about the novel, the rest of it you will have to .work out for yourself. He has two foremen and one of the foremen tells him, "Please, sir, you are becoming too sympathetic to the men." I do not quite understand this psychological motivation myself. The foreman continues to admonish Fenwick. He says, "Your attitude to Poseidon and your attitude to the men dispels all the discipline that the crew should have. The men are beginning to feel that you are soft and they will come and ask you for things and break discipline." Fenwick says: "Well, if they feel that way, that is okay with me. I am beginning to feel that way myself, and I think it is a better feeling than the previous one." And there I will stop in regard to *The Secret Ladder*.

I hope I have made you understand that this is a writer dealing with profoundly important subjects in a bold and original manner that you will not easily find among other novels of the day. The relationship is between Fenwick's everyday existence and Fenwick as he finds an authentic existence, the way in which by getting into the position of "being there" with Poseidon and the rest, he begins to find out what their life really is, his change from feeling that he was coming there to help them, to understand that their opposition to him is in reality authentic and not to be fought down or ignored, all this makes this a highly philosophical novel. Harris breaks easily from all this into philosophical meditation closely allied to the events all within the covers of one novel.

I went the other day to the West Indian Students' Hostel to hear Harris speak on the West Indian novel. Well, in the end we decided that we should print it. I was told I could write an introduction, Learie Constantine has paid for it, and I have the proofs here. Harris is speaking about the West Indian novel and I want to read one extract because we cannot have a talk about Wilson Harris without your hearing something that he says himself. Harris says, "The special point I want to make in regard to the West Indies is that the pursuit of a strange and subtle goal, melting pot, call it what you like, is the mainstream (though unacknowledged) tradition in the Americas. And the significance of this is akin to the European preoccupation with alchemy, with the growth of experimental science, the poetry of science as well as of explosive nature which is informed by a solution of images, agnostic humility and essential beauty rather than vested interest in a fixed assumption and classification of things.''

That I think is the key to Harris. When the pamphlet appears get your own copy and study it. This is what I make of it.

European civilisation for many centuries had a fixed assumption and classification of material achievement and corresponding philosophical conceptions. Harris says that America is not like that. He insists America is not like that, the West Indies are not like that. They have a different attitude to the world, because their whole historical and material experience has been different. But Heidegger, in my opinion, and Jaspers and Sartre, are aware that the European preoccupation or acceptance of the material basis of life, a fixed assumption—that has broken down. That is the significance of Heidegger, Jaspers and Sartre. It began to break down with Nietzsche who said that God was dead and, as Dostoyevsky added, if God is dead then everything is permitted: people, especially people with authority, do anything. The whole European conception of a fixed material assumption of things and a fixed political and philosophical assumption of things—that has broken down. Harris is saying that in the Americas, in Central America and in the West Indies, that has never been. There has never been that fixed assumption of things, that belief in something that is many centuries old and solid. That is why he is saying what I interpret as the *dasein*, the "being there". I find it profoundly important and viable especially for people who live in these territories.

1965

Introduction to "Tradition and the West Indian Novel"

After listening to Wilson Harris's lecture, and reading the script which I at once asked for, I recommended that it be published. I also asked him if he would object to my writing a commentary to be published along with his script. He agreed—I may add, cordially. And I should begin at once by saying why I wished to add a few words of comment to his altogether exceptional piece. (Where I have disagreed with his specific judgments I have told him in person, but that is not my business here.) What I want to do is to show why I think this lecture is one of the most remarkable I have ever heard, both in its application to writing in general and, secondly, not only for the West Indies but coming from the West Indies.

What startled me was that I had been studying existentialism, that modern development in philosophy, and reading the German philosopher Heidegger. I had been reading:

> In what sense however is this most dangerous thing one of man's possessions? Language is his own property. It is at his disposal for the purpose of communicating his experiences, resolutions and moods. Language serves to give information. As a fit instrument for this, it is a "possession". But the essence of language does not consist entirely in being a means of giving information. This definition does not touch its essential essence, but merely indicates an effect of its essence. Language is not a mere tool, one of the many which man possesses; on the contrary, it is only language that affords the very possibility of standing in the openness of the existent. Only where there is language, is there world, i.e. the perpetually altering circuit of decision and production, of action and responsibility, but also of commotion and arbitrariness, of decay and confusion. Only where world predominates, is there history. Language is a possession in a more fundamental sense. It is good for the fact that (i.e. it affords a guarantee that) man can *exist* historically. Language is not a tool at his disposal, rather it is that event which disposes of the supreme possibility of human existence. We must first of all be certain of this essence of language, in order to comprehend truly the sphere of action of poetry and with it poetry itself. How does language become actual? In order to find the answer to this question, let us consider a third saying of Hölderlin's.
>
> We come across this saying in a long and involved sketch for the unfinished poem which begins "*Versohnender, der du nimmer-geglaubt . . .*" (IV, 162ff, and 339ff.):
>> "Much has man learnt.
>> Many of the heavenly ones has he named,
>> Since we have been a conversation
>> And have been able to hear from one another." (IV, 343.)
>
> Let us first pick out from these lines the part which has a direct bearing on what we have said so far: "Since we have been a conversation . . ." We—mankind—are a conversation. The being of man is founded in language.

I have been reading this off and on for some years but it is only since I have felt it urgent, as a marxist, to get myself right on existentialism that I began to pay serious attention. In a critical essay on Heidegger by an American I read that it is a pity that modern students of literature outside of Germany have not paid attention to his analysis of language. For a long time I have been thinking and writing about the origin and influence of language in relation to ourselves in the West Indies, also what happens to us who use a language that originated among another and very different people. Imagine when I sit in the West Indies Student Centre and hear Harris say:

> And this vision of consciousness is the peculiar reality of language

because the concept of language is one which continuously transforms inner and outer formal categories of experience, earlier and representative modes of speech itself, the still life resident in painting and sculpture as such, even music which one ceases to "hear"—the peculiar reality of language provides a medium to *see* in consciousness the "free" motion and to *hear* with consciousness the "silent" flood of sound by a continuous inward revisionary and momentous logic of potent explosive images evoked in the mind. Such a capacity for language is a real and necessary one in a world where the inarticulate person is continuously frozen or legislated for in mass and a genuine experience of his distress, the instinct of distress, sinks into a void. The nightmare proportions of this are already becoming apparent throughout the world.

Whom Harris has been reading I don't know. I sent him at once a copy of my Heidegger and he rapidly replied that he agreed with Heidegger entirely. I have talked with George Lamming on this question of language in the West Indies and he has very definite views on it. These he will, I hope, make clear (and popular) one day. Derek Walcott I know is grappling practically with this problem. The point that shook me was that Harris, grappling with a West Indian problem, had arrived at conclusions which dealt with the problem of language as a whole in the world at large.

The second point that has startled me is Harris's clear recognition that we are the product of a very complicated historical past and all of it is in us *striving or at any rate ready for expression.* We are an adventurous people, ready for anything. We are what we are because we have been what we have been. Take for example Harris on the myth of El Dorado:

> Let us apply our scale, for example, to the open myth of El Dorado. The religious and economic thirst for exploration was true of the Spanish conquistador, of the Portuguese, French, Dutch and English, of Raleigh, of Fawcett, as it is true of the black modern pork-knocker and the pork-knocker of all races. An instinctive idealism associated with this adventure was overpowered within individual and collective by enormous greed, cruelty and exploitation. In fact it would have been very difficult a century ago to present these exploits as other than a very material and degrading hunger for wealth spiced by a king of self-righteous spirituality. It is difficult enough today within clouds of prejudice and nihilism; nevertheless the substance of this adventure, involving men of all races, past and present conditions, has begun to acquire a residual pattern of illuminating correspondences. El Dorado, City of Gold, City of God, grotesque, unique coincidence, another window within upon the Universe, another drunken boat, another ocean, another river; in terms of the novel the distribution of a frail moment of illuminating adjustments within a long succession and grotesque series of adventures, past and present, capable *now* of discovering

themselves and continuing to discover themselves so that in one sense one relives and reverses the "given" condition of the past, freeing oneself from catastrophic idolatry and blindness to one's own historical and philosophical conceptions and misconceptions which may bind one within a statuesque present or a false future.

If you know the outside world and look at and feel the West Indian people (not what you can get out of them but what you can give to them), you can see and feel their past, latent in their contemporary personality—others besides myself call it a search for national identity. That identity conceals or rather constricts an enormous potentiality. We have a history, we don't know it, and we will never know it until we respect ourselves, and relate our present, our past and our future. On this interrelation, Harris is very strong and very clear. Not the least of the virtues of his lecture is that for him the relation between these abstract, you may even say abstruse, matters and day-to-day social, even political life is very clear.

There is only one more point that I wish to take up. Harris obviously thinks that creative originality in literature is a sign, a portent, evidence of creative originality in politics, and in social life. The history of Russian literature during the nineteenth century and Russian social and political life in the twentieth is one irrefutable proof of this. Harris is very critical of the lack of originality—what he sees as remaining bound by the traditional standards of judgement—which he thinks is a characteristic of West Indian literature. I see this question differently but I refuse to argue it here for reasons which I shall make clear in a moment. But when Harris says, "In fact it is one of the ironic things with West Indians of my generation that they may conceive of themselves in the most radical political light but their approach to art and literature is one which consolidates the most conventional and documentary techniques in the novel", when Harris says that, I feel I have to speak. This is a political matter and I have to disagree. Some West Indians may "conceive of themselves" as political radicals. In strict fact during the last twenty years I have never met one, not one. To talk about revolution and nationalisation and the need to create a revolutionary party (on the discredited stalinist model) is merely a senseless aping of the models of East and West. In that there is nothing revolutionary. The instinctive feelings and readiness of the West Indian populations for adventurous creation in all fields is proved among other proofs by the literature these territories produce. Literature as Harris very well sees is not an accident. If it is genuine literature, it expresses more than it knows. For example, powerful on the Jamaican scene is the urge of the Rastafari to find a new life in Africa. Rather fantastic! Not realistic! OK. But Vic Reid writes the finest Jamaican novel so far, about the revolutionary struggle of the Mau Mau in Kenya.

That accident needs some explanation.

Barbados is the West Indian territory where there is the clearest and sharpest social differentiation. George Lamming's novels are permeated by the sense of the role of different classes in West Indian society. His work is an expression of Barbados.

Of the larger territories, Trinidad is the one with the most diversified past, where different foreign influences have been most pervasive, where the sense of insular identity (very strong in Barbados and Jamaica) has been almost non-existent. The result? Trinidadians have written more notable history; we have produced the most remarkable politicians in the West Indies, and in literature the finest study ever produced in the West Indies (or anywhere that I know) of a minority and the herculean obstacles in the way of its achieving a room in the national building—Naipaul's *A House for Mr Biswas*.

British Guiana is the only West Indian territory of space and with easily identified relics of the past. Hence Harris, not only in his theoretical ideas but in his fiction. His novels add a continental dimension to West Indian insular literature.

Enough for the time being. The literature is expressing some very vital reality. I hope I have helped to make Harris easier for West Indians to grasp. That is one trouble. Our novelists, as our cricketers, are recognised abroad for what they are, something new, creative and precious in the organisations and traditions of the West. But what they need is what Heidegger recognised in Hölderlin—a homecoming. Harris should not be confined to London. He should be speaking from end to end of the West Indies.

1965

13

The Making of the Caribbean People

[*This lecture on what James has called "perhaps the strangest community in existence" was delivered in Canada in the summer of 1966, at the Second Montreal Conference on West Indian Affairs.*]

This evening I am to speak on "The Making of the Caribbean People", a people in my opinion unique in the modern world. That is the theme which I will develop. I know nobody like them, nobody like us, both positively and negatively. I'll tell you how I will treat such a tremendous subject. I will begin by stating the kind of opinions that educated people, and well-meaning progressive people, have of us, the Caribbean people. Naturally on such a wide subject, in such a limited time, I will have to be quite precise in the quotations that I give. They are chosen because they have more than passing value. When I have stated what is the general opinion, I shall then proceed to state my own, which is utterly and completely opposed to the opinions held by most educated people, West Indians and non-West Indians. I will do that by going into history and sociology of the West Indian at the beginning of their entry into modern western society. I shall concentrate to a large degree on what took place between 1600 and 1800. When I have established that, then I will move more rapidly through our history and what has been happening since. But I will depend on what has been established in the early part, to be able to move rapidly and easily into matters which are more familiar to us.

First of all then: what is the general opinion held about us by people who are West Indians or who are interested in the West Indies?

I will begin with a quotation from the Moyne Report. A number of excellent English gentlemen and ladies, of broad views, sympathetic to the West Indies, who were sent there by King George V in 1938 on a Royal Commission. They wrote a report which is one of the foremost reports that has ever been made about the West Indies. They were not hostile to the West Indies. They were merely profoundly ignorant of what they were dealing with. Here is a quotation from that report:

> Negroes were taken from lands where they lived no doubt in a primitive state.

I don't know where they got that from because the early Portuguese and the rest who discovered Africa did not find very much difference between the Negro civilisations they met and the great masses of the peasantry they had left at home. In many respects many Africans were more advanced. These commissioners writing the report took for granted that all Africans lived in Africa in a primitive state—but Africans lived in social conditions and were subject to customs and usages which, anthropology increasingly shows, had definite social, economic and cultural value. Well, at any rate, that is much better than what they used to teach twenty or thirty years ago.

The report goes on to say that "their transfer to the West Indies unlike most other large-scale movements of population, did not involve the transfer of any important traces of their traditions and customs, but rather their almost complete destruction." Now it is impossible to produce a sentence that contains more mistakes and more gross misunderstandings and misrepresentations.

The Negroes who came from Africa brought themselves. The Amerindians could not stand the impact of slavery. Chinese came afterwards and couldn't make it: they couldn't do the work. The Europeans tried Portuguese labourers: they were not successful. People of African descent, the African from Africa, made the perpetuation of western civilisation possible in the West Indies. The report says that they left everything behind. But the Africans themselves are the most important and most valuable representatives of their civilisation—that when they came here they brought themselves, something of primary importance, never seems to come to the mind of all these people who write reports.

Now they go on to say that "the Negroes had one function only, the provision of cheap labour on the estates owned and managed by Europeans for the production of their valuable export crops. They lost their language, customs and religions, and no systematic attempt was made to substitute any other." They lost their language, yes. But they rapidly mastered the English, the French and the Spanish languages. So if they lost their language it is necessary to say they had to learn new ones and they learnt them very well. They could do that being the people that they were.

Now this Moyne report is the opinion of a whole body of MPs of various disciplines, and various other persons. These things left their mark—we had been inhumanly treated, as the "primitives" we were. We continued to be. The coming of emancipation gave a strong, if temporary, impetus to such forces as were working for the betterment of the Negro population: Churches and their attempt to teach Negroes Christianity, to read and to write, and to improve their morals so that they shouldn't have so many illegitimate children. That was a primary conception for the betterment of the Negro. I hope before I have concluded to show you how superficial, how entirely false, was this estimate of Negro morals and capability.

Now I want to add to that a statement by no less a person than Professor Arthur Lewis. You will find it in a pamphlet that I have published in Trinidad. It is a statement made to an economic conference, which he addresses as follows: The professors of economics, the economists—so says Professor Lewis—do not know much more on development than the ordinary person does. Economic development depends on saving some of what you have now, in order to improve yourself later. He says, that is all there is to it, there is no special economic theory or economic knowledge required. He says that what is required is the effort and readiness to sacrifice by the great part of the population. And, he concludes, people don't know whether the population, the West Indian population, will make that effort or not. He more than implies that it is a question of doubt as to whether the West Indian population has got that necessary feeling, that impetus to make the sacrifices necessary, for the development of the West Indian economy.

I want to dissociate myself completely from Professor Lewis's view. I have never found that West Indians, when called upon in a critical situation, do not respond. That is their life: I believe that they can't help responding. Beginning as we do in a new civilisation and leaving such elements that they might have brought with them behind, they have always responded to a fundamental and serious challenge. That has been our way of life. That is why we are still alive. What has happened to us is that economic and social forces are sitting upon our backs and preventing us from developing ourselves in vital spheres. Where we have had an opportunity to work freely, there we have shown great distinction. Where we have not shown it is because we have been prevented. It is not the lack of capacity. I want you to understand that. I strongly remove myself from the view expressed by Professor Lewis that it depends on us whether we shall rise to the occasion. If those on our backs get off our backs, we shall be able to rise: we have done pretty well with the burdens that we have always carried and are still carrying.

This whole business consists of criticism and doubts of a "primitive" people. We began with nothing and have learned a great deal, but we still have a lot to learn! That is not my view of the West Indian. I think that we have learned all that it was possible for us to have learned. We have learned far more than other people in similar situations have learned. The difficulties that we have met with, that stood in our way, were difficulties of a breadth and weight which would have crushed a people of less power and less understanding of the fact that we had to do all we could to get somewhere.

Now I want to begin with Lygon's *History of Barbados*. It was written in 1653. You can't begin much earlier. He had been in Barbados up to 1647. The island was populated by Englishmen in the 1620s, and Lygon says that at the beginning, or very soon after, there were eleven thousand white peasant farmers in Barbados. They were on their way to becoming what New England in the United States became later.

But then came the sugar plantations and the Negroes were brought in order to work on the sugar plantations. That was somewhere between 1640 or thereabouts, and Lygon gives this account of what happened to the Negroes who at that time had not been in Barbados more than about ten years. I will give a full account of what he says. Don't think it's a little long: it is very important and means a great deal for our future understanding of the whole three hundred years of *West Indian* history that follows it.

I want to interpolate here that I fully agree with Gilberto Freyre that the African who made the Middle Passage and came to live in the West Indies was an entirely new historical and social category. He was not an African, he was a West Indian black who was a slave. And there had never been people like that before and there haven't been any since. And what I shall make clear is the uniqueness of our history and the unique developments which have resulted.

Back now to Lygon:

> A little before I came thence, there was such a combination amongst them, as the like was never seen there before. Their sufferings being grown to a great height, and their daily complainings to one another (of the intolerable burdens they labour'd under) being spread throughout the Iland; at the last, some amongst them, whose spirits were not able to endure such slavery, resolved to break through it, or die in the act; and so conspired with some others of their acquaintance, whose sufferings were equall, if not above theirs; and their spirits no way inferiour, resolved to draw as many of the discontented party into this plot, as possible they could; and those of this perswasion, were the greatest number of servants in the Iland. So that a day was appointed to fall upon their Masters, and cut all their throats, and by that means, to make themselves not only freemen, but Masters of the Iland.

Now that is the very beginning (and the continuation) of West Indian history. They wanted not only their freedom but to remove their masters and make themselves masters of the island. That is what happened essentially in San Domingo about 150 years afterwards and that is what happened in Cuba in 1958. They got rid of their masters and made themselves masters of the island. Masters isn't exactly the same as Lygon's statement but if I may quote a resilient lawyer: "The principle is the same."

I believe the above to be characteristic of the West Indies and our history. When West Indians reach a certain stage they wish to make a complete change and that is because all of us come from abroad. Liberty means something to us that is very unusual. There were many generations of slaves in Africa, of that we are quite sure. And in Africa they took it and no doubt fought against it at certain times. But when we made the Middle Passage and came to the Caribbean we went straight into a modern industry—the sugar plantation—and there we saw that to be a slave was the result of our being black. A white man was not a slave. The West Indian slave was not accustomed to that kind of slavery in Africa; and therefore in the history of the West Indies there is one dominant fact and that is the desire, sometimes expressed, sometimes unexpressed, but always there, the desire for liberty; the ridding oneself of the particular burden which is the special inheritance of the black skin. *If you don't know that about West Indian people you know nothing about them.*

They have been the most rebellious people in history and that is the reason. It is because being a black man he was made a slave, and the white man, whatever his limitations, was a free subject, a man able to do what he could in the community. That is the history of the West Indies. No hint of that appears in the report of Lord Moyne and if we read any number, not only of government reports but works of economists and historians, some of them West Indians, they have no conception whatever of the people they are dealing with, where and whom we have come from, whom they are dealing with and where we are headed.

To go on with Lygon:

> And so closely was this plot carried, as no discovery was made, till the day before they were to put it in act: And then one of them, either by the failing of his courage, or some new obligation from the love of his Master, revealed this long plotted conspiracy; and so by this timely advertisement, the Masters were saved. Justice Hethersall (whose servant this was) sending letters to all his friends, and they to theirs, and so to one another, till they were all secured; and, by examination, found out the greatest part of them.

Now it is interesting to note that this fellow who betrayed the plot was working with a Justice, Justice Hethersall. Whether he loved his master or some other reason (that is a matter for the psychologists), I don't know. What I think, what I suspect, is that working in the house of a Justice of the Peace, he had acquired a certain respect, a subservience to the conceptions of law and order of the masters of the society which he had just entered. And I say that because we shall see this type constantly reappearing, it is most prominent in West Indian society today: the house-slave. A man is a part of the mass of the population; the mass of the population moves in a certain direction, and for some reason or other, he goes and betrays the cause. We have the West Indian pattern of betrayal from the very beginning.

Lygon continues:

. . . whereof eighteen of the principall men in the conspiracy, and they were the first leaders and contrivers of the plot, were put to death, for example to the rest. And the reason why they made examples of so many, was, they found these so haughty in their resolutions, and so incorrigible, as they were like enough to become actors in a second plot; and so they thought good, to secure them; and for the rest, to have a special eye over them.

Now there in sharp outline at the very beginning is the history of the West Indies. After barely ten years they all of them are knit together not merely by the common bond of colour but far more by a common oppression. They have the majority of people in the island. (I feel fairly certain that it was the sugar plantation and working in it that gave them this possibility. I don't believe they would have been able to organise themselves so well and so clearly in Africa. *That is not important.*) Anyway this thing is planned. Then this person working with Justice Hethersall betrays. He goes and he tells his masters what amounts to: "I am with you, not with them, that is what they are plotting to do."

That is permanent in the history of the West Indies and we shall see that as we go on. Note how the leaders who are caught are incorrigible, they are absolutely determined not to give way in the slightest respect: they have to be executed, all of them, because that is the only way in which their masters could feel safe for the future. That is the history we ought to teach in our schools. That is *our* history, *West Indian* history.

Now why I've chosen that is because I believe that it is symbolical of the whole of West Indian history and as I go on, especially when I come to my special study, *The Black Jacobins*, I shall go into that in some detail. Some of you may believe that you have read the book. I did more than that, I wrote it. But it is only in late years that I am able to understand and to appreciate the full significance of what I wrote in that book. We shall go into that in time.

Now I want to move to another feature which is not understood by these numerous West Indian economists, sociologists, historians and writers. This which I hold up before you is a work called *Merchants and Planters*, by Richard Pares. He is one of the greatest West Indian scholars, a scholar in that he has done a lot of studies and is a man of great learning. (He has not written one book and gone about claiming to be a scholar.) *Merchants and Planters* is a study of the Caribbean and was published for the Economic History Society at the Cambridge University Press. Pares notes that

in all the inventories which are to be found among the West Indian archives it is very usual for the mill, the cauldron, the still and the buildings to count for more than one-sixth of the total capital; in most plantations one-tenth would be nearer the mark. By far the greatest capital items were the value of the slaves and the acreage planted in canes by their previous labour.

So that the greatest capital value (this is about 1760) of the sugar plantation, was the labour of the slaves and the acres they had planted. All sorts of economists do all sorts of studies about the West Indies but they don't know that. They write little studies how this was worth that and that was worth this, and this was worth the other. But that the real value of those economic units was the slaves and the land they had developed by their labour, this escapes nearly all except this English scholar.

Pares goes on to say:

> Yet, when we look closely, we find that the industrial capital required was much larger than a sixth of the total value. With the mill, the boiling house and the still went an army of specialists— almost all of them slaves, but none the less specialists for that.

If you take little away from this meeting and you take that, you will have done well.

There was an army of slaves, but he says they were specialists; they were slaves it is true, but nevertheless they were specialists. That is very hard to grasp. Try hard. This tremendous economy that made so much wealth particularly for British society—it was the slaves who ran those plantations. Note that you get what Pares is saying: the statisticians never write down what was the real value of the important industrial capital of the plantations. And he says (this is terrific):

> They were not only numerous but, because of their skill, they had a high value. If we add their cost to that of the instruments and machinery which they used, we find that the industrial capital of the plantations, without which it could not be a plantation at all, was probably not much less than half its total capital.

I hope there are some economists here who have done research in this field, who will stand up and take part in the discussion; about what they have written, or to be more precise, what they have not written.

It takes an Englishman to write this. And here let me, in advance, correct a misunderstanding very prevalent today. I denounce European colonialist scholarship. But I respect the learning and the profound discoveries of Western civilisation. It is by means of the work of the great men of Ancient Greece; of Michelet, the French historian; of Hegel, Marx and Lenin; of Du Bois; of contemporary Europeans and Englishmen like Pares and E. P. Thompson; of an African like the late Chisiza, that my eyes and ears have been opened and I can today see and hear what we were, what we are, and what we can be, in other words—the making of the Caribbean people.

Pares goes on to say:

But when we examine specifications of the negroes, we find so many
boilers, masons, carters, botswains of the mill, etc., that we cannot
feel much confidence in our categories, especially when we find
individuals described as "excellent boiler and field negro."

So that about 1766 Negroes ran the plantations. That is what
this scholar is saying. A man is described as excellent boiler and
field Negro, this prevents us from putting such persons on either
side of the line. He not only worked in the fields but he also did
the necessary technical work. Further complication arises from
the fact that specialist jobs were awarded to the sickly and the
ruptured. The sickly or the ruptured were given the technical
jobs to do—note the spread of technical skill.

That gave me, and I had read it elsewhere, an entirely different picture of the kind of civilisation that was in existence in
the West Indies well before the French revolution of 1789. I have
found other evidence elsewhere and it seems to me that they, the
slaves, ran that society; they were the persons responsible. If
they had been removed the society would have collapsed. That
is perfectly clear in certain writings about Trinidad and Tobago.
But the West Indian economists, the West Indian sociologists,
the West Indian historians; they write but I have never met any
one of them who understood that, and I would be very glad if
either here, or if you feel ashamed about it, in private, you will
let me know, one or two of you, why this had to be done by an
Englishman, an English scholar. I want to put it as sharply as
possible. Slaves ran the plantations; those tremendous plantations, the great source of wealth of so many English aristocrats
and merchants, the merchant princes who cut such a figure in
English society (and French too, but we are speaking of English
society). Those plantations were run by the slaves. That is what
Pares is saying. Slave labour was not an advanced stage of
labour, but those plantations created millions and from top to
bottom slaves ran them.

And now we are able to understand one of the greatest events
in the history of the West Indian people which I will now spend
some time upon in the light of what we have said of the earlier
part. It will deal with the San Domingo revolution. I wrote the
book, *The Black Jacobins.* I studied that society very closely but
it is only of late years with my acquaintance with the West Indian people and actual contact with them, political and in some
degree sociological, that I have learned to understand what I
wrote in this book. And I have learned to understand it because
as I read educated persons writing about the West Indies, it
becomes clear that they have no understanding whatever of the
West Indian people.

I will take an excerpt here and there and spend a word or two
on each, but I prefer to deal with the extracts themselves. The
first one is from Fortescue, the historian of the British Army.

And Fortescue writes what happened to the British expedition to San Domingo in 1792. This is the sentence I want you to bear in mind. This was the war in which England was fighting for its life against revolutionary France. And Fortescue says, the secret of England's impotence for this first six years of the war may be said to lie in two fatal word—San Domingo. Fortescue puts the blame on Pitt and Dundas, who had full warning that on this occasion they would have to fight not only poor, sickly Frenchmen, but the Negro population of the West Indies. Yet they poured their troops into these pestilent islands, in the expectation that thereby they would destroy the power of France, only to discover, when it was too late, that they had practically destroyed the British Army.

Now I have done some teaching, a great deal of teaching: I was a member of that noble army of martyrs for twelve years and I have met many students who knew all about the Battle of Hastings, the Battle of Waterloo, the Battle of the Great Armada. Some of them were pretty bright on Blank in the Battle of Blank, but that the British Army was destroyed by slaves in San Domingo, and England was impotent for the first six years of the greatest war in history up to 1914, they simply don't know anything about that. I wonder how many of you know that. I wouldn't press it any further.

Now an important thing is that the slaves worked collectively on the sugar plantation and I am going to read a statement now which shows what that had made of them.

A few years after the revolution began (it began in 1791 and this is about 1796), a French official, Roume, notes the change in the people.

> In the North [that is where the great sugar plantations were, in the great North plain] they came out to sustain royalty, nobility and religion against the poor whites and the patriots. But they were soon formed into regiments and were hardened by fighting. They organised themselves into armed sections and into popular bodies, and even while fighting for royalty they adopted instinctively and rigidly observed all the forms of republican organisation.

This is in 1796, only five years after the revolt.

> Slogans and rallying cries were established between the chiefs of the sections and divisions and gave them points of contact from one extremity of the plains and towns of the North to the other.

Over one-third of the island of San Domingo. This was not a few, but the mass.

> This guaranteed the leaders a means of calling out the labourers and sending them back at will. These forms were extended to the districts in the West Province, and were faithfully observed by the black labourers, whether fighting for Spain and royalty or for the

republic, Roume assured Bonaparte that he recognised these slogans, even during the insurrection which forced him to authorise the taking of Spanish San Domingo.

This was some years afterwards. Now I wonder what conclusions you draw from this self-mobilisation and self-discipline of a West Indian population. The conclusion I draw is the absolute impertinence and stupidity of a Colonial Office, which, as late as 1950, was wondering whether the people of Trinidad should have freedom or not, or whether they should have five members or more in the Legislature or how many in the Executive; playing a game of checkers they put one member and they see how it goes; then they put two and wait a bit; and they put another one, but he did not do so well so they take him away. And that is the kind of business, that is what they were doing, they said, to train the people for democracy. But look at our people in 1796. They were illiterate: Toussaint used to say that two-thirds of them had made the Middle Passage and could not speak a word of French. They knew a few words of patois. But they worked on sugar plantations. They were masters of the technical necessities of the plantation, and when the time came they were able to organise themselves over the whole of the North Plain, and their leaders could call them out and send them back home merely by the use of political slogans. Any population which could act in this way while only a few years from slavery was fitted for full parliamentary democracy 150 years afterwards.

British colonial officials have understood nothing about the development of colonial peoples. They have stood in the way of their forward movement from colonial status to freedom. The people who understand this had to go to jail. Gandhi and Nehru went to jail for any number of years. Nkrumah went to jail. Dr Hastings Banda went to jail. Nyerere went to jail. All of them, and that priest from Cyprus, he went to jail also. So you notice that they didn't learn about democracy in British schools, they learnt it in the jails into which the British had put them; and from those jails they taught the population and taught the Colonial Office what were the realities of independence. I don't mind what nonsense the British historians and economists write. But our writers, our West Indian writer, he is the man I am concerned with. He does not seem to understand anything of what I am saying to you here.

Toussaint, about 1801 or 1802, came to a conception for which the only word is genius. He wrote a constitution for San Domingo and he didn't submit it to the French government. He declared in the constitution that San Domingo would be governed by the ex-slaves. French officials asked him: what is the place of the French government in this constitution? He replied, "They will send commissioners to talk with me"—and that was all he would say.

His plan was absolute local independence on the one hand, but on the other hand French capital and French commissioners to establish the relation. He begged them to help him develop and educate the country, and to *send a high official from France as a link between both governments. The local power was too well safe-guarded for us to call it a protectorate.* All the evidence shows that Toussaint, working alone, had reached forward to that form of political relation which we know today as dominion status. This was forty years before the famous report on Canada, forty years before the Durham report. Toussaint said, we must have absolute independence but we admit the sovereignty of France; France must send educators, officials, and a commissioner who will speak with me. In this political proposal he was far beyond politicians and officials of the time. This point they were only to reach in 1932 at Ottawa, when they accepted the complete independence of the colonies, with a High Commissioner to speak with the local governments of Canada, of Australia, etc. Over and over again I am aware in these early days of struggles by these early West Indians, that they laid down lines which could be followed without too much difficulty by their descendants, but for the obstacle of their political education by the Colonial Office. (Toussaint knew and introduced a literacy campaign.)

You may think that Toussaint L'Ouverture was an exceptional person. So he was. But you will see the same tremendous spirit, energy and political creativeness in Marcus Garvey, George Padmore, Frantz Fanon, and other West Indians shall we say "too numerous to mention" or "too near to home"? That is the breed. Until the Colonial Office gets hold of us to educate us.

But listen to this typically West Indian passage. It is about Toussaint again. I quote from *The Black Jacobins*:

Firm as was his grasp of reality, old Toussaint looked beyond San Domingo with a boldness of imagination surpassed by no contemporary. In the constitution he authorised the slave-trade because the island needed people to cultivate it. When the Africans landed, however, they would be free men. But while loaded with the cares of government, he cherished a project of sailing to Africa with arms, ammunition and a thousand of his best soldiers, and there conquering vast tracts of country, putting an end to the slave-trade, and making millions of blacks "free and French", as his constitution had made the blacks of San Domingo. It was no dream. He had sent millions of francs to America to wait for the day when he would be ready. He was already 55. What spirit was it that moved him? Ideas do not fall from heaven. The great revolution had propelled him out of his humble joys and obscure destiny, and the trumpets of its heroic period rang ever in his ears. In him, born a slave and the leader of slaves, the concrete realisation of liberty,

184 C. L. R. JAMES

equality and fraternity was the womb of ideas and the springs of power, which overflowed their narrow environment and embraced the whole of the world. But for the revolution, this extraordinary man and his band of gifted associates would have lived their lives as slaves, serving the commonplace creatures who owned them, standing barefooted and in rags to watch inflated little governors and mediocre officials from Europe pass by, as many a talented African stands in Africa today.

That was Toussaint, the West Indian, who having established a base at home showed himself the ancestor of Garvey, Padmore and Fanon. They had to go abroad to develop their West Indian characteristics. One West Indian who did not have to go abroad to carry out his West Indian ideas was the one who had built himself a base at home—Fidel Castro.

Let me repeat the end of that quotation:

But for the revolution, this extraordinary man and his band of gifted associates would have lived their lives as slaves, serving the commonplace creatures who owned them, standing barefooted and in rags to watch inflated little governors and mediocre officials from Europe pass by as many a talented African stands in Africa today.

I wrote that in 1938. I am very proud of it. There were not many people thinking in those terms as far back as 1938. There are not enough who are thinking in those terms today.

Let us go on with these extraordinary people, these West Indians. They won their freedom in 1803. Up to 1791 they had been slaves. All this was done within twelve years. They defeated a Spanish army of some 50,000 soldiers, a British army of 60,000 soldiers, and another 60,000 Frenchmen sent by Bonaparte to re-establish slavery. They fought Bonaparte's great army and drove it off their land.

Now for the making of our people since these glorious and creative days. Some of you, I have no doubt, are profoundly aware of the savage ferocity of some of the West Indian rulers today to the populations who have put them in power. In 1966, this is appearing in island after island in the Caribbean. What we have to do is to see the origin of this, its early appearance at the very moment when freedom was won. That will give us the historic fact and the historic origins of the fact. I shall confine myself to the period after Toussaint had been captured and sent away, and General Leclerc has been compelled to employ the Negro generals as members of his staff to help keep "order". Then the news came that the old colonial régime, slavery and mulatto discrimination, had been restored in Guadeloupe. The insurrection among the mass of the population in San Domingo became general.

What we have to do now is to see first the behaviour of the mass of the population, the rank and file, the man in the street, the ordinary peasant, the agricultural labourer. And on the other hand, the behaviour of those who, formerly slaves, had now become generals, high officials, and members of the governing body.

This is how the masses behave. The masses from whom the masses of today (and some of us here) are descended. Back to *The Black Jacobins*:

> With a skill and tenacity which astonished their seasoned opponents, the little local leaders not only beat off attacks but maintained a ceaseless harrying of the French posts, giving them no peace, so that the soldiers were worn out and nerve-wracked, and fell in thousands to the yellow fever. When the French sent large expeditions against them they disappeared in the mountains, leaving a trail of flames behind them, returning when the weary French retreated, to destroy still more plantations and carry their attacks into the French lines. Running short of ammunition, the labourers in the mountains around Port-de-Paix attacked this important town, drove out the garrison, killed the whites, burned the houses that had been rebuilt, and took possession of the fort with 25,000 pounds of powder. Who comes to capture it? Maurepas, who had commanded in the district and had so valiantly driven off the attacks of Humbert, Debelle and Hardy. He and the French, with a vigorous counterattack, recaptured the fort, but "the insurgents with incredible activity . . . men, women and children, all had got back to the mountains more or less heavily laden." The masses of the North plain ran to put themselves under the guidance of these new leaders.

Now we leave these heroic people and will go straight on to what I call the old gang, those who had become generals, administrators and part of the new government. They would not join the new revolution, but joined with the French government to suppress the revolutionaries. They had become house-slaves of the most subservient kind. Here is what I had to write immediately after that last passage describing the heroism of the mass:

> All that old gang would do was to threaten Leclerc. Some of the blacks who had been slaves attempted to purchase their freedom from their former masters. These refused and singled out as their private property high officials and officers, men who had shed their blood on the battlefield and served with distinction in the administration. Christophe told General Ramel that if he thought slavery was to be restored, he would burn the whole of San Domingo to the ground. A black general dining with Lacroix pointed to his two daughters and asked him, "Are these to go back to slavery?" It was as if they could not believe it.

The whole house-slave character of these new masters of the sweets of government is summed up in the observation of a

French historian who was part of the French expedition:

> But no one observed that in the new insurrection of San Domingo, as in all insurrections which attack constitutional authority, it was not the avowed chiefs who gave the signal for revolt, but obscure creatures for the greater part personal enemies of the coloured generals.

This subservience to a ruling class by new rulers is rampant all over the Caribbean today, and I understand it much better when I read and get it into my head that after just ten years of freedom and becoming masters of San Domingo, that was the way they behaved to the emissary sent by Bonaparte. They were totally and completely subservient and it took a man like Dessalines, an absolute barbarian, to lead the people finally to their freedom. Dessalines could not write: the name of many a Haitian general had to be traced for him in pencil for him to trace it over in ink. But he was the one who could lead the rebellious mass of the population. All the educated ones, all those who were not so educated but who had sat for a while in the seats of power, they were prepared to submit to any indignity in order to remain, not with power but merely the symbols and the profits of power.

I have two more quotations, one written fifty years later by a soldier who had fought against them, and one written at the time by General Leclerc, the brother-in-law of Napoleon, who was in command of the expedition. General Lemmonier-Delafosse (who believed in slavery) wrote in his memoirs:

> But what men these blacks are! How they fight and how they die! One has to make war against them to know their reckless courage in braving danger when they can no longer have recourse to stratagem. I have seen a solid column, torn by grape-shot from four pieces of cannon, advance without making a retrograde step. The more they fell, the greater seemed to be the courage of the rest. They advanced singing, for the Negro sings everywhere, makes songs on everything. Their song was a song of brave men and went as follows:
> "To the attack, grenadier,
> Who gets killed, that's his affair.
> Forget your ma,
> Forget your pa,
> To the attack, grenadier,
> Who gets killed, that's his affair."
> This song was worth all our republic songs. Three times these brave men, arms in hand, advanced without firing a shot, and each time repulsed, only retired after leaving the ground strewed with three-quarters of their troop. One must have seen this bravery to have any conception of it. Those songs shouted into the sky in unison by 2,000 voices, to which the cannon formed a bass, produced a thrilling effect. French courage alone could resist it. Indeed large ditches, an excellent artillery, perfect soldiers gave us a

great advantage. But for many a day that massed square which marched singing to its death, lighted by a magnificent sun, remained in my thoughts, and even today after more than 40 years, this majestic and glorious spectacle still lives as vividly in my imagination as in the moments when I saw it.

And finally General Leclerc wrote to his brother-in-law Napoleon Bonaparte:

We have in Europe a false idea of the country and the men whom we fight against.

That was written by a defeated general over 150 years ago. Today, 150 years after, not only in Europe and the United States, but in the very West Indies itself, there is a false idea of the country in which our people live and the quality of the people who live in it.

These are my ancestors, these are my people. They are yours too, if you want them. We are descendants from the same stock and the same kind of life on the sugar plantations which made them what they were. Faced with certain difficulties, we would respond in the same way. That seems to be inherent in people who have made the Middle Passage and had to learn all that they can and build a new life with what they gathered from the standards, the ideas and the ideologies of the people and the new civilisation in which they live. But I repeat: We had brought ourselves. We had not come with nothing.

I do not think it was at all accidental that after a dozen years of fighting these men showed themselves equal to the soldiers of Napoleon, the finest army Europe had then known. They are our people. They are our ancestors. If we want to know what the ordinary population can do, let us know what they have done in the past. It is the way of life, not blood. The Negro people in the Caribbean are of the same stock as the men who played such a role in the history of their time. We are the product of the same historical past and the same type of life, and as long as we are not being educated by the Colonial Office (or the stooges of the financial interests), we shall be able to do whatever we have to do. We have to remember that where slavery was abolished by law, the great mass of the Negro slaves had shown that they were ready to take any steps that were necessary to free themselves. That was a very important step in the making of the Caribbean people.

We now have to move on to more modern times, and we shall be able to do that more confidently and easily because what we are, both positively and negatively, is the result of what we have been. I shall use two examples, the example of Trinidad and the example of Barbados. Trinidad first. I shall use this to explain the particularity of the insular history of the different islands. We know that Trinidad produced the most remarkable politician of the British West Indies during the twentieth century, Arthur Andrew Cipriani. Now, where did he come from? In Trinidad we had a number of Frenchmen who came to the island in the last years of the eighteenth century. First of all they were able to find a source of economic progress independent of the sugar estates. They worked cocoa estates, therefore were independent of the sugar magnates and of the colonial officials. They were, some of them, men of great culture, and fully able to stand up against the domination of sugar planters and colonial officials. They had a language of their own, in addition to their economic independence. They had a religion of their own, they were Roman Catholic and therefore were able to feel a differentiation between their religion and the Protestant religion of the British domination. Therefore, while they shared to some degree the superior status and opportunities that all local whites had, they were constantly aware of themselves as a body of people distinct from, and even opposed at times to the British colonial caste. That was the origin of the independent political attitude that Cipriani took from the beginning of the war in regard to the opportunities for West Indian self-assertion that the war of 1914–18 opened to the West Indian people, at least in the general opinion of the times. So we get it clearly. Cipriani was able to take the stand he did because the French Creoles had a long tradition of independent economic life and social differentiation.

That to begin with. But there was more to Cipriani. I remember seeing the soldiers who went to the war of 1914–18. Many of them wore shoes consistently for the first time. To the astonishment of everybody (I believe not excluding the men themselves and Captain Cipriani), they became soldiers who were able to hold their own in the complicated techniques of modern warfare and the social relations that accompany it; to hold their own with soldiers not only from Britain, but from some of the most advanced countries of the Commonwealth. Cipriani never forgot that, never. From that time he advocated independence, self-government, and federation on the basis that the West Indian rank and file, "the barefooted man" as he called him, was able to hold his own with any sort of people anywhere. He had seen it in war, a stern test. That was the basis of his ceaseless agitation from island to island in the British Caribbean, mobilising labour against capital for independence and federation. So you see that Cipriani was no historical accident. That he was able to discover the tremendous qualities of the Caribbean population (with this I began) was due to the fact that history had presented him with political opportunities unfolding the capacities of a highly developed people. These soldiers were the descendants of Toussaint's army.

Now another example, Barbados. Barbados, one of the most highly developed, most highly civilised territories in the extra-

European world. You will have noticed that of the middle-class people in the early years of political activity, there was only one member of the black middle class who took a prominent and in fact very important part. That was Sir Grantley Adams. And while I do not wish to make Grantley and the fine work he did merely a product of historical circumstances, I have to say that of the Caribbean territories, Barbados alone had an unbroken tradition of political activity and actually had a House of Assembly. In Barbados therefore there was something for Grantley to join. He had to sacrifice a great deal. At times his life was in danger. But we have to know, that in those revolutionary days, nowhere else did any member of the black middle class enter into politics. Today a whole lot of them are very noisy politicos, the way is very easy, you get a good salary, you can become a minister, and you can go to England and be entertained by royalty! But, Cipriani and Grantley Adams started before World War II. In those days there was nothing but work and danger.

And now I come to my final contention. As late as 1945 the number of people in the Caribbean who had the vote was less than five per cent. I say that if we look properly at who and what we were, we were long ready for self-government and independence, most certainly by 1920. And I go further, and I say that by delaying the achievement of self-government, having to appoint a Royal Commission after the upheavals of 1937–8, and by the mean and grudging granting to so many the vote, so many to become ministers, and all the palaver and so-called education by which the British government claimed that it trained the West Indian population for self-government, a terrible damage was inflicted upon us. In reality, our people were miseducated, our political consciousness was twisted and broken. Far from being guided to independence by the 1960s, from 1920 onwards, for forty years the imperialist governments poisoned and corrupted that sense of self-confidence and political dynamic needed for any people about to embark on the uncharted seas of independence and nationhood. We are still without that self-confidence and that dynamic today. We lack them because for the last half-century, we were deprived of making the Caribbean people what our history and achievements had made possible and for which we were ready. That then is my conclusion. They have not educated, they have mis-educated us, stood in our way, piled burdens on our backs. Let me quote one of our most profound analysts:

> Free is how you is from the start, an' when it look different you got to move, just move, an' when you movin' say that it is a natural freedom that make you move.

That is George Lamming, than whom no one has a clearer view of words like independence, freedom, liberty. . . .

Still we have made history. As evidence of what we can make of ourselves, I need only add some of the names our people from the Caribbean have inscribed on the pages of history. Here I shall give a list of names, a list without which it is impossible to write of the history and literature of Western civilisation. No account of Western civilisation could leave out the names of Toussaint L'Ouverture, Alexander Hamilton, Alexander Dumas (the father), Leconte Delisle, José Maria de Heredia, Marcus Garvey, René Maran, Saint-John Perse, Aimé Césaire, George Padmore, Frantz Fanon, and allow me to include one contemporary, a Cuban writer, Alejo Carpentier. I do not mention the remarkable novelists whom we of the British Caribbean have produced during the last twenty years. I end this list by a name acknowledged by critics all over the world as an unprecedented, unimaginable practitioner of his particular art—I refer, of course, to Garfield Sobers.

1966

14

Peasants and Workers

[*First published in the November 1971 issue of* Radical America, *this is a major excerpt from* The Gathering Forces, *written in 1967 as a draft for an unpublished document marking the fiftieth anniversary of the Russian revolution. Sections of it were written in collaboration with Martin Glaberman, William Gorman and George Rawick.*]

A three-way division of affairs among Russia, China, and the United States dominates world politics today. Two nations out of these three are governed, according to their official declarations, by the theories and practices of marxism-leninism. The human consciousness must inescapably satisfy itself with answers to the questions: What exactly is this all about and how did it come to be? Has it always been so, and, if not, when and how did such a state of affairs take place?

Prospects of war and peace, budgets, armies, parties, elections, trade and cultural exchanges, the United Nations, and the Third World of emerging nations, are all entangled. Hundreds of millions cover their eyes and, sick of the dehumanisation of civilised society, shut off news of interminable and unsolvable conflict between Russia and China on the one side, and American attempts to dominate the world on the other.

What is being awaited is a consummation of what began with the breakup of the Eastern Front in World War I: the arrival of the populace politically on to the streets of Petrograd and Moscow. The October revolution of 1917 was the initial landmark on the landscape of war and revolution, mass initiative and class repressions, self-liberating efforts and alienating mystifications. A breaking point in human existence began in October 1917 and now awaits resolution. After Stalinism, Khrushchevism, and the bewildering profundities of Chairman Mao, the present generation is suffused with the desire to arrive at the terminal point of the twentieth-century political upheavals.

In the same Russia today, October is celebrated by self-congratulations accompanied by displays of the latest missiles, tanks, and rockets. The United States—while still declaring how it deplores the rise of Bolshevism—compares the mellowness of the present Russian leaders with the intransigence of the Chinese. Furthermore, an event which, upon its happening, had made bright man's hopes is now used as an occasion to insist that the great majorities of the populations cannot alter or improve their conditions of life.

Fifty years ago, the October revolution made mankind aware of the task placed in the hands of the proletariat: destroying the accepted, constantly increasing evils of capitalist society. Today there has emerged a new force to join the proletariat, comprising hundreds of millions. This force is engaged in the struggle to rid contemporary society of the incubus which weighs upon it and which threatens to destroy mankind itself by fratricidal struggles for power. This force is the people of the Third World, whose liberation is possible only by the destruction of the economic and cultural domination of imperialism. For us who celebrate the fiftieth anniversary of the October revolution this political emergence of the Third World is a culmination of what emerged from theory into reality in October 1917.

What is new in our analysis will concern itself above all with the emergence of this new form which struggles to complete what the October revolution began. But it is necessary, first and foremost, to understand what was the October revolution, what it did and what it did not do.

War is the mother of revolution. Everywhere revulsion was the logical response to three years of trench mud and carnage, only in Russia did world war give birth to completely volcanic social reorganisation. Strict objectivity compels not a mere listing of reasons but a statement of premises.

The largest factory known in the world anywhere in the year 1917 was the Putilov works in Leningrad. The co-ordinate labour of that factory involved 40,000 people. Other factories surrounded it in the same district. Capital had put them there. The backwardness of transport in the large mass of land area that is Russia geographically concentrated the forces of the Russian workers socially. The Russian autocracy and its secret police, fearful of the slightest liberalising influences from European civilisation, set up the strictest barriers as a means of self-protection and self-perpetuation. This in turn gave to the Russian working class a certain inner freedom from inhibiting traditionalism and organisational fixity, and mere imitation of the rest of Europe. There was no exclusivism of trade unions, arbitration machinery, grievance umpires, or pettifogging about "equity".

Compared to Russian society as a whole, the number of industrial workers was small. The bulk of the workers were one or two generations away from the land, from social isolation on the vastest countryside in all the world. But the working class was fresh. It was as if the inner class life of the American working class had begun with the CIO, or that of their British working-class brothers had begun with the movement of shop stewards.

Class power, combined with the creative appropriation by the Russian intelligentisa of the discoveries of Western civilisation before and particularly after 1789, was the specific potential of the new industrial working class. Class paralysis in the face of the traditional brutishness of the Russian aristocracy capped by a Tsar was the specific immediate reaction of the small Russian bourgeoisie. They were dominated, in their minds if not completely in fact, by foreign capital.

Both bourgeoisie and working class were small in peasant Russia. The future could not even believe in itself in that war period of a royal family guided by the monk Rasputin at the centre of power.

The intelligentsia, which, unlike that of other countries, did not automatically ally itself with the class above, moved through the exacting discipline of the politics of an approaching revolution to define its relation to the new working class.

Viewed from the standpoint of the development of civilisation—mankind's capacity to understand itself and its prospects—the work of the Russian intelligentsia constitutes one of the wonders of the world. The brilliance of the intellectuals was due to their European strivings at a time when German philosophy, French literature, and British politics were stagnant. The transition from the nineteenth to the twentieth century in what is broadly called culture is in the great achievements of the phenomenal Russian intelligentsia. In drama, novel, ballet, poetry, literary criticism, musical expressiveness, they transformed the relations of the nineteenth to the twentieth century. The constitutive elements of an entire epoch were created. No proof in the conventional meaning of that word will be offered here. In the dialectic of the actual development, including the politics of the later stage, that of the degeneration of the 1917 revolution, politics offers the historical proof.

One more point must be made. The entrance of bourgeois economy into Russia did not so much weaken as accentuate the caste character of Russian social life. It is comparable to how in the United States the very triumph of the powerful captains of industry refastened more perniciously the manacles and even the lynch mob's rope to the Negro emancipated by the Civil War. Class reinforced itself administratively as caste. Russia was familiarly known to the world as the prison house of peoples. This was not only because its pre-1917 existence was the closest to a police state that period could recognise. It was so because the variety of people and ethnic groups within the country itself were forbidden the use of their own language or native institutions.

We can thus help to resolve the mystery as to why October is Russian. Its resistant intelligentsia was European, its working class small but with a concentration unique in European history, its minorities lived in the recesses of the inner colonialism of Tsarist power. This all together was the nurturing ground of what is called Bolshevism. When the war came in 1914, despite the fact that a full theoretical understanding had to await Lenin's great achievements during the war, these Bolshevik enclaves did not succumb as did the social democracy everywhere to imperialism, the bourgeoisification of skilled workers, the corruptions of the parliamentary system, the great war of all the nation states.

There was a corresponding development in the relationship between the working class and its representative party, which found the source for its strength in the experiences of the factory and the workers' districts. The revolutionary creations and the experiences of 1905 were the curtain raiser for the victory of 1917. The defeat of the military pretensions of the Tsar in the 1904–5 war against Japan stimulated the workers—as the defeat of rulers has stimulated the oppressed populations since time immemorial—to the measures which went far beyond anything Western Europe had known: the general strike, the political general strike, and finally the creation of councils—the soviets.

When the soviet appeared it consisted of one representative for every five hundred workers in a factory. The peasants, organised in the army, started to form soviets for themselves. The rapid formation of the soviets, lightning-like progress of strikes, and armed extension of struggle tell us things which no experts on the theory of the powerlessness of permanently alienated populations dare even to think. Soviets and general strike did not wait upon any party. Parties attached to the cause of the working class had to adapt themselves to soviets while no wise giving up the aspirations to democratic rights and elections of representatives to government in the familiar bourgeois manner. 1917 provided the final curtain to the historical stage opening in 1905. The ruling class no longer had any claim of leading the Russian nation or even showing any capacity of disciplining its own hollow personnel. Soldiers fled the front and the trial of strength began.

Both the present American and Russian rulers believe that the Bolshevik Party made the revolution; the former hold this idea with regrets, and the latter with grandiose self-adulation. The same glaring mental, that is, political, defect displays itself in all sectors of opinion both from those for and those against the Russian revolution.

Thus, those small vanguard groupings of political radicals who have never had the taste of power ascribe the wonders of its arrival to the power of correct slogans. But Peace, Bread, and Land were not the blare of an advertised uprising. The critical element was a population poised upon split-second's notice to act upon its impulses, not in the everyday sense, but to rescue society from the bottomless pit of trench warfare and state corruption. Slogans make aspirations more palpable, but it is a self-prepared people that make fundamental revolution.

February 1917 witnessed the abdication of the Tsar and the formation of what Lenin himself described as the freest republic the world had ever known. The working class was seeking to abolish itself as a mere component cog in the machinery of production, the soldiers were struggling to end the corrupting role in the machinery of war, and the serfs were permeated with the desire to make themselves into an independent yeomanry such as Russia had never seen before. Freedom could no longer be a matter of right. It was the content of human-social activity, above all politics. When you have such large-scale social experience, infinite in its immeasurability—millions in and out of the battlefront, or out on strike, parading their power through the major streets of cities, transport and communication broken down so that the most ordinary routines of life become a matter to be settled on the spot as necessity dictates—then the establishment of new social ties becomes the most natural and inevitable thing in the world. Sailors of battleships were nestling in the Neva near Petrograd; soldiers had not only deserted, they were moving around on the streets of a major metropolis testing out for what and for whom their military experiences had truly prepared them. It produced the dominant simplicity of the revolutionary politics and even the finished style of its leading politician, that familiar homeliness of Lenin's utterances.

Lenin's style constitutes an enigma and even conspiratorial mystery to what parades itself before our eyes now as social science. Today this science goes round and round with its talk of the paradoxes of the Russians and the inscrutabilities of the even more distant Chinese. The meaning of the social interventions and social transformations of ordinary men and women in the midst of social revolution social scientists evade, leading them to create these mysteries, which lie at the heart of the scientific disciplines created and recreated in confusions.

Kerensky, one of the men of February 1917, may have been a fool to believe he could crate the Russian people back into World War I. More notable for 1967 is the vacillation and self-contortion of the whole section of the intelligentsia. They had tied the fate of Russia to its working class. They proved feckless when it came for the moment to establish the workers, now armed, as the government of the problem-laden, vast, and exhausted Russian society, cut off from Europe and having to depend upon its own internal social resources. The reluctance of Lenin's own co-workers on that famous Central Committee to adopt the position of seizing the power, of turning February into October, was not cowardice or timidity. The politically trained intelligentsia was not any kind of effete aristocracy.

Its problem—the modern problem—is elsewhere. It is that the bourgeoisie have proven hopelessly ineffectual through depressions and war and calamitous crises of every kind. Only the workers remain to create a human society. But the intelligentsia, which considers itself the repository of everything civilised, must by the very nature of the accumulation of social relations through the centuries as well as immediately all around

it, consider the working population to be incapable of facing
and solving the problems of governing whole areas of economic,
political, and social life.

Lenin was the embodiment of the best virtues of the Russian
intelligentsia. This great Russian intelligentsia was European in
mental scope, exacting in correctness of formulation and
procedure, contemptuous of autocracy and hateful of the
pogrom mentality which in the eyes of the world was Mother
Russia. But there was a negative as well. An intellectual element
of the population so conditioned to exile, so tenuous in its hold
on national realities, so ephemeral in regard to its own experience in the practicalities of government, when once
congealed into a party apparatus and thereby transformed from
isolated individuals into the shadow of the state power it hopes
to become, must inevitably turn into—particularly in caste-
ridden Russia—an obstacle when the proletariat is ready to
assert the full measure of its power.

Why then did Lenin succeed in spite of them? Not mere individual uniqueness but concrete universality provides the shape
of the answer. Aside from being prepared by research and
debate on the class character of Russian revolution, aside from
the overwhelming homeliness and explicitness of his own
political make-up, aside from the self-discipline that political
struggle inheres in individuals as well as in groups, Lenin knew
the political alternatives as few people have been pressed and
shaped to know them. For in the midst of that eight-month span
between February and October, the whole backwash of Russian
society and Russian history was preparing to drown the
population in the ageless mud of Russian barbarism.

What Lenin knew, and what he knew the soldiers, workers,
and peasants knew at the very first hand, was the fist of a
Kolchak and a Kornilov, the naked barbarism of the counter-
revolution. He knew what native barbarism could do and what
mere oratory about freedom could not do. On this he deluded no
one because he did not deceive himself as so many highly intelligent people have done not only before Hitler and Mussolini
and Stalin but increasingly afterward. The seizure of political
power by the working class, the shattering of all centres of
authority was to prevent the making of politics into that
specialised type of gangsterism so prevalent today that its
existence marks off the world before World War I from the way
we now live.

Besides the specificity of staying the whip of the counter-
revolution, the genius of that much-abused Bolshevism of Lenin
is that it added both to the vision and science of revolutionary
politics more than all the political science courses in all the
world's schools will ever be able to stare at plainly, let alone
master as knowledge. Capitalist economy and the great mystery
of the commodity over which Marx wrestled for so many pages

was to become a matter of specific measures of workers' discipline and national public accounting. Large-scale funds were to be wrested from the parasitic owners by the self-motivated peasants. Only they could do that. Housing, in the absence of new construction, was to be provided by the occupation of unfilled, unused houses in overblown mansions by homeless tenants. Only they could do that. International diplomacy consisted of the signing away of territories according to the will of the population living there. We cannot go on with this list indefinitely except to say that it is all this which distinguished Bolshevism from its opponent Menshevism.

It is this which distinguishes Bolshevism from all those to this very day and the day after tomorrow who believe that trench warfare for millions is possible, atomic bombs are possible, anti-missile missiles are possible, flights to the moon are possible, atomic disintegration of cities is possible, assassinations of political leaders are possible, all of these are not only possible but actually inevitable, whereas the proletarian seizure of political power is—impossible. It is this which provides the decisive dividing line between self-activity and mere chasing around, the "rat race" in short, on an international plane the gulf between human and subhuman modes of political release. Marxism in the nineteenth century demonstrated how the new society is nurtured even amidst the poisonous bosom of the old. Leninism contributed its originality and force to the notion of social-economic reconstruction as the true *a priori*, the sole *a priori* of all revolution for the twentieth century.

In the Civil War in Russia, the revolution had defeated the White armies that had been sponsored and supported by West European states, Japan, and the United States. With the defeat of these armies Soviet power now confronted the immense task of reconstructing the national economy in such a way that the new social relations of the revolution would reproduce themselves as viable self-activated institutions. Around these the work activity of the masses of men, women, and youth could be grouped. In order to comprehend these struggles of the last years of the revolution, we must pay very careful attention to the specific problems and events.

"A great universal agrarian revolution was worked out with an audacity unprecedented in any other country, and at the same time, the imagination was lacking to work out a tenth-rate reform in office routine" [Lenin, *Selected Works*, volume 9, page 396]. Although workers are masters of detail labour, certain tasks were shifted to professional administrators, or non-professionals aspiring to administer. The habits and methods of the Tsarist bureaucracy were continued and deepened by the thousands of carryovers from the old régime and the thousands of new arrivals who copied and furthered their ways.

In all countries the state sees itself as mediator between various sections of the people. That Russian administrators saw their own position that way is quite certain. The problem in the crisis of 1921–23 was not that the party had to grip together the two halves of the "scissors", the gap between socialised workers and individualised peasants. That anyone still believes this was the heart of the matter is the consequence of certain bureaucratic thought patterns, the heritage of tendencies which Lenin had set himself against.

Lenin in his last years counterposed to state and party the development of the cultural level of the whole population, through policies designed to get the direct involvement of the working population, urban and rural, in the solution of problems. Lenin never believed that there would be any completion of the building of socialism under conditions which approached pre-literary culture on the one side and the fragmented productivity of labour on the other. His approach was that of education but of the kind never seen elsewhere in the world at any time.

The working population had the power: landlords, capitalists, Tsarists, and foreign powers all knew that. But how to develop it? Lenin tied reconstruction of the economy to education. Trade unions were to educate the workers toward that voluntary self-discipline which guarantees a constantly higher productivity. Agricultural co-operatives were to transform a peasantry, conscious of their attainment of individual possession of the land, into free associations of producers on the countryside.

The main task, Lenin said, was "first, of learning, second, of learning, and third, of learning, and then of testing what we have learnt so it shall not remain a dead letter, or a fashionable phrase (and, it is no use concealing it, this often happens among us), so that what we have learnt may become part of our very beings, so that it may actually and fully become a constituent element of our social life" [*Selected Works*, volume 9, page 389]. Culture would be taken away from the exclusive position it occupied in old Russia.

But, Lenin continued, "I know that it will be hard to follow this rule and apply it to our conditions. I know that the opposite rule will force its way through a thousand loopholes. I know that enormous resistance will have to be offered, that devilish persistence will have to be displayed, that . . . the work in this connection will be hellishly hard" [*Selected Works*, volume 9, page 389].

What went wrong in 1923 was that the opposite rule did force its way through a thousand loopholes, leading to a flight from the task of developing a new, revolutionary sophistication completing the transformation of a population set in motion by the revolution. And this was the base for the most extreme atrocities of Stalin which are now known to all the world.

The party of the Russian revolution did not only fail at this new deep attempt to arouse the social resourcefulness of the population. It abdicated that realm entirely. It fled from it. Until this day such notions as Workers' and Peasants' Inspection, whereby every citizen, particularly the women, in Lenin's memorable phrase, were to examine regularly and systematically and audit the concrete affairs of the Soviet administration; trade unionism as the schooling of workers toward a communist society in which all state coercion disappears; agricultural co-operatives voluntarily formed by the populace in all areas of Russia, are all roundly abused or purposefully ignored, even by the most radical of radicals.

After the Civil War, after the triumph of one party over all others, this flight from the deepening of the revolutionary involvement of the populace accelerated. It was given its signal expression in the trade-union debates of 1920–21. These debates announced the birth of modern state capital: the rise of governments so total, so peremptory in their attitudes, that they throttle the very notion of mass revolutionary initiative. The large parties which were presumably formed to act on the grievances of large sections of the people became transformed into the disciplinarians of workers, peasants, and all other revolutionary forces.

The particular conflict in 1921 involved Trotsky as chief commander of the victorious Red Army and a small union of Water Transport Workers. Out of this initial conflict came Trotsky's thesis about the subordination of the trade unions to party and state. Trotsky called for "shaking up" the trade unions. Tomsky, the member of the Central Committee of the Bolshevik Party most concerned with trade-union affairs, fought this off as an attempt at the militarisation of the labouring force and of its sole protective organisation, the trade unions.

Lenin took the side of Tomsky, and in the next few months it was the Bolshevik Party and not the trade unions which was shaken up by rampant factionalism. In the isolation of the working class in a peasant country combined with the isolation of a workers' Russia in a bourgeois world, it was apparent that everything accomplished up to then was in absolute peril. "The Russian found consolation for the bleak bureaucratic realities at home in unusually bold theoretical constructions, and that is why these unusually bold theoretical constructions assumed an unusually one-sided character among us" [*Selected Works*, volume 9, page 397].

The solution to the problem of the Russian revolution was not, as Trotsky demonstrated, in brilliant formulations about more democracy at home in Russia and world revolution abroad. Nor was the solution the liberal theory of a multi-party state.

Lenin modestly noted, but with great powers of anticipation, what would inevitably happen when the mass intervention that was the Russian revolution would begin to go downhill: "Our social life combines within itself an astonishing degree of fearless audacity and mental timidity" [*Selected Works*, volume 9, page 394]. This mental timidity was in the face of a population that had experienced for itself Soviets, insurrection, and civil war. By swelling the membership of the trade unions, the exhausted working class of an economically exhausted Russia was showing its recognition of where the threat of administrationism had reached and that they were prepared to do battle with it. The main obstacle was the very brilliance of one-sided Russian intellectualism functioning as the political leadership. In reaction to that kind of one-sided bold theoretical construction we have the emergence of Stalin.

Stalin, the party policeman, showed that he had no patience, and that the straitened economic circumstances of post-Civil War Russia allowed for no patience, with the one-sidedness of Russian intellectualism. Instead he chose the most self-specialising aspect of the modern state—the secret police and their penetration into all environs of political activity.

The inherent antagonism which stalinism offered to the activity of free human personalities can be seen most specifically when we examine the following lines of Lenin, among the last lines ever to flow from his pen: "Much that was fantastic, even romantic, and even banal, in the dreams of the old co-operators is now becoming the most unvarnished reality. . . . Our co-operatives are looked down upon with contempt, but those who do so fail to understand the exceptional significance . . . from the aspect of the transition to the new order by means that will be simplest, easiest, and most intelligible" [*Selected Works*, volume 9, page 403].

Lenin is speaking here specifically about the peasantry being educated toward co-operation. In the same years he took the position that the trade unions must be schools of the workers which would not only be institutions for the self-protection by the workers against a bureaucratic state apparatus; they would also, as the positive result of struggle, turn into schools of communist management. And for the youth Lenin was insistent on learning, testing the learning by practice, and furthering the practice by increase of learning.

After the twenty million membership of the soviets had coalesced with the party or had fallen away entirely from mass participation in government, the task of finding another way forward preoccupied Lenin. "But this again is the most important thing. It is one thing to draw up fantastic plans for building socialism by means of all sorts of workers' associations; but it is quite another thing to learn to build it practically, in such a way that every small peasant may take part in the work of construction" [*Selected Works*, volume 9, page 403]. The conclusive word is "every".

Trotsky was eager for propaganda of the most extreme sort, propaganda combined with purely administrative party orders, army orders. The Soviet technicians were preparing themselves for the day of plans and production quotas. In the meantime Stalin was preparing his blows against specific individuals in the party. The result of all this, in the absence of a unified policy delineated by Lenin, was that the dictatorship swallowed the whole of society. That was Stalin whose arrival tells us of the consequences of an opposite policy and power.

Malenkov, Khrushchev, Brezhnev, and Kosygin all have talked of trying to undo what Stalin constructed. What stalinism established will undo them, and all other heralds of some nebulous great internal reforms in Russia.

Socialised workers of Petrograd and Moscow, socialised peasants of the Russian Army, made the greatest social change the world has ever known. The failure to carry through the same penetration into mass impulse afterward, and at an even higher pitch of social tension, blocked the reconstruction of Russia as a new civilisation.

We are often told that Lenin, the man who anticipated and warred against learning as a "dead letter, or a fashionable phrase" produced, or by means of his doctrine produced, a Joseph Stalin. This is revealed for the false notion it is both by the words of Lenin himself and by the figures of how many leninists Stalin had to kill, the way he had to kill them, the pages that had to be torn out of history books, the sentences that had to be torn out of editions of Lenin's own writings.

Even the work of a Trotsky and his magnificent polemical war could not restrain the spread of the *idée fixe* that leninism produced stalinism. Only comprehension of what took place in October, and of what took place in its failure, can break up that idea in the manner that it deserves on this historic occasion.

Such a comprehension is assisted by the internal setting of the world in which we live today. Lenin anticipated it: "At the same time, precisely as a result of the last imperialist war, a number of countries—the East, India, China, et cetera—have been completely dislodged from their groove. Their development has completely shifted. . . . The general European ferment has begun to affect them, and it is now clear to the whole world that they have been drawn into a process of development that cannot but lead to a crisis in the whole of world capitalism" [*Selected Works*, volume 9, page 398].

These lines of 1923 tell us, at least in general, more about the world in which we now live than do most of the pages of tomorrow morning's newspaper. Not the gift of prophecy, but the social weight of the Russian peasantry plus the underdeveloped character of the Russian economy, enabled Lenin to see what was emerging. The Russian experience poses the problem of reconstructing all of contemporary society along the most modern, sensible lines: the intertwining of the movements of the peasantry with those of the proletariat and all other revolutionary forces. No underdeveloped country has as yet been able to escape what was once called the "Russian question". The critical components of 1922–23 are today the preoccupations of leaders and led, the organised and unorganised, small organisations and large parties, academic scholars and the most ordinary men and women of the street and work place.

The reader will note that we are constantly talking about struggles, conflicts, the attempts of classes to dominate one another or break through to something new. This is supposed to be a special viciousness introduced into history by Marx and Lenin, ending in the inevitable bloodthirstiness and savagery of stalinism. This is not only untrue, it is stupid.

Marx insisted from the beginning that he had not invented the class struggle, that he had not conjured it up as an idea or as a mere interpretation of historical actuality. Various others had done that before him and even more so afterward. Among the most specific additions that Marx made to social thought was while there had always been class conflicts, with the arrival of the workers at the industrial base of society, a class had come upon the scene which as the culmination of its struggle would abolish all classes and any notion of society as being in any way built upon class differentiation.

Deep in the evolution of European philosophy there was this concept of a life-and-death struggle for every single human being, in which each is engaged from the very beginning of his consciousness of the world. In the main it has been the prime purpose of political leaders, and of their philosophers, to deny any such general truth, even to indict it as criminal, while at the same time employing such a notion of life-and-death human struggle when it serves their specific purposes, as for example in a war. Before entering into the questions involving the world's peasant peoples, we must examine two quotations on this subject, one from a classic of philosophy, and the other, equally well-acknowledged, from sociology, the science of society.

First Hegel. In the extracts that follow, extracts that will be discussed as we go on, Hegel is dealing with the phenomenology of mind and he is saying what are the mental processes of people in society. He deals with the mental processes of the master and the slave, of the man in charge of an economic development and the man who is working for him:

> The presentation of itself, however, as pure abstraction of self-consciousness consists in showing itself as a pure negation of its objective form, or in showing that it is fettered to no determinate existence, that it is not bound at all by the particularity everywhere

characteristic of existence as such, and is not tied up with life. The process of bringing all this out involves a twofold action—action on the part of the other (the person over there) and action on the part of itself. In so far as it is the other's action, each aims at the destruction and death of the other.

This is what has been taking place in Detroit and elsewhere in the United States, and throughout the world. It says: in so far as it is the other's action—other—two separate people—the relation between them, each aims at the destruction and death of the other.

But in this there is implicated also the second kind of action, self-activity; for the former implies that it risks its own life.

The question is that in a class relation life is risked, and Hegel says a fundamental part of a relation of one section, one man to the other, and Marx and others have applied it to classes, is the fact that they are ready at a certain stage, the relation demands a fight to the death. Your life has to be risked.

The relation of both self-consciousnesses is in this way so constituted that they prove themselves and each other through a life-and-death struggle.

In other words, the different sections of society cannot work out any system and cannot find out what they are to each other and what they are to themselves unless they reach a stage where they are fighting to the end and life and death are involved.

They must enter into this struggle, for they must bring their certainty of themselves (you have to find out what you are), the certainty of being for themselves, to the level of objective truth, and make this a fact both in the case of the other and in their own case as well.

They have to fight to know what they are. They have to fight to know what they are going for. They have to fight to the death to know what the other fellow wants. And it is only under these conditions that some understanding of full self-consciousness is reached.

And it is solely by risking life that freedom is obtained.

Otherwise you don't know. There are places where, he says, you live a sort of superficial life, and then:

Only thus is it tried and proved that the essential nature of self-consciousness is not bare existence, is not the merely immediate form in which it at first makes its appearance, is not its mere absorption in the expanse of life. Rather it is thereby guaranteed that there is nothing present but what might be taken as a vanishing moment—that self-consciousness is merely pure self-existence, being-for-self. The individual, who has not staked his life, may, no doubt, be recognised as a Person; but he has not attained the truth of his recognition as an independent self-consciousness. In the same way each must aim at the death of the other, as it risks its own life thereby; for that other is to it of more worth than itself; the other's reality is presented to the former as an external other, as outside itself; it must cancel that externality. The other is a purely existent consciousness and entangled in manifold ways; it must view its otherness as pure existence for itself or as absolute negation. [Hegel: *Phenomenology of Mind*, page 233]

We have been dealing with the relation between master and slave. Now he goes on to the bondsman. The master has one form of existence, the slave has another. And now Hegel says:

But again, shaping or forming the object has not only the positive significance that the bondsman becomes thereby aware of himself as factually and objectively self-existent. [page 238]

It is in shaping the object for the master that the bondsman becomes aware of himself as factually and objectively self-existent.

This type of consciousness has also a negative import, in contrast with its first moment, the element of fear. For in shaping the thing it only becomes aware of its own proper negativity. [page 239]

In working at the business it realises its own insignificance, its own weakness:

Its existence on its own account, as an object, through the fact that it cancels the actual form confronting it. But this objective negative element is precisely the alien, external reality, before which it trembled. Now, however, it destroys this extraneous alien negative, affirms and sets itself up as a negative in the element of permanence, and thereby becomes for itself a self-existent being. [page 239]

By changing this thing in front of it and working for the master and being the person who handles it, it thereby becomes a self-existent being.

In the master, the bondsman feels self-existence to be something external, an objective fact; in fear self-existence is present within himself; (but) in fashioning the thing, self-existence comes to be felt explicitly as his own proper being, and he attains the consciousness that he himself exists in its own right and on its own account.

The man is the slave to the master, and the self-existence of the consciousness of the slave is in reality the master. However they have reached the stage by fighting it out to the death, each understands the other and something begins. Now, however, he has to handle the goods which his master is going to enjoy and he is afraid of the master because he has to handle this thing and do it well. He realises in his self-consciousness that the master is in reality the master of everything. But in shaping the thing and taking part in making it into something else, he then realises his own self-consciousness as an independent being.

If we penetrate this bit of Hegel, we can come to understand the bitter but inevitable nature of the struggles that go on in the world, and have gone on. From this we can comprehend the nature of the struggle of classes which Marx took from a commonplace observation to a profound and world-significant universal philosophical comprehension.

The life and death struggle that Hegel talks of appears in the bitter character of peasant wars from those in Germany in the sixteenth century to the guerrilla struggles in Latin America and Vietnam today. It characterises as well the struggle of those who are some mere decades away from peasant existence, such as the Negro people of the United States.

What Hegel expostulated as philosophy for the individual thinker Marx proceeded to advance as the movement of social bodies. Marx wrote:

> What I did that was new was to prove (1) that the existence of classes is only bound up with particular, historic phases in the development of production; (2) that the class struggle necessarily leads to the dictatorship of the proletariat; (3) that this dictatorship itself only constitutes the transition to the abolition of all classes and to a classless society. [Marx-Engels: *Selected Correspondence*, page 57]

Those lines were written in 1852; they were pushed to a conclusion in twentieth century terms by Lenin:

> A new source of great world storms opened up in Asia. The Russian revolution was followed by the Turkish, the Persian, and the Chinese revolutions. It is in this era of storms and their "repercussions" on Europe that we are now living. Whatever may be the fate of the great Chinese Republic, against which the various "civilised" hyenas are now baring their teeth, no power on earth can restore the old serfdom in Asia or wipe out the heroic democracy of the masses of the people in the Asiatic and semi-Asiatic countries. [*Selected Works*, volume 11, page 51]

For Lenin this all confirmed the class nature of political struggle and thinking about the political future, about the "Historical Destiny of Marx's Doctrine", the title Lenin uses for the previous quotation and the next:

> The Asiatic revolutions have revealed the same spinelessness and baseness of liberalism, the same exceptional importance of the independence of the democratic masses, and the same sharp line of division between the proletariat and bourgeoisie of all kinds. After the experience of both Europe and Asia, whoever now speaks of non-class politics and non-class socialism simply deserves to be put

in a cage and exhibited alongside the Australian kangaroo. [*Selected Works*, volume 11, pages 51–2]

What once pertained to Europe is now of Asia and of much more. The life-and-death struggle described in a classic philosophical work is in reality class politics, the class politics that encompasses the world. At a time when society as a civilised entity is endangered by social stratification which calls itself democratic or liberal or socialist, we are compelled to reconsider those moments of participation of the peasant masses which help account for whatever civilisation we still have.

The name of Solon is still to be found in the newspapers and the school texts as a personification of political wisdom. What he did was to set Greece on the road to what is legitimately claimed to be the most remarkable achievement of civilisation. He involved the peasantry in the revolution which broke the power of the landed aristocrats. Trade and industry of the elemental kind was substituted, but the peasantry took the great role open to it by bringing about the new régime and what we now know of as "the glory that was Greece", especially that startling concentration of civilised accomplishment that was Athens.

In Rome there took place the great revolution led by the Gracci. It failed, but peasants right through the peninsula of Italy insisted that citizenship could no longer belong only to the inhabitants of the city of Rome, but should be the possession of the peninsula as a whole. Under the Roman Empire, many historians believe, it was this notion of a universal citizenship which was extended to all the free inhabitants of the Empire that was crucial in maintaining that remarkable political achievement. Indeed, the very concept, citizenship, in Rome came to be associated with the very reality of civilisation itself. It is important to remember this today.

What followed in the late Middle Ages was continuity along a similar line. The reason for the failure of such highly advanced centres of civilisation as the city-states of Florence and north Italy was that they were unable to incorporate the peasantry of the surrounding areas. It proved impossible to maintain the polarisation of urbanised artistic, economic, and social sophistication at one end with rural idiocy, superstition, and isolation at the opposite extreme. The city-state had to give way to capitalistic society, a monarch heading the whole nation, supported to a substantial degree by the feudal landowners. The failure of the prologue to modern society, the attempt of the city-states of Italy (and indeed those of the Low Countries) at popular democracy was based on the failure to involve the peasant masses.

The first great modern revolution was the one that owes more to the peasantry than to any other section of society. The yeoman farmers of England in the English revolution of the seventeenth century were the basis of the finest army that Europe up to that date had known; it first and foremost ensured the success of that revolution. Secondly, the army in discussions with its leader, Oliver Cromwell, produced as a political formation the Levellers, the leaders and spokesmen who formulated the "Agreement of the People" in its various forms. These laid down the relevant principles of democracy, the popular, democratic content of which has not yet been fulfilled in any modern country. Thus, the yeomanry was not only the fundamental mass leverage of the overturn of the ancient monarchy and its accompanying feudalism; it also put forward clear and distinct political ideas which must be the basis of any socialist society.

From the vantage point of the extensive Russian peasantry, Lenin repeatedly explained that you cannot have socialism without carrying democracy to its extreme, a concept impossible to understand in a historically concrete way unless one begins with the party of the Levellers.

Everyone knows that it was the peasant revolution which helped to break the power of the French aristocrats. But there is something else which the majority of people do not know. All over France, village communes consisting of peasants and agricultural workers organised together and formed the various federations which became the different districts of which France is composed today. While Paris spearheaded the revolution, the new France was built on the federation established by the actions of the populace in the countryside.

We believe that this achievement of the peasantry in establishing what we know as modern France needs to be solidly established today when the peasants of the world have once again laid claim to the making of history and the advancement of civilisation, this time not on a city, or national, but on a world-wide scale. It is not accidental that this tremendous historical event is registered in a piece of writing by Michelet, the famous historian of the French revolution. Michelet writes:

> This opposition becomes completely insignificant in the midst of the immense popular movement which was asserting itself everywhere. Never since the Crusades was there such a shaking up of the masses, so general, so deep. In '90 the impetus of fraternity, now the impetus of war.
>
> Where did this impetus begin? Everywhere. No precise origins can be fixed for these great spontaneous acts. In the summer of 1789 during the terrorism of the brigands, the scattered population, even those of the hamlets are afraid of their isolation: hamlets are united with hamlets, villages with villages, even the city with the country. Confederation, mutual help, brotherly friendship, fraternity, this is the idea, the title of these pacts. Few, very few, are as yet written

down. At first the idea of fraternity is limited. It involved only
neighbors, and at most the province. The great federation of
Brittany and Anjou still has this provincial character. Convened on
26 November, it achieved its purpose in January. At the centre of
the peninsula, far from the main highways in the lonely little town
of Pontivy, the representatives of 150,000 national guards are
meeting. Only the horsemen wear a common uniform, red jackets
with black lapels; all the others distinguishable by their pink, purple
and suede lapels, et cetera, recalled at this same gathering the
diversity of the cities which sent them. In their coalition, to which
they invited all the municipalities of the kingdom, they nevertheless
insisted upon forming a permanent family of Brittany and Anjou,
"whatever new departmental division may be necessary for the
administration". They established a system of correspondence
between their cities. In the general disorder, in the uncertainty in
which they find themselves due to the success of their new order,
they arrange at least to be organised separately.

In the less isolated countries, at the crossing of large routes,
especially on the rivers, the pact of fraternity takes on a wider scope.
Under the old régime with the multitude of toll charges, and internal
customs, the rivers were merely limits, obstacles, fetters; but under
the rule of liberty they became the main routes of circulation, they
put men in contact with ideas, with feelings, as well as with commerce.

It is near the Rhone, two leagues from Valence, in the small
market town of Etoile, that, for the first time, the province is
renounced; fourteen rural communes of Dauphine unite and embrace the great French unity (29 November 1789). A very effective
reply from these peasants to the politicians and to the Mouniers who
appealed to provincial pride, to the spirit of partition, who were
trying to arm the province of Dauphine against France.

This Federation, renewed at Montelimart, is no longer only
Dauphinoise, but is mixed with several provinces from both banks.
Dauphine and Vivarais, Provence and Languedoc. This time,
therefore, they are French. Grenoble sends people there of its own
accord, in spite of the municipality, in spite of its politics; she no
longer cares about her role as capital, she prefers to be part of
France. All together they repeat the sacred oath which the peasants
have already sworn in November: "No more provinces! the
Nation!" And to help each other, to feed one another, to pass the
corn from hand to hand along the Rhone (13 December).

The work of rural people in transforming society and
eradicating ancient ills was continued in the American Civil
War. White farmers and black former slaves intervened to bring
American civilisation to a new height. In the first half of that
conflict the farmers of the American northwest opposed the
extension of slavery into the free states and territories. These
farmers played a crucial role in the creation of a new political

party, the Republican Party, dedicated to free states and territories.

In the final decisive years of that war, the slaves themselves flocked to the Northern Army to guarantee the unity of the country and to safeguard and deepen their own emancipation. The stage was being set for something in the next century.

Not only do the present generation of Afro-Americans, themselves a few generations away from Southern soil, rural people undergoing the new impact of urban life and industrial capitalism, battle for equality in every sphere of life. They demand in reality the outline of an entirely new America. Rural people in their transition to urban life have nurtured the pre-condition of a new ordering of the constitutive elements that make America.

In the twentieth century the Russian peasants took the stage. It required the Russian peasantry of two revolutions, 1905 and 1917, plus the counter-revolution of the 1920s, to enable us to see clearly in experience that is now thoroughly international. Stalin was forced in his drive for mastery not only to destroy the Bolshevik Party, to stifle free intellectual and artistic development and behead, shackle, and fetter the working class. He had to subjugate the peasantry to ensure his domination of all that had been the product of the Russian revolution, a domination which enabled him to defeat that revolution in a way that all the reactionary armies had not been able to do. Stalin, with his eyes set on the necessity of economic development of backward Russian society as a whole, unloosed a war upon those he called "kulaks"—an insulting word referring to the middle layer and the well-to-do among the agricultural population. He sent millions of peasants, torn away from their lands by military power, to Siberia.

At the very same time, in the turn from the port cities of Shanghai and Canton to the peasantry in the interior that took place in 1927-28, the Chinese Communist Party made its own turn—but in an opposite direction. At first it went into the interior of the country for tactical reasons, to escape the per-secutions opened upon it in the cities. Mao Tse-tung was theoretically unprepared for the intricacies of the agrarian question. But the objective situation was such, and the readiness of the peasants for self-arming so ingrained in the Chinese countryside, that while paying lip service to Stalin, the Chinese communists began to root their own party situation in the struggles against landlordism.

The fruit of all this was Chinese national independence and the troubles this has given the bourgeois powers of the West and the traditional communist movement ever since. Without the peasant associations of China, which did not wait for their formation upon any Communist Party, all this could not have come about. The peasantry was announcing its entry into world politics. What may have happened to the Chinese revolution after the consolidation of national independence is another question. But the achievement of national independence by a peasant army stands as an unquestionable fact by all willing to see.

The Indian national struggles after World War I followed something of the path whereby the Russian intelligentsia went to the peasant mass a century before. The Indian leader, Gandhi, made his name and fame by emulating the life of the peasant and engaging in all kinds of activities which would capture the peasants' imagination. Even those who called themselves socialist in India, would, by the late 1930s, attempt to carry the whole peasantry with them in the effort to expel the British. Gandhi found a unifying tactic in the refusal to pay taxes, the peasants drove the struggle forward to include assaults on the landlords and moneylenders.

It was the intervention of war which moved the mass of the sharecroppers into the new struggle. The Japanese had invaded East Bengal, peasant committees began to administer affairs in the village and order justice there. Undoubtedly among the vital reasons that the British imperial authorities were prepared to leave the sub-continent that is India and Pakistan was the determination of the peasants to engage in uncompromising struggles which no amount of diplomatic conferences with Indian Congress Party leaders could in any way obviate. An organic social rupture was taking place in the length and breadth of Asia with the masses of peasants as its centre and political independence as its viable result.

Perhaps there is no more singular illustration of the power of the peasantry than the world impact of Vietnamese peasants. The Vietnam peasants have in effect now mobilised whole sections of the American population and immobilised whole sectors of the American state. The Vietnamese as a people live in an industrially primitive civilisation revolving around the cultivation of rice and the isolation of a village-based social structure. Yet they are facing the tremendous power of the United States with an energy, an endurance, and a heroism which cannot be exceeded. Napoleon, the greatest man of military affairs of the last centuries, faced it in Spain, he faced it in peasant Russia, he faced it in San Domingo. And today the Vietnam farmer shows us what the peasantry contains in itself.

Africa is in many ways key to the understanding of the role of the peasants in a world order in transition. The first new, independent state to be established on that continent was Ghana. The rise of Nkrumah in Ghana was ultimately determined by the peasant population in both political and social terms. While Nkrumah built a certain base for his political party in the major city of Accra, it was his tireless campaigning in the most outlying parts of the country among the rural people which produced the situation where the once all-powerful Colonial Office had to bring him out of jail to govern. No one else could govern the country. The population, ready, as Nkrumah has written, for anything, had seen to that.

The closeness of the city people to the peasantry in Ghana created the objective environment for the unification of the mass of the population, in both city and country. The market women who have for centuries united town and country through well-established domestic marketing arrangements, the internal migration of people, and the sophistication of the coastal population, provided the bridge to the more distant rural population.

Nkrumah was able to respond to this readiness of the population, this closeness between town and country, and to express the aspirations of the total population. But more than this, he was the most vocal spokesman for African unity, for the notion of a Pan-African movement—the continental unity of peasant peoples.

We have now surveyed the role of the peasantry throughout the world, and have dealt with the reactionary prejudice that it will take hundreds of years before supposedly backward masses are brought up to the level of supposedly advanced peoples. Historical example after example show that the popular mass need only see the possibilities of a new society and the possibilities of assistance, not domination, of the advanced technical knowledge of the world: within fifteen or twenty years we can have a totally different world society.

Political independence is only, however, the first step in a long and difficult process. Now must come the working out of the difficult internal problems, the work relations, the connections between town and country, the utilisation of popular resourcefulness. The mess left by the colonial powers, still not by any means totally out of the picture, must be cleared up.

The work and slim writings of a leader of the movement for independence in Tanganyika, D. K. Chisiza, offer the most concrete and penetrating analysis of the problem before Africa—and indeed the rest of the former colonial territories— that we know. Chisiza, unfortunately killed in an automobile accident when barely thirty, provides that kind of understanding that the architects of the new Africa must have.

The great strength of Chisiza's analysis lies in the fact that it begins and ends in the spirit of concern with the ninety per cent of the population which is rural and tribal. It is through this emphasis that he avoids the abstract treatment typical of old-fashioned autocracies and modern bureaucracies. While aware of the general problem of Africa in the midst of the cold war and the dangers of atomic annihilation, neo-colonialist economic control, and intervention by way of political intrigue and mercenary armies, Chisiza keeps his sights aimed at the transformation of the African tribalist into an industrial citizen. The uniqueness of his analysis and its general unavailability not only in Europe and America but in Africa as well, fully justifies an extensive quotation from his work in this document. The following is taken from his *Realities of African Independence*, published in 1961.

Men flock in from rural areas to take up jobs in industrial enterprises. They are taught certain skills. But no sooner is the training over than they decide to return "home". Thus money, time and valuable effort will have been wasted on training men who will keep no track with industry. Worse still, when these men return to the industrial centres for another bout of employment, there is no arrangement to get them back to the jobs for which they were trained. The result is that they take up new jobs for which they have to receive new training. But before long the process is repeated all over again, the men turn their backs on industry and head for "home". Governments which have schemes for training foremen, charge hands, mechanics, artisans, and other skilled or semi-skilled workers face precisely the same, and no less a problem. This will probably prove to be one of the most intractable problems confronting African governments.

The question must be asked: Why is it that Africans from rural areas find it difficult to sink roots in industrial centres? Why won't they settle down to regular industrial employment? There are six answers to this question:

(a) Because they feel lonely in urban areas. An African who has been brought up in an extended family system, under which family ties are very strong, cannot bear to be away from his family and relations for long. He is subjected to a loneliness which comes close to being a torture. Those who are brought up in a horizontal family system may not fully appreciate its intensity. But it is there—real, intense, merciless.

(b) Because towns subject them to a sense of insecurity. Tribal life revolves around the institution of "mutual aid and co-operation" from which people derive a tremendous sense of security. Like land, it is the equivalent of banks, savings, insurance policies, old age pensions, national assistance schemes, and social security. This "mutual aid and co-operation" is non-existent in towns because urban communities are made up of people drawn not from one but from numerous tribes—conglomerations in which the institution cannot survive even if it were introduced.

(c) Because they have obligations to their people "back home" which can be fulfilled only in person. The people who come to work in industrial centres are at once children of their parents, fathers, husbands, brothers, and uncles. According to African custom, they must therefore look after and take over the responsibilities of their ageing parents: they must periodically build houses for themselves and "the old people"; they must initiate their male children in the customs and traditions of their tribes; and they must discharge their duties as husbands—all of which cannot be done from afar.

(d) Because they find it trying to adjust themselves to the mode of life of urban areas. Town life bears little resemblance to the life they lead in rural areas. In fact it is a wonder that they are able to put up with the complexities and vicissitudes of urban life for as long as they do. The gap between the two ways of life is so wide that one can cross it permanently only at the risk of protracted psychological discomfiture. It is a far cry from the world of the hoe, deer hunting, war dances, canoe regattas, and moral rectitude to that of the conveyor belt, tennis, tango, and promiscuity.

(e) Because a good many of them feel that one cannot bring up children properly in towns. Juvenile delinquency, hooliganism, prostitution, marriage instability, greed, and individualism which characterise life in urban areas are revolting to rural peoples. That is why those of them who are forced by circumstances to ask their wives to join them in towns, send their children "back home" to be brought up in the traditional way.

(f) Because their goals are realised quickly. Men who come to towns have definite goals in mind. It may be the purchase of a sewing machine, a plough, a bicycle, clothes, or kitchen utensils. They may be trying to raise money to enable them to build brick houses or to settle cases or to pay taxes. As soon as the goals are achieved it is deemed time to put odds and ends together and head for home.

All these reasons combine to compel the rural African to return to the rural areas "where men are men and women are proud of them".

What makes these detailed analyses exemplary in their perceptiveness is that they correspond to the problems of peoples trying to make their way everywhere. From the original entry of the Russian peasantry into the forefront of political experience to the emergence of modern Africa, the overriding central issue has been the division between town and countryside, between ever-centralising bureaucrats and the resourcefulness of local initiative.

Here is the problem in the Russian revolution at the eve of the long dark night of its deterioration and degeneration. Lenin is speaking:

Under certain conditions the exemplary organisation of local work, even on a small scale, is of far greater national importance than many branches of central state work. And these are precisely the conditions we are in at the present moment in regard to peasant farming in general, and in regard to the exchange of surplus products of agriculture for the manufacture of industry in particular. Exemplary organisation in this respect, even in a single volost, is of far greater national importance than the "exemplary" improvement of the central apparatus of any People's Commissariat; for our central apparatus has been built up during the past three and a half years to such an extent, we cannot improve it quickly to any extent, we do not know how to do it. Assistance in the more radical improvement of it, a new flow of fresh forces, assistance in the successful struggle against bureaucracy, in the struggle to overcome this harmful inertness, must come from the localities, from the lower ranks, with the exemplary organisation of a small "whole", precisely a "whole", that is, not one farm, not one branch of the economy, not one enterprise, but the sum total of economic relations, the sum total of economic exchange, even if only in a small locality.

Those of us who are doomed to remain on work at the centre will continue the task of improving the apparatus and purging it of bureaucracy, even if in modest and immediately achievable dimensions. But the greatest assistance in this task is coming, and will come, from the localities. [*Selected Works*, volume 9, page 191]

That phrase, "Those of us who are doomed to remain on work at the centre", is the ultimate wisdom, the need, the overwhelming desire of the greatest student of human affairs that any government has ever known. His mastery of philosophy, political economy, and politics could find its climax and fruition only in going to work among the peasants in a Russian village.

What has happened in relations between Russia and the United States over the last dozen years is of primary significance for us. American power has accommodated itself to Russian power because the threat of working-class revolution against stalinist power is more frightening than the competition with modern Russia. While the conflict has not ceased, it has been carefully controlled. This new stage in the relationship was marked by the October of 1956, the Hungarian revolution. This was a revolution of the entire Hungarian population, led by the working class, against Russian occupation and the Communist Party dictatorship. In the past in the cold war between America and Russia, the American government responded quickly and forcefully to what it considered the challenge of "international communism". But it met the rising of the Hungarian working class in the face of tremendous military odds with the insistence that the repression of Hungary was an internal matter of the "Warsaw Pact" signatories. America acquiesced in the slaughter of the Hungarian proletarian revolution, a revolution that marked the furthest stage of the revolutionary development of the modern working class. In it the working class demonstrated that it could dispense with political parties and rely solely on the power of its direct organisation in workers' councils at the point of production. This workers' power was too great a threat to American capitalism; American capitalism did not mind that Russian tanks defeated it.

Today the American and Russian working classes stand as the heirs of the Hungarian workers of 1956. Therefore, only an analysis of the interpenetration of Russian and American working classes can allow us to see the way out of the tensions that portend the making of World War III.

In 1917 the largest and most modern factory in the world was the Putilov works in Saint Petersburg. The social organisation to correspond to that, however, was not in Russia at all. It was at the plant of the Ford Motor Company in Highland Park, Michigan. The Russian workers overthrew Tsarism, and then the capitalist government of Kerensky, in order to take possession of the Putilov works and all the rest of Russian industry. But the social order which they were revolting against, and which they were to face again in another form, had reached its highest development at Ford.

Ford had introduced the assembly line to raise labour productivity to new heights. But the assembly line raised more than productivity. It raised the alienation and fragmentation of workers to new heights. And so Ford introduced a new social organisation to correspond to the technical organisation of the assembly line. This was the Ford Service Department, which organised a totalitarian control over the lives of Ford workers, at work and at home, which was to become notorious for its viciousness, for its corruption, and for its pervasiveness. Combined with the ultimate in alienation and control was—the Five-Dollar Day. This was evidence right at the start of a new stage of capitalist production that the intensification of exploitation was no longer to be synonymous with low wages.

What the Ford system was, was the embryonic form, limited to one company and one community, of fascism or totalitarianism. When the Ford system of production became the universal one in all industrial nations, the attempt to impose the Ford social system also became universal. It was successful in Italy. It was successful in Germany. And it was the system which Stalin turned to in order to destroy the conquests of 1917 and to industrialise Russia at the expense of the Russian workers. Harry Bennett's Service Department on the grand scale—the GPU, organiser of purges, organiser of assassinations, organiser of slave labour camps.

In one sense, the fact that the peak of capitalist social organisation had been reached in the United States and not in Russia was a sign of the weakness of the Russian working class. Although the Putilov works was the largest in the world and contained under its roof the largest concentration of workers ever assembled until that time, Russian industry as a whole was small and weak. And the Russian working class was small and weak. Not, of course, in relation to Tsarism, but in relation to the needs of a modern industrial civilisation.

The American working class, despite the greater intensity of its exploitation in 1917 and in the years that followed, proved powerful enough to prevent the imposition of the Ford social system, that is, fascism, on the nation as a whole. The attempts to impose totalitarian order and regimentation on the nation, especially after the explosions of the depression days, were continuous. Fascist organisations were formed and reached considerable strength in some instances. And the interest in promoting an imposed social peace on the nation through totalitarian instruments reached into the New Deal cabinet of Franklin Roosevelt. But the outburts, the strikes, the sitdowns, the political organisation proved stronger than the counter-revolution and what emerged was welfare state capitalism instead of totalitarian state capitalism.

Now, after fifty years, we have come full circle and Russian and American workers once again share a fundamentally similar situation. In the Soviet Union it took the organisation of labour itself, the Communist Party, to impose the brutal discipline required by the needs of capital. The organisation of labour transformed into its opposite, the instrument of capitalist discipline in production. In the United States too, although in more moderate form, the old social order proved inadequate to control and regiment the working class and one of the consequences of welfare state capitalism is that that task is more and more assumed by the organisations of labour, the unions. (In England the process is even more visible in the Labour Party.) Here, too, the organisation of labour is transformed into its opposite, the instrument of capitalist discipline in production. And old Henry Ford knew what he was doing; his pattern is imitated to this day. He knew that he had to combine the carrot with the stick, the Five-Dollar Day with the Service Department. So the union contracts of today combine the high wages and fringe benefits with the increase of discipline and intensification of the speed-up.

In 1917 it was still possible for different parts of the world to travel different roads. Today that is no longer true. What Russian workers will find it necessary to do, or what American workers will find it necessary to do, will also be done by their fellow workers on the other side of the world.

The Russian working class travelled a rocky and tortuous road from 1917 to 1967. In 1917 the Russian workers were unable to end the contradiction between economics and politics. They mastered politics and formed soviets. But they did not succeed in mastering economics. They proved too small, too backward, too isolated to manage production. As a result they were driven back. The battles of the Civil War took a tremendous toll. Thousands of the workers who had made the revolution fell in battle. The physical plant of Russian industry deteriorated with the result that the working class itself was scattered with an additional loss of productive skills. Skilled workers unable to work at their trade because of lack of equipment or of materials drifted into black market trade or back to the farm or accepted unskilled work. The final blow was the stalinist counter-revolution which annihilated the rank-and-file militants, the factory leaders, the worker-Bolsheviks.

In 1917 the Russian workers put an end to Russian feudalism. A decade later (1928) Stalin introduced the first Five-Year Plan to impose a capitalist discipline on the workers. But it was an almost new working class, driven from the farms through the forced collectivisation of agriculture which was intended both to supply the workers and to feed them. In 1928 the aim was the largest possible mass of labour through the subordination of the workers to the specialists in general. By 1931 industrialisation had reached the point where exploitation could be intensified by increasing the pay of individuals through the institution of the piecework system. By 1935 this is developed into fully blown stakhanovism, the piece worker as individual hero, the competition between workers. In this brutal way was in-dustrialisation introduced to state capitalist Russia and illiterate peasants transformed into disciplined workers. In 1936 the new stalinist constitution codified the new system and established the "intelligentsia"; that is, the experts, the party leaders, the managers as the new capitalist class.

The power of the small Russian working class of 1917, its overthrow of Tsarism and its control of the state, called forth the absolute extreme of totalitarian terror to overthrow it and then to dominate and discipline the new Russian working class. By the time of World War II, Russian industrialisation had reached the point where the machinery itself could begin to discipline and organise the workers. Piecework becomes more systematised in the form of competition between factories.

The major turning point is 1943. This is the year of the conversion to the conveyor belt system. It corresponds to the theoretical admission, in Leontiev's *Political Economy in the Soviet Union*, that the law of value operates in the Soviet Union. But the conveyor-belt system indicates more than a technical level of sophistication. It indicates that a modern industrial proletariat has been formed, far in advance of the Russian workers of 1917. And the class struggle begins to develop as the workers attempt to organise their resistance to the intense ex-ploitation. It begins in Vorkuta and the slave labour camps before the death of Stalin, and then spreads to all of Russia. Stalin's death and the relaxation of the oppression conceals the fact that the change in rulers did not cause the thaw but merely corresponded to the pressures of the workers.

At the Twentieth Congress of the Russian Communist Party in 1956, in a speech to which no one paid any attention because it was public (unlike the secret speech denouncing Stalin), Khrushchev points out that "there is a great deal of disorder and confusion in the system of wages and rate-fixing. . . . Cases of wage levelling are not uncommon. On the other hand, payment for the same type of work sometimes differs between various bodies, and even within a single body. Alongside the low-paid workers there exists a category of workers, a small one it is true, in whose wages unjustified excesses are tolerated.''

What this means, of course, is that the Russian workers have succeeded in establishing the informal shop-floor organisations of struggle, known in all industrial countries. They have been able to make a mockery of the national plan and to force adjustments in wages (and, of necessity, working conditions) on a shop or department basis.

The stage that the modern industrial proletariat of a totalitarian state capitalist nation has reached was indicated negatively by Khrushchev. It was indicated positively by the Hungarian revolution, where the opposition between economics and politics was finally overcome. Hungary shows where the Russian working class has in fact reached, able to manage society both politically and economically.

In the United States the fantastic growth of the chemical industry and the development of the electric motor made possible the introduction of the continuous assembly line. Huge complexes such as the Ford plant were made possible by the new source of power which was portable within the plant and freed production from the need to be close to water power. They were aided, in the early stages of the chemical industry, by the finer grades of steel and other products made possible by the application of electricity and chemistry to machine production.

The result in the United States was a tremendous expansion of the working class, aided by World War I, and almost immediately the explosion of the class struggle. The period of the twenties, the so-called prosperity years, begins with the great steel strike of 1919 and the Seattle general strike, and ends in the Great Depression. It is a period, not of class peace, but of class war. But with the crushing of the steel strike the state and all the instruments of political power are clearly seen as the direct servant of capital. The workers, adept at using their economic power, find themselves unmercifully beaten back by the political (and military) power arrayed against them. In the United States, as in Russia, the workers are taking the needed time to learn about themselves, about the new forms of production, about the forms of organisation adequate for their situation.

With the Great Depression this bursts forth in the formation of the CIO and the introduction of the sitdown strike. In the sitdown, the workers take their first long step toward control of production and, thereby, the elimination of the contradiction between economics and politics as it confronted the American working class. In their origin as spontaneous outbursts started without the approval and against the wishes of the leaders of the new unions, the sit-downs already foretell the fundamental split between workers and union leaders that is the hallmark of the labour movement today. And just as the workers' revolution of 1917 brought forth totalitarian state capitalism to suppress it, so the workers' revolt of the 1930s also brought forth the massive intervention of the state in the form of welfare state capitalism to suppress it. All of the labour and social reforms of the New Deal were designed to provide orderly bargaining through representatives supervised by the state and to put an end to workers' representing themselves in sit-downs and wildcats. The massive uprising of the 1930s had finally broken through the separation of economics and politics, but because it was not complete, because it ended in unions instead of control, the workers were able to transform American politics but not to control it.

The period of World War II is the period of the codification of the social legislation of the New Deal. The fusion between unions and government is made complete. The workers make one last attempt to break it in the immediate postwar years, and when the first round of postwar strikes has only limited success (winning the sliding scale of wages in the auto industry) both sides in the conflict move in new directions. American industry in the early fifties embarks on a massive programme of automation to free itself from the restrictions imposed on it by the workers (and made possible by the technological advances during the war in military products). The workers begin the necessary reorganisation to correspond to the new form of production. In 1955 they indicate what that new form is. In the massive wildcats against a union settlement in auto, the workers put forward their own "specific local grievances" which, in their totality, show the desire of workers to control production and demonstrate their total separation from the union. No longer will the union be the instrument to make significant social gains. Quite the contrary, through the union-company contract, the union becomes the instrument of capital, maintaining discipline in production, maintaining labour peace.

In the United States, by a different road and in modified form, the labour organisation (the union) becomes the organiser of production corresponding to Russian state capitalism under which the labour organisation (the Communist Party) becomes the organiser of production. The American working class too, although coming by a different road, has reached the point where it is demonstrating its capacity to govern production and society in its own name. The Hungarian revolution becomes the hallmark not only of the Russian working class, but of the workers of any industrialised country, above all, of the United States.

In 1917 the Russian workers demonstrated mastery over politics but failed in economics. The American workers were the most advanced economically but were beaten down politically. Fifty years later, both have achieved the maturity, the organisation, the freedom from bureaucratic domination to make the final leap, the socialist revolution.

1967

15

Black Power

[*Subtitled "Its Past, Today and the Way Ahead", this is the text of a lecture delivered in London in August 1967, and was published by the Marcus Garvey Institute in the USA. In James's words, "it is an attempt to clarify a concept which at that time meant so many different things to so many different people."*]

Mr Chairman, Ladies and Gentlemen, Black Power. I believe that this slogan is destined to become one of the great political slogans of our time. Of course, only time itself can tell that. Nevertheless, when we see how powerful an impact this slogan has made it is obvious that it touches very sensitive nerves in the political consciousness of the world today. This evening I don't intend to tell you that it is your political duty to fight against racial consciousness in the British people; or that you must seek ways and means to expose and put an end to the racialist policies of the present Labour government. If you are not doing that already I don't see that this meeting will help you to greater political activity. That is not the particular purpose of this meeting though, as you shall hear, there will be specific aims and concrete proposals. What I aim to do this evening is to make clear to all of us what this slogan Black Power means, what it does *not* mean, *cannot* mean; and I say quite plainly, we must get rid, once and for all, of a vast amount of confusion which is arising, copiously, both from the right and also from the left. Now I shall tell you quite precisely what I intend to do this evening. The subject is extremely wide, comprising hundreds of millions of people, and therefore in the course of an address of about an hour or so, we had better begin by being very precise about what is going to be said and what is not going to be said.

But before I outline, so to speak, the premises on which I will build, I want to say a few words about Stokely Carmichael: I think I ought to say Stokely because everybody, everywhere, calls him Stokely which I think is a political fact of some importance. The slogan Black Power, beginning in the United States and spreading from there elsewhere, is undoubtedly closely associated with him and with those who are fighting with him. But for us in Britain his name, whether we like it or not, means more than that. It is undoubtedly his presence here, and the impact that he has made in his speeches and his conversations, that have made the slogan Black Power reverberate in the way that it is doing in political Britain; and even outside of that, in Britain in general. And I want to begin by making a particular reference to Stokely which, fortunately, I am in a position to make. And I do this because on the whole in public speaking, in writing (and also to a large degree in private conversation), I usually avoid, take great care to avoid placing any emphasis on a personality in politics.

I was reading the other day Professor Lévi-Strauss and in a very sharp attack on historical conceptions prevalent today, I saw him say that the description of personality, or of the anecdote (which so many people of my acquaintance historically and politically live by) were the lowest forms of history. With much satisfaction I agreed: I have been saying so for nearly half a century. But then he went on to place the political personality within a context that I thought was misleading, and it seemed to me that in avoiding it as much as I have done, I was making a mistake, if not so much in writing, certainly in public speech. And that is why I begin what I have to say, and will spend a certain amount of time, on one of the most remarkable personalities of contemporary politics. And I am happy to say that I did not have to wait until Stokely came here to understand the force which he symbolises.

I heard him speak in Canada at Sir George Williams University in March of this year. There were about one thousand people present, chiefly white students, about sixty or seventy Negro people, and I was so struck by what he was saying and the way he was saying it (a thing which does not happen to me politically very often) that I sat down immediately and took the unusual step of writing a letter to him, a political letter. After all, he was a young man of twenty-three or twenty-four and I was old enough to be his grandfather and, as I say, I thought I had a few things to tell him which would be of use to him and, through him, the movement he represented. I will now read to you parts of this letter:

> I was glad to hear you because I wanted to know for myself what had lifted you up to the pinnacle on which you now stand. It is a pinnacle and one that is very rare in my experience or even historically. You are just twenty-four and you are not only one of the people on the American continent who is to be reckoned with, but you are a world-famous figure. At twenty-four. That fact is something very special and seems to offer immense possibilities both for the cause and the advancement, or rather I should say the development, of the personality. I am profoundly aware of the dangers of being in such a position at such an early age. I propose therefore in this letter to deal of course with the movement, because everything depends on that, but also with the specific dangers that beset you as a leader, perhaps the most prominent leader today, of this great movement in the United States.

I then explained why in particular I had been so struck by him. The letter continues:

One of my most important and pregnant experiences is my experience both personal and otherwise of West Indians and people of West Indian origin who have made their way on the broad stage of Western civilisation. Some of them I knew very well personally and others I have studied, am very familiar with their work, and have systematically added to my information and knowledge about them from people who knew them well. They are Marcus Garvey, George Padmore, Aimé Césaire, Frantz Fanon. These are West Indians who have played a role on the world political stage that is not even properly understood by their own people. One of the tasks I have set myself is to make people understand what these men have done and their significance in world politics. In a substantial respect I am one of them, although I have not played the concrete role that they have played: I say that I am one of them because it means that I understand the type very well. And you are one. I suspected it when I was reading some of your writings and having heard you I am absolutely certain of it. Let me briefly state at once some of the points that brought this home to me with extreme force, particularly at that meeting.

We need not go further into that now. I went on to say (it was a rather lengthy letter) that there were certain doubtful points in his speech which he should bear in mind. I went on further to indicate in the letter that there were grave weaknesses in the whole Negro struggle in the United States; for one, that it lacked a sound historical and theoretical basis. And I suggested to him, that if he did not see his way to initiate this study himself, he should see to it that others take it up and take it up seriously. *So large and far-reaching a struggle needed to know where it was, where it had come from, and where it was going.*

I received a reply in which he took up the points I had made and said he recognised their importance. That was in March and April of this year, 1967. The year has not ended and now he speaks with a scope and a depth and range of political understanding that astonishes me. That the Stokely whom I heard in March and whose conspicuous political ability and character I recognised (that is why I wrote to him) in less than a year should have developed into the political leader we are hearing and seeing, this to me is a testimony not merely to him but to the speed with which the modern world is moving politically. I have to add that much that I shall now say to you I knew before, but I could never have said it in the way that you will hear, unless I had been able to listen and to talk to the new Stokely, the Stokely that we have been hearing.

Now, Black Power. A political slogan and yet not a political slogan: rather a banner. We see that at once the moment we look at previous statements which have captured the political imagination and guided the activity of people all over the world during past centuries and up to today. I shall take some of the best known ones and that will enable us to put Black Power in the proper place to which it belongs.

You remember about the middle of the eighteenth century Rousseau's statement with which he began his famous book *The Social Contract*? "Man was born free and is everywhere in chains." Listen to it again: "Man was born free and is everywhere in chains." It was written two hundred years ago and yet today, in classes in political philosophy, in universities all over the world, in articles and books that are daily published, the debate rages: what did Rousseau mean by saying that man was born free and is everywhere in chains? Some people draw the conclusion about Rousseau that he was the originator of the totalitarian state, others that we have not yet reached the kind of democracy which he had in mind. It is not our business this evening to come to any decision about that (although I know where I stand). The point is that the phrase has been a banner under which men have struggled for liberty and freedom, a phrase under which that struggle goes on today. Without Rousseau's "Man was born free and is everywhere in chains", the world would be a poorer place.

Let us take another statement almost two hundred years old, the statement by Jefferson that "We hold these truths to be self-evident, that all men are created equal . . . that they are endowed by their Creator with certain inalienable rights . . .", the beginning of one of the most famous documents in history, the Declaration of Independence of the United States, declared in Congress on the fourth of July 1776. Self-evident! Jefferson had a nerve. Nothing like that was "self-evident" anywhere. In Britain, all over Europe, all over Asia, all over the known world, people were being overned by kings who were supposed to have been placed on the throne by God; there were nobles, aristocrats; there were the clergy with special rights, in every part of the known globe. In the United States itself there was a solid mass of people who did not believe that even in the United States all men were created equal. Yet Jefferson had the nerve to begin the famous document by saying that this was a truth that he held to be self-evident, i.e. everybody could see it. At the time there were very few people who accepted it. To this day there are vast numbers of people who don't believe it. Nevertheless it is one of the greatest political statements ever made. It is a banner by which and under which tremendous struggles have been waged for liberty, for democracy, for democratic freedom. I hope that you are following me in my view that it is only by placing it historically that we can begin to see what Black Power signifies and avoid gross and dangerous blunders. In fact, it is not a slogan at all. Rather it is a banner for people with certain political aims, needs and attitudes, a banner around which they can rally, a banner which I believe many millions already today see and in the not too distant future will see, as the symbol of a tremendous change in life and society as they have known it.

Let us now leave these slogans (I prefer to think of them as banners) and go directly to the origin and ancestry of this world-shaking movement, Booker T. Washington. For, yes, it is with Booker T. Washington that we have to begin. Today the name of Booker T. is not often mentioned in regard to the development of Negro struggles. Most often people mention with a certain disdain his famous concession, or I can call it his infamous capitulation to race prejudice in the South. It is part of the history of the Negro and of the history of the United States that Booker T., in a famous speech in Atlanta, Georgia, told the South:

> In all things purely social we can be as separate as the five fingers, and yet one as the hand in all things essential to mutual progress.

Today we ought to be able to see first that Booker T. Washington faced a situation in which he was seeking desperately for a way out, and he could see no way out except capitulation. But Booker T. did something else. He said that Negroes should prepare themselves for the work of artisans and labourers: everybody could not be a scholar or do a skilled clerical job; the Negro had to prepare himself for manual labour. But, added Booker T., he sould also seek to educate himself in the humanities. So it was that Tuskegee, which was the centre of Negro education in the South for many years, became a great pioneer of modern education, i.e. education for the members of a modern community, education of body and mind for manual and intellectual labour. So that today Booker T. Washington's *method* of education, *forced upon him by race prejudice*, has become an educational ideal which is more and more widely accepted as a necessity for the world in which we live.

But Booker T. is also remembered for the fact that he drew upon himself a devastating attack by another great pioneer in Negro struggles, Dr W. E. B. Du Bois. Du Bois marked a great stage in the history of Negro struggles when he said that Negroes could no longer accept the subordination which Booker T. Washington had preached. On it Booker T. had built a base not only for himself but for a certain type of Negro educator and social functionary. Dr Du Bois declared the absolute right of the Negro for whatever task he was fitted. And we can see how history changes in that, looking at the qualifications and weaknesses of American Negroes in his day, Du Bois championed specifically the Negroes of "the talented tenth", that tenth of the Negro community which he believed was already fitted to exercise fully the qualifications it had already attained. We can see how history moves when we understand that this, which was a legitimate demand by one of the great pioneers of Negro emancipation, would today be repudiated by Stokely and all supporters of Black Power. They do not seek to advance claims, rights for one-tenth of the present Negro population of the United States. They say that it is this tenth of the Negro population which has been and is being given special positions which corrupt it and act as a deadweight on the development of the great mass of the Negro people as a whole. So that "the talented tenth" in the days of Du Bois fifty years ago represented an advance, while today it is the main enemy of all those who fight under the banner of Black Power.

But if we wish properly to understand *the advanced position which Stokely Carmichael and the advocates of Black Power hold today*, we have only to see that Dr Du Bois was not a man whose reputation rested only on the fact that he was one of the great leaders of Negro emancipaaipation. Not only white journalists have thus circumscribed him. I have had to protest to leading people in the coloured community in the United States about what they said when Du Bois died. I am glad to say that I had had the opportunity to point out that in organising the National Association for the Advancement of Coloured People and founding its periodical *The Crisis*, Dr Du Bois took the lead in making the United States and the world recognise that racial prejudice was not a mere matter of Negroes being persecuted but was a cancer which poisoned the whole civilisation of the United States. Secondly, in the Pan-African Conferences that he organised all over the world, he first made people in the United States and elsewhere recognise that Africa could not be left in the state of stagnation and exploitation in which it had entered the twentieth century. Thirdly, in his study of the American slave trade and in his studies of the Civil War he was undoubtedly one of the most penetrating and effective historians of his time: there is no noteworthy American historian writing today and during the last fifty years who does not owe a tremendous debt to Du Bois's work in history. So that in all these respects he was far more than "a leader of our people". In fundamental respects he was a generation in advance of most American thinking of his time and he is one of the great citizens of the United States in the twentieth century. We must bear that mistake in mind and not make it again as we are on the way to doing in regard to the advocates of Black Power. *Think of this seriously, please.*

Now the foundation having been firmly laid, we can move a little faster. Next on the list is Marcus Garvey, of whom we need say only a few sentences. Before Garvey the great millions of Africans and people of African descent simply did not exist in the political consciousness of the world in general, of the general public, and of politicians in particular. After less than a decade this Jamaican had placed them there. He had placed them there in a manner that they could never be removed again. Garvey had placed them not only in the consciousness of the oppressors but as a constituent part of the minds and aims of the great mass of Africans and people of African descent.

We can now go still faster. After Garvey came Padmore, who added a new dimension. Padmore was the originator of the movement to achieve the political independence of the African countries and people of African descent. That is why he is increasingly known as the Father of African Emancipation. So that a certain stage of African emancipation had arrived, very soon after the independence of Ghana, by actually achieving political independence, i.e. rule by local and native politicians over large areas.

There follows automatically the rise and significance of the activities and writings of Frantz Fanon. We must see Fanon as the political activist and writer who is saying that now we have actually achieved independence we have to fight against not only the old imperialism creeping back: we have to carry on a desperate all-out struggle against those native leaders who may have fought for independence. Many do not represent the forward movement of the underdeveloped peoples to some new stage of economic and political progress. Says Fanon: after independence those become the enemy. We do not see Fanon correctly if we do not see him as a natural development after what Padmore represented, and Padmore as the political stage of the wide avenue opened by Du Bois and Marcus Garvey.

It is only now that we are able to see what Stokely and the advocates of Black Power represent. They stand on the shoulders of their ancestors. I have not mentioned all. For example, I have had to leave out Aimé Césaire, the man of Negritude, and I have had to leave out Malcolm X, that great fighter whose potentialities were growing so fast that his opponents had to get rid of him by plain murder. So then, it is now that we can see what Stokely and the concept of Black Power represent.

Stokely and the advocates of Black Power stand on the shoulders of all that has gone before. To too many people here in England, and unfortunately to people in the United States too (you remember I had mentioned this in my letter to Stokely), too many people see Black Power and its advocates as some sort of portent, a sudden apparition, as some racist eruption from the depths of blank oppression and black backwardness. It is nothing of the kind. It represents the high peak of thought on the Negro question which has been going on for over half a century. That much we have to know, and that much we have to be certain other people get to know.

Now, as in any political manifestation on a world scale, there is involved not only a general principle. As far as any particular country is concerned, we have to see it not only in its general but in its particular application. Now you notice that Booker T. Washington was from the South of the United States. W. E. B.

Du Bois was South and North, everywhere, and in the world outside: his was a universal mind. But the West Indians, Garvey, Césaire, Padmore and Fanon, all worked abroad, away from home, and much of their work, in fact most of it, was concerned with Africa. And taking advantage of this immense political experience which has been accumulated, and the advanced stage of American society, we find that it is in the United States that the Negro struggle has advanced and is now taken to the highest peak it has ever reached. For note that whereas the others on the whole concentrated on Africa and peoples of African descent, in the voice of Stokely we can hear that they are laying the basis of a mortal struggle to the death for what black people believe to be their rights.

They have further extended that struggle to what they call the Third World. By that phrase, the Third World, they embrace what is today the majority of mankind. There are people who say that the Stokely they heard in England here, and the Stokely they have read about is racist. The falsity of that, or if not falsity, its dishonesty, can be easily exposed. You all have heard him say that as far as he is concerned Tshombe is a white man. Black though his skin may be, he is the servant of what Malcolm X called the white power-structure. He tells us specifically that the concept of the Third World includes the population of Latin America. He says specifically that they are not in the majority coloured but he includes them in the Third World. How can one call this racism except through ignorance or malice? And he embraces the concept of the Third World under the slogan Black Power because blacks are the ones who have suffered longest and most from the crimes of imperialism.

Furthermore, there are special conditions in the United States to some of which I shall now draw your attention. First there are districts in the South where the Negroes are prevented from exercising the elementary rights of parliamentary democracy by the guns which the white racists keep pointed at their heads. The advocates of Black Power say that they intend (if necessary by using guns) to restore to the blacks in these areas the political power which is theirs by right. Secondly, they say what has long been noted and commented upon in the United States, that as the whites have moved out to the suburbs, the centres of all the big cities of the United States are increasingly populated by Negro majorities. This is a source of power which they propose to organise, and use as key positions in the struggle for Negro rights in the United States as a whole. Note and note well how precise is their concrete use of the term Black Power. And finally, the Negro people in the United States are not a people of a backward colonial area; they are Americans in what is in many ways the most advanced country in the world. The kind of impact the Negroes are making is due to the fact that they constitute a vanguard not only to the Third World, but con-

stitute also that section of the United States which is most
politically advanced.

So for the time being, that is what we know. I hope we know
it. That is what Black Power means, and when we consider
where that banner is being advanced and held aloft, and the kind
of people who are carrying it, we can recognise that it is a banner
which has come to stay, a banner which the twentieth century
will need in the great efforts it will need to overcome the crisis
that imperialist domination has imposed upon the whole world.
Not only upon the Third.

So far I have been dealing with what we know *or what we
ought to know*. That is, I now inform you, the answer to the first
of the three famous questions asked by Kant: "What do I
know?" The second question is "What must I do?", and here I
will take the liberty of reminding you of another profound
warning by a famous philosopher: *every determination is a
negation*. That is to say: every time you do something, every
time you *determine* on something, you *do not do* something else.
That is very important for us here. The things that I believe we
ought to do are very much in opposition to the things we ought
not to do. They are, I would suggest, two in number.

Number one, we support the fighters for Negro rights and for
Black Power in the United States. That means we *do not*
apologise or seek to explain, particularly to British people (and
in particular to British marxists), or give any justification or
apologise for whatever forms the struggle in the United States
may take.

It is over one hundred years since the abolition of slavery. The
Negro people in the United States have taken plenty and they
have reached a stage where they have decided that they are not
going to take any more. Who are we here to stand, or rather to
sit in judgment over what they decide to do or what they decide
not to do? I want to take in particular Mr Rap Brown, who
makes the most challenging statements, is prepared to challenge
American racial prejudice to the utmost limit of his strength and
the strength of the Negroes who will follow him. Who are we to
say, "Yes, you are entitled to say this but not to say that; you are
entitled to do this but not to do that"? If we know the realities
of Negro oppression in the USA (and if we don't we should keep
our mouths shut until we do), then we should guide ourselves by
a West Indian expression which I recommend to you: *what he
do, he well do*. Let me repeat that: what the American Negroes
do is, as far as we are concerned, well done. They will take their
chances, they will risk their liberty, they will risk their lives if
need be. *The decisions are theirs*.

A word more about Rap Brown. Whether he is what "they"
call a racist, or he is not one, does not interest me at all. I am
interested in Rap Brown as a political leader. And I know what
Rap Brown is doing. He is not a Garveyite: Garvey's doctrine

was quite suitable for his time. What Brown is doing is this: He is taking care that the total rejection of second-class citizenship, the single-mindedness, the determination to fight to the death if need be, which now permeates the Negro movement, will not be corrupted, modified, or in any way twisted from its all-embracing purpose by white do-gooders and well-wishers of whom the United States is full. Even when whites go down to the South to face blows and bullets from the Southern police and gangsters, the Negro movement finds that they cause difficulties which impede the struggle. If you want to know the facts about this you will have to go and look for it in the August 1967 number of the Negro magazine *Ebony*. There they are stated in full. And there you will see certain sections of the movement declare that they do not want white people in their organisations. It is not racism, it is politics, and the rapidity with which they are learning politics is proved by the masterly solution of this problem that they have arrived at. They say to whites who want to fight. "We welcome the addition of your forces to the struggle. But there up in the North, in your own town, there are areas where a Negro is not allowed to own a house or even to rent. There is an opportunity to fight American race prejudice. You want to fight? Go *there* and fight *there*. We can manage down here without you."

No, that is not racism. Racism is on the decline in the United States. Yes, on the decline. Years ago you used to have white people fighting against black people. Not today. Stokely insists and all the evidence points to the fact that what is taking place in American city after American city is black people fighting against the *police*. In other words, they are challenging an ancient enemy which is one wing of the state power. That is not racism. That is revolutionary politics.

They will decide and we support. But if we do that we do not do something else. We do not go around seeking to explain away what they have done, or to prove that they are not good marxists in that they are not waiting for the American proletariat to move. We know the first thing we must do, and that tells us what we do not do.

The second thing is that we miss no opportunity to make the British public and the public at large know that we consider the life and safety of Stokely Carmichael to be in the greatest danger in the United States. A number of people here, and all over the world, realise that the simple way out for the racists in the United States (or the men of peace, peace at any price) is to murder him out of hand. They did it to Malcolm X, and today the progress of the struggle, building on what Malcolm X began, makes Stokely a person who is a mortal danger to those who wish to preserve the old way of life of the United States. We have not only to let the people in the United States know what we think, but we have to let the people know, and understand, that Stokely is not a person to be shot at by trigger-happy racists, or by deep thinkers who believe that the best black man is a dead black man. Let us, therefore, to personal friends and acquaintances, to unions, to whatever political parties we belong, let us tell them that it is their duty to register, by resolution and motion, the fears that all have for Stokely's safety; and so make those in the United States who want to kill him realise that such an action will make the public opinion of the world question not only the attitude of America to the coloured races, but the American attitude to elementary democracy and respect for the human person. We can do no better than take note of what Fidel Castro said about Stokely's safety at the closing of the OLAS Conference:

> And our people admire Stokely for the courageous statements he has made in the OLAS Conference, because we know that it takes courage to do this, because we know what it means to make such statements when you are going to return to a society that applies the most cruel and brutal procedures of repression, that constantly practises the worst crimes against the Negro sector of the population, and we know the hatred that his statements will arouse among the oppressors.
>
> And for this reason, we believe that the revolutionary movements all over the world must give Stokely their utmost support as protection against the repression of the imperialists, in such a way that everyone will know that any crime committed against this leader will have serious repercussions throughout the world. And our solidarity can help to protect Stokely's life.

Castro is a revolutionary, one of the greatest revolutionaries history has ever known, but the sentiment that he there expresses, you can participate in and take action upon even though you may be a Liberal or, it is not impossible, a Conservative. And we in Britain have a special task to perform in regard to the role that Stokely is playing. I want to read for you a notable piece of historical literature which, though written nearly two hundred years ago, was never so much apropos as it is today. It is a proclamation by the King of England for suppressing rebellion and sedition. It reads as follows:

> Whereas many of our subjects in divers parts of our Colonies and Plantations in North America, misled by dangerous and ill designing men, and forgetting the allegiance which they owe to the power that has protected and supported them; after various disorderly acts committed in disturbance of the public peace, to the obstruction of lawful commerce, and to the oppression of our loyal subjects carrying on the same; have at length proceeded to open and avowed rebellion, by arraying themselves in a hostile manner, to withstand the execution of the law, and traitorously preparing, ordering and levying war against us: And whereas, there is reason to

apprehend that such rebellion hath been much promoted and encouraged by the traitorous correspondence, counsels and comfort of divers wicked and desperate persons within this realm: To the end therefore, that none of our subjects may neglect or violate their duty through ignorance thereof, or through any doubt of the protection which the law will afford to their loyalty and zeal, we have thought fit, by and with the advice of our Privy Council, to issue our Royal Proclamation, hereby declaring, that not only all our Officers, civil and military, are obliged to exert their utmost endeavours to suppress such rebellion, and to bring the traitors to justice, but that all our subjects of this Realm, and the dominions thereunto belonging, are bound by the law to be aiding and assisting in the suppression of such rebellion, and to disclose and make known all traitorous conspiracies and attempts against us, our crown and dignity; and we do accordingly strictly charge and command all our Officers, as well civil as military, and all others our obedient and loyal subjects, to use their utmost endeavours to withstand and suppress such rebellion, and to disclose and make known all treasons and traitorous conspiracies which they shall know to be against us, our crown and dignity; and for that purpose, that they transmit to one of our principal Secretaries of State, or other proper officer, due and full information of all persons who shall be found carrying on correspondence with, or in any manner or degree aiding or abetting the persons now in open arms and rebellion against our Government, within any of our Colonies and Plantations in *North America*, in order to bring to condign punishment the authors, perpetrators, and abetters of such traitorous designs.

Given at our Court at *St James's* the twenty-third day of *August*, one thousand seven hundred and seventy-five, in the fifteenth year of our reign.

GOD *save the* KING.

Now the curious thing about that piece is that it had in mind George Washington, Jefferson and others, as the men who were being rebellious and seditious. Today, however, the very same proclamation can be signed by Harold Wilson, the Labour Party Prime Minister of Great Britain. In banning Stokely Carmichael from re-entry into Great Britain, he is acting in the identical spirit with which George III issued this proclamation, and helped the people of the United States towards independence. And with Harold Wilson we have to link another Prime Minister, Eric Williams of Trinidad and Tobago. Instead of being proud that Trinidad and Tobago was the birthplace of so distinguished a citizen of our age, Williams hastened to follow in the footsteps of George III and Harold Wilson, and has declared Stokely's presence in the country where he was born to be undesirable. To Williams no doubt it is.

We have lived to see a statue of George Washington in the heart of London. History moves very fast these days, and we may yet live to see Stokely, not only welcomed in Britain, but given the honour of a public statue. That, I am sure, is not as extravagant as some of you might think. Remember: history moves very fast these days and can quickly leave the dull behind. I doubt if we shall hear of Stokely getting married to a daughter or any relation of the Secretary of State (and in any case, that is Stokely's business, not ours). But this much I can say with confidence, that today, over half the world, Stokely, not as anybody's son-in-law but as the Secretary of State for the United States, would be more welcome than the gentleman who today obscurely fills that high position.

Now we come to Kant's last question. The first one, you remember, was: what do I know? Second: what must I do? And now, third: what may I hope? And here I have to deal with a personal experience which I shall share with you. Needless to say, it is completely political. I went to the US from England in 1938 and found them in a rare confusion as to what a marxist policy should be on the Negro question. What for them, as marxists, was a difficult social situation was further complicated by the fact that the stalinists for years had been preaching that marxism demanded the advocacy of an independent Negro state within the confines of the US. And the trotskyist movement from top to bottom, at home and abroad, simply did not know where it stood in regard to this fundamental question for a socialist party in the US. I had no difficulty whatever in telling them what I was quite certain was the correct policy. And this I knew not because I was a Negro, not because I had studied closely the situation in the US. No. From the very beginning I put forward what I conceived to be a very simple, straight-forward leninist policy.

I had studied Lenin in order to write *The Black Jacobins*, the analysis of a revolution for self-determination in a colonial territory. I had studied Lenin to be able to write my book on *World Revolution*. I had studied Lenin to be able to take part with George Padmore in his organisation that worked for the independence of all colonial territories, but particularly the territories of Africa. I therefore was in a position from the very beginning to state my position and to state it in a discussion that some of us had with Trotsky on the Negro question in 1939.

The position was this: the independent struggle of the Negro people for their democratic rights and equality with the rest of the American nation not only had to be defended and advocated by the marxist movement. The marxist movement had to understand that *such independent struggles were a contributory factor to the socialist revolution.* Let me restate that as crudely as possible: the American Negroes in fighting for their democratic rights were making an indispensable addition to the struggle for socialism in the US. I have to emphasise this because it was not only a clarification in the darkness of the trotskyist movement on the Negro struggle in 1938–39. Today, 1967, I find in Britain here a confusion as great as I found in the US in 1938, and nowhere more than among the marxists.

Now I am going to quote for you one statement by Lenin in which he states the basis of his argument. His actual political programme you will find in the resolutions which he presented to the Second Congress of the Third International on the question of self-determination, and in that resolution specifically you will find that he mentions the Negroes in the US. But the basic argument which was the foundation of Lenin's policy is stated many times in the debates that he carried on before 1917 on the right of nations to self-determination, and I will quote particularly from his sharp observations on the Irish rebellion of 1916:

> To imagine that social revolution is conceivable without revolts by small nations in the colonies and in Europe, without the revolutionary outbursts of a section of the petty bourgeoisie *with all its prejudices*, without the movement of non-class-conscious proletarian and semi-proletarian masses against the oppression of the landlords, the church, the monarchy, the foreign nations, etc . . . to imagine this means *repudiating social revolution*. Only those who imagine that in one place an army will line up and say, "we are for socialism", and in another place another army will say, "we are for imperialism", and that this will be the social revolution, only those who hold such a ridiculously pedantic opinion could vilify the Irish rebellion by calling it a "putsch".

Lenin is very angry and though often very sharp he is not often very angry. He explains how the Russian revolution of 1905 came:

> The Russian revolution of 1905 was a bourgeois-democratic revolution. It consisted of a series of battles in which *all* the discontented classes, groups, and elements of the population participated. Among these there were masses imbued with the crudest prejudices, with the vaguest and most fantastic aims of struggle; there were small groups which accepted Japanese money, there were speculators and adventurers, etc. *Objectively*, the mass movement broke the back of tsarism and paved the way for democracy; for that reason the class conscious workers led it.

Now it is necessary to continue straight on with Lenin, because he seems to me to have had some experience, some feeling, that people would not understand what socialist revolution was. And this is one of his sharpest passages. I give it to you in full so that you may see how strongly he feels on what is for him a vital constituent of the phrase, but the way in which he underlined what he considered absolutely necessary to the understanding of what a socialist revolution was:

The socialist revolution in Europe *cannot be anything else* than an outburst of mass struggle on the part of all oppressed and discontented elements. Sections of the petty bourgeoisie and of the backward workers will inevitably participate in it—without such participation, *mass* struggle is impossible, without it *no* revolution is possible—and just as inevitably will they bring into the movement their prejudices, their reactionary fantasies, their weaknesses and errors. But *objectively* they will attack *capital*, and the class conscious vanguard of the revolution, the advanced proletariat, expressing this objective truth of a heterogeneous and discordant, motley and outwardly incohesive, mass struggle, will be able to unite and direct it, to capture power, to seize the banks, to expropriate the trusts (hated by all, though for different reasons) and introduce other dictatorial measures which in their totality will amount to the overthrow of the bourgeoisie and the victory of socialism, which, however, will by no means immediately "purge" itself of petty-bourgeois slag.

Now the moment Trotsky agreed that the independent Negro struggle for its democratic rights was part of the way to the social revolution, the trotskyist movement accepted it. They accepted it but I don't think they really understood it. At any rate, in 1951 my friends and I broke irrevocably and fundamentally with the premises of trotskyism, and as independent marxists, we advocated this policy, this leninist policy, on the Negro question, and we believed that at any rate we understood this question thoroughly. We did not know what this policy contained in it. I began by telling you that early this year I listened to Stokely Carmichael and was immediately struck by the enormous revolutionary potential which was very clear to me. But I had no idea that before the end of the year I would hear from him the following:

We speak with you, comrades, because we wish to make clear that we understand that our destinies are intertwined. Our world can only be the third world; our only struggle for the third world; our only vision, of the third world.

Stokely is speaking at the OLAS Conference, and the Negro movement in the US, being what it is, he makes very clear that this movement sees itself as a part of the Third World. But before very long he says what I knew was always inherent in his thoughts, if not always totally plain in his words. I wish you to appreciate the gravity and the weight which a man who speaks as Stokely has been speaking must give to the following words:

But we do not seek to create communities where, in place of white rulers, black rulers control the lives of black masses and where black money goes into a few black pockets: we want to see it go into the communal pocket. The society we seek to build among black people is not an oppressive capitalist society—for capitalism by its very nature cannot create structures free from exploitation. We are fighting for the redistribution of wealth and for the end of private property inside the United States.

In the opinion of myself and many of my friends no clearer or stronger voice for socialism has ever been raised in the US. It is obvious that for him, based as he is and fighting for a future of freedom for the Negro people of the US, the socialist society is not a hope, *not what we may hope*, but a compelling necessity. *What he or any other Negro leader may say tomorrow, I do not know.* But I have followed fairly closely the career of this young man, and I leave you with this very deeply based philosophical conception of political personality. He is far away out, in a very difficult position, and I am sure there are those in his own camp who are doubtful of the positions he is taking, but I believe his future and the future of the policies which he is now advocating does not depend upon him as an individual. It depends upon the actions and reactions of those surrounding him and, to a substantial degree, not only on what you who are listening to me may hope, but also on what you do.

1967

16

Discovering Literature in
Trinidad: the 1930s

[*This essay on the origins of West Indian creative writing was published in the July 1969 issue of* The Journal of Commonwealth Literature. *James himself, with his short stories and especially the novel* Minty Alley, *was a participant in those origins, of which he says: "It is a matter of historical importance what we aimed at and what reception we met with."*]

I don't know much about West Indian literature in the 1930s—there wasn't much to know. But at any rate I want to give some idea of how I grew up in the thirties and became the kind of writer that I am. I want to make it clear that the origins of my work and my thoughts are to be found in Western European literature, Western European history and Western European thought. To avoid misunderstanding, I must say that I think the people of the underdeveloped countries accept me and feel that I have had a lot to say that is valid about the underdeveloped countries. That is important. But what I want to make clear is that I learnt this quality in the literature, history and philosophy of Western Europe. I didn't *have* to be a member of an underdeveloped country, though I know a lot of people who are, and yet don't know anything about those countries. I didn't *have* to be an exploited African. It is in the history and philosophy and literature of Western Europe that I have gained my understanding not only of Western Europe's civilisation, but of the importance of the underdeveloped countries. And that is still my outlook.

The atmosphere in which I came to maturity, and which has developed me along the lines that I have gone, is the atmosphere of the literature of Western Europe. In my youth we lived according to the tenets of Matthew Arnold; we spread sweetness and light, and we studied the best that there was in literature in order to transmit it to the people—as we thought, the poor, backward West Indian people. I want to tell you what journals I used to read, together with other writers and some other people—there were very few of us. To my house, on my subscription, came *The Times Literary Supplement*, *The Times Educational Supplement*, *The New Statesman and Nation*, *The Observer*, *The Sunday Times*, *The Daily Telegraph* (when Rebecca West wrote in it), *The Evening Standard* (when Arnold Bennett wrote in it—I think Tuesday and Thursday), *The Criterion*, *The Nation*; from the United States *The New Republic*; from France *Mercure de France* and the *Nouvelle Revue Française*; also the *Musical Review* and the *Gramophone*. That

was what Alfred Mendes and I, and the rest of us, read and
circulated; I didn't take these from the library. I took other
books from the library—these I subecribed to. I didn't learn
literatare from the mango-tree, or bathing on the shore and
getting the sun of the colonial countries; I set out to master the
literature, philosophy and ideas of Western civilisation. That is
where I have come from, and I would not pretend to be
anything else. And I am able to speak of the underdeveloped
countries infinitely better than I would otherwise have been able
to.

We live in one world, and we have to find out what is taking
place in the world. And I, a man of the Caribbean, have found
that it is in the study of Western literature, Western philosophy
and Western history that I have found out the things I have
found out, even about the underdeveloped countries.

In the 1930s there were a number of us in the West Indies who
were to become writers—in Trinidad, myself and George
Padmore (we were boys together, and used to bathe in the Arima
River, underneath the ice factory); in Martinique there was
Aimé Césaire. We hadn't the faintest idea that the time would
come when we would be in the forefront of the revolution for
African independence. Among my contemporaries was Grantley
Adams, who is now a very distinguished citizen. When I was
talking to him a few years ago, he told me that before he left
Harrison College he had read Homer, Hesiod, Euripides,
Sophocles and Aristophanes, and he was a great master of
Aeschylus; he could read Greek almost as well as he could read
English. That is the way he was educated, and later he went to an
English university and studied law. That was the way that
generation was brought up. That's how we became what we are,
and if Grantley is a man about whose career one has reser-
vations, he still has very much to his credit. Now Aimé Césaire, I
believe, had much the same sort of education in the Victor
Schoelscher school in Martinique. Then he went to Paris and
something happened to him which is very notable about all of
us—he joined the Communist Party. George Padmore joined
the Communist Party. I joined the trotskyite movement. We
were educated not only in the literature and material life of
Western civilisation, but we also became marxists and were
educated by marxism. To the end of his days Padmore remained
a marxist.

There were some of us who were not black men. There was
Carpenter the violinist. There was Alfred Mendes. There was a
tall, handsome boy, a very able boy, called Frank Evans, a white
boy. There was Daly who had an extremely sharp wit, and was
lightskinned. There was De Boissière. There was Albert Gomes.
We went one way; these white boys all went the other way. We
were black and the only way we could do anything along the
lines we were interested in was by going abroad; that's how I

grew up. De Boissière* went to Australia and wrote two books. Daly has gone, I don't know where. Frank Evans—fine person, great literary skill—gone, I don't know where. Carpenter was a fine violinist and a great student of musical criticism. But George Padmore and I, and, in similar circumstances, Aimé Césaire, and in his way Grantley Adams (because Grantley was an unusual black man as there was a parliament he could join, and outside of Barbados there wasn't one)—if we wanted to write and do something, we had to go abroad. We couldn't make it at home. Mendes and I had work published before we left, but that was because distinguished people came to the island, we were introduced to them as "literary persons", and they took our work away and gave it to editors; that's how I was first published.

Albert Gomes told me the other day: "You know the difference between all of you and me? You all went away; I stayed." I didn't tell him what I could have told him: "You stayed not only because your parents had money but because your skin was white; there was a chance for you, but for us there wasn't—except to be a civil servant and hand papers, take them from the men downstairs and hand them to the man upstairs." We *had* to go, whereas Mendes could go to the United States and learn to practise his writing, because he was white and had money. But we had to make our money. I came to Europe because Learie Constantine told me: "You come. I'll see that you go on all right. I'll see that nothing happens to you." It reminds me of what Khrushchev said at the Twentieth Party Congress, when he claimed that Stalin used to do this and used to do that, and they asked him, "But if that is so, what did *you* do?" And he answered, "Boys, it was tough." That was the general atmosphere, and all of us black writers in the Caribbean went that way, suffered from that.

My father's experience illustrates what circumstances were like in the West Indies. In a West Indian island in those days there would be certain small towns and villages where the schoolmaster was an important person. Next to him were the Anglican parson and the Catholic parson, but the third stage was the teacher. If you wanted to know what was happening in the British Parliament, or if you wanted to know about the revolution in Turkey, or if you wanted to know what was happening in Barbados, or who had written this or that book, or what books Dickens had written, or who Henry VIII was, or what Magna Carta was—whatever it was, you came to the local teacher to find out. And if he didn't know, he went to the two parsons, and if they didn't know—well, nobody knew. That was the intellectual life of a rather narrow area. But the local teacher recognised his responsibility. There is a

---

*Ralph de Boissière, *Crown Jewel* and *Rum and Coca-Cola*.

wonderful list of black teachers in Trinidad. My father was one.
I knew them well. There was E. B. Grosvenor, there was Nelson
Comma, there were the two Regises, there was Napoleon
Raymond, there was old De Suse—a whole bunch of them,
including my godfather, Mr Poyer, and the man who married
my aunt, Mr Richard Austin. These men have made the
Caribbean what it is today. If I get the opportunity to go back to
the West Indies, I shall write about them. They taught you
everything you needed to know: reading, writing, arithmetic,
proper behaviour, good manners, how you were to wear your
clothes—everything. Those teachers educated the present
generation of Caribbean people who are now between fifty and
sixty years of age. Few today remember them. I knew all of them
extremely well, and it is from their world that I and Grantley
Adams and George Padmore have come, so that from early on
we had a sense of intellectual and moral responsibility to the
community—it was the atmosphere in which we grew up.

Now you can analyse up to a point, and beyond that you just
have to guess. But there is one case that I can speak about—the
writer George Padmore, because he was not only a politician, he
wrote. Padmore's father was a man named Alfonso Nurse. And
Mr Nurse was an intellectual, an intellectual of the generation
before me. My father was one too, although he read few books,
but he was first in his class of student teachers. (My mother was
the reader and all the books she used to read and put there; some
she used to tell me not to read, but I read them all.) Mr Nurse
knew my father very well, and we were friendly, the parents and
the children. Some person said that the children in Trinidad
should be educated in agriculture. So a Professor Carmody, a
white man (I don't know where he got his professorship from,
but he was a man of science), taught a group of teachers
agriculture. Alfonso Nurse learnt this agriculture very quickly
indeed. He learnt it so well that he was made an agricultural
instructor and inspector to teachers who were to teach the
children modern agriculture to help the economy. But Mr Nurse
was a reader and he read about science and related matters.
Some controversy started in the newspapers and he wrote a long
letter to the paper and signed his name: "James Alfonso Nurse,
Agricultural Inspector", or something of the kind. Professor
Carmody ripped hell and said that Nurse had no right to do
that—who was he to write on science and so forth? Finally Mr
Nurse told him to go to the devil, and promptly resigned his
inspectorship. That was the sort of man Padmore's father was.

Furthermore, he broke with the Christian religion and became
a Black Muslim, the only one I have ever heard about in
Trinidad. That was about 1900. I have never seen another house
in Trinidad like his: he lived in a small room about ten feet
square covered with books on every side. I knew no other man in
the Caribbean who read so much, or so many books; he was a

truly learned man. Whenever you wanted to know something, Mr Nurse knew it. That's where George Padmore came from. My father and mother were much the same type of persons, although nobody touched the religious audacity and the wide range of knowledge of Mr Nurse. He was exceptional and he produced an exceptional son. But that was the atmosphere in which we grew up, and though there were white boys among us, they were not compelled to do what we had to do to get somewhere.

James Anthony Froude, friend and executor of Carlyle, great English historian, took it upon himself to pay a visit to the West Indies and, when he returned, to write a book about the West Indies. It is quite clear that he had decided what he would write before he went. This book created a great deal of hostility in the Caribbean, and people wrote in the press about it. But a black schoolmaster, Jacob Thomas, decided to write a book about it in reply, called *Froudacity, West Indian Fables Explained*. I want to give an extract from it in order to illustrate further the mentality in which I grew up, which was our inheritance of over a century. Jacob Thomas's English is as good as Froude's, in many places better:

> Thus far we have dealt with the main questions raised by Mr Froude on the lines of his own choosing, lines which demonstrate to the fullest how unsuited his capacity is for appreciating, still less grappling with, the political and social issues he has so confidently undertaken to determine.
>
> In vain have we sought throughout his bastard philosophising for any phrase giving promise of an adequate treatment of this important subject. We find paraded ostentatiously enough the doctrine that in the adjustment of human affairs the possession of a white skin should be the strongest recommendation. Wonder might fairly be felt that there is no suggestion of a corresponding advantage being accorded to the possession of a long nose or of auburn hair. Indeed, little or no attention that can be deemed serious is given to the interest of the blacks as a large, and, out of Africa, no longer despicable section of the human family, in the great world problems which are so visibly preparing and press for definitive solutions.

Clearly, Marcus Garvey was not an accident. The moment Jacob Thomas had to write, this was the way he thought, and it was along these lines that all of us who were black thought. Those who were not black had the same education and were interested in books and music as we were, but they could go elsewhere. If you were black, you had to stay where you were, or go abroad to get an opportunity.

Jacob Thomas also wrote:

> The intra-African negro is clearly powerless to struggle successfully against personal enslavement, annexation, or volunteer (or fight

for) protection of his territory. What we ask, will in the coming ages be the opinion and attitudes of the extra-Africans: ten millions in the Western hemisphere, dispersed so widely over the surface of the globe, apt apprentices in every conceivable department of civilised culture. Will these men remain for ever too poor, too isolated from one another, for grand racial combination, or will the naturally opulent cradle of their people, too long a place of violence and unholy greed, become at length the sacred watchword of a generation willing and able to conquer or perish under its inspiration. Such large and interesting questions it was within the province and duty of a famous historian, laying confident claim to prophetic insight, not to propound alone but also definitely to solve. The sacred power to forecast, however, has been confined to finical pronouncements regarding those for whose special benefit he has exercised it, and the childish insults of the blacks whose doom must be sealed to secure the precious result which is aimed at. In view of this ill-intentioned omission we shall offer a few cursory remarks bearing on, but not attempting to answer, those grave inquiries concerning the African people; as in our humble opinion these are questions paramount to all the petty local issues finically dilated upon by the confident prophet. . . . Accepting the theory of human development propounded by our author, let us apply it to the African race.

I feel I could have written that way under the same circumstances. That is our tradition. And it was there a hundred years ago. This man was not educated abroad; I doubt if he went to a secondary school. But his is the West Indian type of mind. By the thirties some of us were feeling our way to something, but we had to leave. After the Second World War those who began to feel that they had some possibility had also, *of necessity*, to leave. What I want to make clear is that all of us were writers of a certain type. All of us had this literary tradition; all of us had the European training; all of us wrote in the definite tradition of English literature. For us in the thirties there was no literature otherwise. And if I am not mistaken, although here I am open to correction, all those who began writing after 1945 were also in this tradition. The most notable one is Mr Wilson Harris. He writes as one educated in a German university, and has studied the philosophy of Heidegger and Jaspers, and to be writing English as if his native language were German. Not that the language is not fine English, but he has exactly the terms and outlook of German philosophy, especially of the present generation—what I mean is that it is in the European tradition. I know that I and my contemporaries have been writing in the European tradition, and that we still do, and as I read those who started after 1945 I think I see the same thing happening. But here I want to make a sharp break.

At the present time I have discovered in two writers of the

Caribbean—Earl Lovelace and Michael Anthony—a new type of West Indian writer. They are not writing with all the echoes and traditions of English literature in their minds. As I see them (and I know the West Indies and particularly Trinidad very well), they are native writers in the sense that their prose and the things that they are dealing with, spring from below, and are not seen through a European-educated literary sieve, as some of the finest writing in the West Indies up to today has been. I hope nobody takes that in the wrong sense. For I believe that Herman Melville, in my opinion the greatest writer that the New World has ever produced, also saw writing in terms of the European literary tradition. The man who broke that and began to write from the native American tradition was Mark Twain, and Hemingway says plainly that American prose began with Mark Twain, with *Tom Sawyer* and *Huckleberry Finn*. I can't say that it does, but I know what he means. And I have begun to see a new type of writer, a new type of prose, a different type of work, that is not the result, as Melville's work was, of a tremendous absorption of the European literary tradition. I have seen it in Michael Anthony, and it is remarkable work, very fine, and something new, and native in the best sense of the word. Lovelace also, in *When Gods Are Falling*, is a writer of this kind.

When I wrote *Beyond the Boundary*, I told in the first part of my early life and how I grew up. I remember that Vidia Naipaul wrote me a letter in which he said: "I have only read half of the book so far but I want to let you know at once I am extremely glad because it lets these English people know who and what we West Indians are."

Saint-John Perse and Césaire and others broke away from the tradition, and a lot of their work was work which sought to get rid of the domination of the life of the Caribbean—and of life in Europe which had made the life in the Caribbean—all of them, white, black, brown, all of them are that way. They want to get out of it, but you don't get out of a linguistic tradition so easily.

Lastly, I want us to look beyond the Caribbean, at English literature generally in the twentieth century. At the end of the nineteenth century the great figure (and a man whose writing I respect a great deal) was Rudyard Kipling. And Kipling was trained in the Punjab. The early stories, which in my opinion are his finest, were published in a Punjab paper. He was not British. Then we have three writers from the United States who have had an enormous influence on English literature: Henry James, Ezra Pound, T. S. Eliot. Foreigners. We have another foreigner, one of the most foreign of foreigners, Joseph Conrad, who has written a novel which I regard as unsurpassed in the twentieth century, *Nostromo*. He was a Pole. And then we have that tremendous body of Irish writers: Bernard Shaw, W. B. Yeats, James Joyce, Sean O'Casey, J. M. Synge. They dominate

English literature. So, when you look at English literature in this century, it is foreigners who are important, men who know the language and can take part in the civilisation, but are not part of it, who are outsiders and looking at it from outside. The only English writer of the lot who can stand up is D. H. Lawrence—and he couldn't live in England at all.

Now I am emphasising our relationship with Western civilisation, with Western philosophy, with Western literature. That's the way I grew up, but I'm not saying others have to grow up that way, for they will grow up as they please. But I am pointing out that because we have the same language as the British and the outline of our civilisation is based on theirs, we are in the same situation that has created the great writers of the twentieth century. We are members of this civilisation and take part in it, but we come from outside. And that is why those Irish and American writers and Joseph Conrad have dominated English literature this century. I believe that at the back of the success our writers are gaining (for which there are many reasons) is the fact that we are part of the civilisation, we can come here and live here, we can stay abroad and understand the civilisation, but we don't really belong. And it is when you are outside, but can take part as a member, that you see differently from the ways they see, and you are able to write independently.

1969

17

Learie Constantine

[*This is one of two contributions (the other, on Garfield Sobers, appears in* The Future in the Present*) to an anthology entitled* The Great All-Rounders *(Pelham Books, 1969), edited by John Arlott. James says: "I wrote about Constantine in a more familiar manner, in the old style in which we wrote about cricketers, because I knew him personally extremely well, I knew the style of cricket he played. It was quite different from the style that Sobers played since they were of two different ages."*]

Constantine is probably the only all-rounder in cricket who could win his place in a Test side by fielding alone. That will not be easy to demonstrate on the page of a book. In baseball, errors and brilliant playing in the field are statistically recorded; not yet in cricket. Not as difficult but not very easy to record is the place he has won in other spheres of this great and important game: both on and off the field he did not leave the game where he found it. To very few has it been given to do this.

Constantine is not a Test cricketer who played in the leagues. He is a league cricketer who played Test cricket. It is not enough to do justice to league cricket. Justice must be seen to be done. League cricket today is what he made it. As far back as 1963 I referred to the coverage of league cricket by the national Press as "caves, dark and unfathomed". It was only in 1965 that *Wisden* extended its section on league cricket. We shall therefore begin with league performances of this greatest of league cricketers.

Here are the figures of Constantine's play during his great years in the Lancashire League, 1929–37. In the nine seasons that he played with Nelson, they were league champions on seven occasions, runners-up twice. His first season, in 1929, broke all records, for £2,380 was paid in gate records to watch this great professional play with a great team. A higher record was created in away matches, for these gates totalled £2,659. Of course, Nelson were again champions. Learie in his final analysis had scored 820 runs (average 34.16) and taken 88 wickets at 12 runs each.

Although Nelson were only runners-up in 1930, he headed their batting and bowling averages, with 621 runs (average 38.81), and 73 wickets at a cost of 10.46 each. Nelson won again in 1931 and, added to this victory, the Worsley Cup. Learie's figures read: 961 runs (average 51), 91 wickets (average 9.54).

In 1932, the figures were: 476 runs (average 22.66), 91 wickets (average 8.15). In 1933 but for missing two matches (to play with the West Indies team) he would surely have done the double unheard-of in this league, of 1,000 runs and 100 wickets. Only four wickets short, his final analysis was: 1,000 runs (average 52.63), 96 wickets, (average 8.5). In 1934 Nelson won both cups. Learie's analysis was 807 runs (average 40.17), 104 wickets (average 8.12).

In 1935, victory again. Although Learie missed seven matches, his analysis was: 493 runs (average 30.81), 79 wickets (average 10.5). It was victory again in 1936; Learie's final figures being: 632 runs (average 33.26), 86 wickets (average 11.22). 1937 was his final year. Little short of thirty-five years of age, his final Nelson analysis read: 863 runs (average 43.15), 82 wickets (average 11.41).

The concentration on Learie's figures (in relation to league cricket in Lancashire it would be wrong, unhistorical, not to call him "Learie") . . . the concentration on the figures is not simply a biographical and historical need. Constantine has written extensively on the game, few cricketers more, and wherever possible I shall let him speak for himself. In an illuminating chapter on league cricket in his first book he analyses the role of the professional in a league side. He draws in detail his special functions and value but ends by saying: "If even the professional is the essence of selfishness, and thinks only of doing well for himself, it will pay him in the end to study and help his side as much as possible; for it is with them that he has to play and no one man can consistently beat eleven others at cricket. It is a case of him who wishes to save his soul first losing it."

The figures are biographically important for another reason. So acute a critic as Sir Donald Bradman has expressed the belief that Constantine was the success he was in league cricket because he could turn the fortunes of a Saturday afternoon match by quarter hours of fierce fast bowling and brilliant hitting. Those figures and the record in general show nothing of the kind. I saw a good many of those league matches. The cricket was tense and often it was tough. It was agreed among the players that it was harder to get a hundred wickets in the league than in county games. But tight as the cricket was, happenings were always bursting through. And I repeat here one recorded by the Nelson journalist to whom I am indebted for these figures:

> One year Nelson required only a victory over Enfield, in the last match of the season to enable them to retain the league cup. The Lancashire League officials came to Nelson, and sat down to witness a comfortable Nelson victory. Making full use of the glorious uncertainty, the Enfield team beat Nelson, and then raced back to the pavilion, to get the rare privilege of a look at the cup. But they were yards late. The cup and officials were speeding off to Church in a taxi. Todmorden, having beaten Church, were the new champions.

Constantine had visited England in 1923. He had come with a modest reputation. He left with little more than a promise of great things to come. Then came the 1928 visit. He scored more runs than any other member of the team, and also headed the bowling averages. In first-class games alone he scored 1,381 runs at an average of 34.52, and took 107 wickets at a cost of 22.95 runs each wicket. But even this remarkable performance, although without parallel for over a generation by any visiting fast bowler (except for J. M. Gregory in 1921) was relegated to mere statistics by something that both the public and the professors hailed with equal enthusiasm as a new dimension of play on the field. There had been and were great all-round fieldsmen. No one had so dominated this department of cricket wherever he was placed, or decided to place himself, slip, short leg, or in the covers. We have to stay here a while and place great fielding in general, and Constantine's fielding in particular, where it belongs. I do not believe it has been done before and if even it has been it is worth doing again.

We cannot do better than place ourselves in the shadow of that luminary of English life and English prose. William Hazlitt. With his usual directness Hazlitt tackles the question of the use of the term "great" in relation to physical performers. There are passages and persons it would be sacrilegious to paraphrase.

> A great chess-player is not a great man, for he leaves the world as he found it. No act terminating in itself constitutes greatness. This will apply to all displays of power or trials of skill, which are confined to the momentary, individual effort, and construct no permanent image or trophy of themselves without them. Is not an actor, then, a great man, because "he dies and leaves the world no copy"? I must make an exception for Mrs Siddons or else give up my definition of greatness for her sake.

You might think that this writer of casual essays was, as is the habit of this type of writer, merely expressing a personal preference, being what the Americans call "cute". No such thing. Hazlitt is deadly serious. Elsewhere we find him saying at length what he thought of Mrs Siddons and why:

> But to the retired and lonely student, through long years of solitude, her face has shone as if an eye had appeared from heaven; her name has been as if a voice had opened the chambers of the human heart, or as if a trumpet had awakened the sleeping and the dead. To have seen Mrs Siddons was an event in everyone's life. . . .
> Though the distance of place is a disadvantage to a performance like Mrs Siddons's Lady Macbeth, we question whether the distance of time at which we have formerly seen it is any. It is nearly twenty years since we first saw her in this character, and certainly the impression which we have still left on our minds from that first exhibition is stronger than the one we received the other evening.

The sublimity of Mrs Siddons's acting is such, that the first impulse which it gives to the mind can never wear out, and we doubt whether this original and paramount impression is not weakened, rather than strengthened, by subsequent repetition; if we have seen Mrs Siddons in Lady Macbeth, only once, it is enough. The impression is stamped there for ever, and any after-experiments and critical inquiries only serve to fritter away and tamper with the sacredness of the early recollection.

If only Hazlitt had reported cricket matches. (He wrote fabulously on boxers and on a great fives-player.) But in his writing you glimpse some representation of what people see when they are dazzled by the sunburst (especially in the bleak English weather) of a great cricketer at his best, and particularly of a fieldsman. In 1928 people learnt to come to see Constantine field and to this day some have never forgotten what they saw. I know I have never forgotten single episodes I have seen at cricket: a great number by Constantine, batting, or bowling, or fielding. It is a conception I am trying to drive home: one day in 1954 at Sheffield I saw an England fast bowler bowl a length ball to Freddie Trueman. What spirit moved through that strong-willed, strong-armed bowler of fast balls I do not know, but he drew himself up to his full height, put his left foot forward in a most majestic manner and taking the ball on the rise drove it through extra-cover (nearer to mid-off), for a classical perfection of a four. His follow-through was just high enough to make the stroke a drive and not a forward-stroke. Having finished his stroke he remained poised just long enough to show that he knew he did not have to run. Whereupon he returned to normality, this being for him an old style number ten or eleven who might or might not connect with his sporadic heaves at the ball. The point about Constantine's fielding is that you came to the ground and looked at him expecting the moment of artistic truth and were rarely disappointed.

But more than that. That year he could register indelibly on the spectator's consciousness on the field, with bat and with ball, right through a three-day match. Against Middlesex he went in at 79 for 5. In twenty minutes he had scored 50 and 86 in less than an hour. Then in 6.1 overs he took 6 wickets for 11 runs. In the second innings West Indies were 121 for 5. He hit 103 out of 133 in an hour, 50 of them in eighteen minutes. All through the season he was performing similarly. It is sufficient to say of this series of displays that they defied the accepted logic of past history. That year the only outstanding player with any pretensions to pace who did the double was Maurice Tate who took 165 wickets and scored over 1,400 runs. But whereas Tate bowled well over 1,500 overs Constantine bowled little over 700. He took thirty catches. Tate was a tremendous cricketer, definitely a greater bowler than Constantine. But I do not think that any or many single efforts by him made the shattering registration on the consciousness and memory of the spectator which Constantine repeatedly did through a whole season. Figures here positively distort the actuality.

We restore perspective by noting that in 1928 Constantine failed in the last three Test matches, failed that is to say as batsman and bowler. In 1929–30 in the West Indies, he took 18 wickets with his fast bowling in four Tests. His batting was again moderate but his fielding at slip and short-leg reached heights never attained by him before or after. The account of that, however, must wait. He went to Australia in 1930–31 and though his figures were good they were not particularly striking. However, he did not fail to make spectators realise that they were watching a cricketer the like of which they had never seen before. The Australian authorities asked him for a photograph to place among their special collection of great players.

By 1933 Constantine had mastered the technique of batting and bowling in the League. But for playing with the visiting West Indies team he would have done the double. He took, you remember, 96 wickets and made 1,000 runs with an average of over 50. This was the seasoned cricketer who now re-entered the first-class game in England. He played in very few matches. Against Yorkshire at Harrogate he had 5 for 44 and 4 for 50, getting Sutcliffe for 2, Holmes for 0, Leyland for 9 (in the second innings for 10); in the whole match 9 wickets for 94 runs.

Previous to this he had come down to play for West Indies against MCC. Thousands came out to see the man of 1928. He took four wickets for 88 runs including Hearne for 12, Hendren for 6, and D. R. Jardine for 7. In the second innings he hit 51 out of 66 in 27 minutes. But it was in the single Test match that he played at Manchester that Constantine, the Test batsman, appeared. He made 31 out of 36 in the first innings; the West Indies after 226 for 2 collapsing for 325. In the second innings West Indies were 2 for 132 and finally staved off defeat by reaching 225. Constantine had saved the situation by a hard hit 64 made in 50 minutes. I know that he was spoiling for the fray in the last Test at the Oval and he complains that he was manipulated out of it. In 1934–35 in the West Indies, he was at his best. He played in only three of the four Tests but took 15 wickets at a cost of 13.13 each and made runs steadily, usually when they were badly wanted.

The next height scaled by Constantine—he always gave me the impression that he was scaling or about to scale new heights— was his re-entry for a season's play with the West Indies team of 1939. What Constantine did in 1939 can best be expressed by an experience with his fellow warrior in many a hard-fought field. I was talking to George Headley in Jamaica in 1965 and the conversation, one of the strangest that I have ever had on cricket, went something like this.

"Tell me, George, do you remember any innings that you have played that you think of with special pride and satisfaction?"

Headley's face was that of a man who was asked if he remembered the day that he was born. "No," he said, "I don't remember any of them. I just played these innings as they came."

"Nothing. George? Not even the century in each innings at Lords?"

"No," he replied, his face still a blank.

I was intrigued. "Tell me," I said, "is there any innings played by anybody that stands out in your mind?"

"No," he said slowly, trying his best to help me. "Frankly I don't remember any of them specially. I have seen a lot of good innings but none stands out."

I decided to force him to the wall.

"Is there anything at all in your career which stands out as something you cannot forget?"

His face lightened and he became not only enthusiastic but excited. "Yes," he said, "most certainly. I often remember how Learie, the fast bowler I used to know, changed his style in 1939 and became a slow to medium bowler as effective as he had been when bowling fast. That is the thing about cricket that I remember most."

I had the sense not to push the matter any further. George Headley is a very honest and a very sincere man and what he had told me showed not only his own attitude to the game that he had played with such distinction, but the impact that Constantine made upon not only spectators but upon players.

In 1939, bowling a mixture of medium pace and slow, with googlies, and of course the inevitable fast one, Constantine ended with the following: 651.2 overs, 67 maidens, 1,831 runs, 103 wickets, average 17.7.

These are among the most remarkable figures ever achieved by any visiting bowler in England. Especially for a man of thirty-seven who eleven years before, as a fast bowler, had taken his hundred wickets in the following terms: 723.3 overs, 131 maidens, 2,456 runs, 107 wickets; average 22.95.

A cursory review of the figures of visiting bowlers who have taken a hundred wickets convey unexpected relations, even oddities out of which Constantine's figures emerge not only with brilliance but with an abiding solidity. Take O'Reilly in 1938 and R. J. Crisp of South Africa in 1935. In 1938, W. J. O'Reilly bowled 709.4 overs, 215 maidens, 1,732 runs, 104 wickets, average 16.65. In 1935, Crisp: 690.5 overs, 105 maidens, 2,096 runs, 107 wickets, average 19.58. In 1934, O'Reilly and Grimmett each took 109 wickets. But where more than one bowler has taken that number of wickets, too much has to be taken into account before any too obvious conclusions can be drawn. To take their hundred wickets, however, O'Reilly needed 870 overs and Grimmett 985.4. Constantine took his 103 wickets in 651 overs. We have to go back to a great bowler of pre-1914 to find comparable figures: Hugh Trumble in 1902 (six ball overs), took 137 wickets at the low cost of 14.2 runs per wicket and needed only 912 overs, just above Constantine's wicket every six overs. However, 1902 was a notoriously wet season, made to order for bowlers of Trumble's pace and spin.

The figures of other West Indies bowlers are worth remembering and comparing. In 1933, E. A. Martindale, the West Indian fast bowler, carrying the main responsibility for piercing a heavy phalanx of English batsmen, emerged with 668 overs, 109 maidens, 2,161 runs, 103 wickets, average 20.98. For the fast bowler's business, despatching batsmen with promptitude, these figures are almost identical with Constantine's. Nothing, however, approaches Charlie Griffith's figures in 1963. His 119 wickets fell in 695 overs, a batsman every six overs, and the cost was incredible: 12.82 runs per wicket. To complete the overall outline, add the following for the West Indies team in 1966. Between them Griffith, Sobers, Gibbs and Hall took 195 wickets and to do so needed 1,962 overs, ten overs for a wicket. Apart from the deceptiveness of figures in themselves, it must be repeated that there are all sorts of imponderables which have to be taken into account, not only the year's weather but the quality and type of batting that the bowlers faced. One point, however, can be responsibly added. Robertson-Glasgow, summing up the season of 1939, in *Wisden* of 1940 reported that an experienced observer had given a considered opinion that the first dozen or so of English batsmen in 1939 were in sum the equals at least of his own time, that is about 1905–14. Robertson-Glasgow went on to say that the old freedom of stroke-play had returned. Perhaps this it was that helped Constantine's slows to get his wicket every six overs. It would be too invidious to detail the many batsmen heading the averages for their county whom Constantine's slows dismissed for little or nothing. It was a correspondent of *The Times* who noted that no other bowler was more expert at diddling batsmen out. That he had learnt in the league.

Constantine played some league cricket afterwards but we need not go into that. Two years after 1937 war broke out. He was occupied with war work and there was no league cricket again until 1946. He played for various league clubs but at no time did he attempt or could he reach the standards he had set in the Nelson years. That much he knew and although he gave great service to various clubs in other leagues, the Nelson years were the beginning and end of a period, one of the historic periods of English cricket.

It would be a mistake to ignore the fact that the glamorous spontaneity of Constantine's cricket did not have behind it an exceptionally shrewd and penetrating judgement of the generalities and refinements of play on the field. Take what would appear to be above all, an explosion of hand and eye and energy—the marvellous catches. I have never seen or heard of a series of catches such as Constantine took in Trinidad against the MCC team in 1930. Some of the catches were literally created by the fieldsman. George Gunn brought to the West Indies his habit of walking down the pitch to meet a ball just as it pitched. He did this once. The second time as he started to go down Constantine, at second slip, moved fast and began walking side by side with him: Gunn did not completely control the stroke: he edged the ball slightly, the catch was a dolly and Constantine picked it up one-handed. I presume that such a response to his adventurous habits had never happened to Gunn before. That alertness was behind many of the catches. I used to watch the great Bradman playing to Verity before he had begun to score. During that initial period, more than once I saw Bradman nervous, playing forward very shakily to Verity's leg-break and edging the ball slightly towards the offside in the direction of point. Once that had happened Bradman was at once, as if by magic, completely master of himself. But after seeing the uncertain stroke off Verity and the ball drop two or three feet from the edge of the bat I said to myself, "If Constantine was on that side you would play Verity differently or you would be caught for 0."

Many of the famous catches were so subtly created, that even to a not unskilled observer, the process could only be known afterwards when Constantine himself explained. Hendren is 98 on the matting wicket in Trinidad. Achong is bowling to him slow to medium left hand and as is natural on the old style coconut matting he is turning the ball slightly from the leg. Constantine knows the tension which Hendren, at 98, probably feels. He is standing in the gully and he instructs Achong, his junior, to keep the ball just outside the off-stump at a good length and not to attempt anything else. Achong obeys implicitly and Hendren remains at 98. Standing in the gully, his eyes glued on Hendren, Constantine notices that Hendren, before getting down to face Achong once more, takes a quick glance at the wide spaces between gully and second slip. Achong bowls the same ball as before. Hendren cuts to pierce the gap he has spotted between Constantine at gully and second slip, only to see that Constantine has anticipated the stroke and is making what is apparently an easy catch from not a bad but an ill-judged stroke. I saw the incident and the whole thing had been done so discreetly and unobtrusively that I did not know what had happened until I was told. Hendren, however, knew and before he left the wicket expressed his appreciation to Constantine in language not violent but personal, quite personal.

Some more of the brain which directed the brawny West

Indies playing in Kingston. Constantine is captaining the side, the official captain being ill. West Indies are well ahead in runs. The problem is to get the England team out in time, in particular Leslie Ames who is in the 90s and completely master of the bowling. Constantine knows he has to get Ames out and he goes to the slow left arm bowler and tells him what he must do. "Keep your length. Drop the ball on the off-stump breaking away as you have been doing. I am going to go and stand at silly mid-off a few feet away. Now, mind you, keep the length with the little bit of turn from leg that you are getting. Ames is going to get his century. The moment he gets it he is going to be looking for a chance to open out and especially to move me. Then bowl a ball over the good length but moving in to him with the arm. He is going to drive. The ball will hit the inside edge of the bat and I will have a chance to pick him up. But mind you when I am standing there I am taking my life in my hands. You do exactly as I tell you and we will see."

Constantine stood at silly mid-off. Ames made his century. The bowler pitched up the ball moving in with the arm. Ames believed his chance had come; came forward and drove. He did not connect squarely but hit with the inside edge, Constantine threw him up and the match was won. A year or two ago I saw Constantine recalling the incident to Ames at Lords. And both of them revelled in the memory.

This standing where a full hit by a powerful batsman can seriously hurt plays a part in one of Constantine's most spectacular catches. It was in 1933 in the Test at Manchester, where a Lancashire crowd saw Learie catch R. E. S. Wyatt one-handed practically under the bat at short leg. Constantine was standing there for Martindale's attempt at body-line. Martindale pitched short, and Constantine began to move away looking to defend himself, not to catch anything but to avoid being damaged by a powerful stroke from a good batsman and bad ball. But as he was going he kept his eye on Wyatt and spotted that Wyatt was mistiming the stroke and could not possibly do anything serious to the ball. He therefore returned to his position. Wyatt hit the ball much too late, and Constantine stuck up one hand and pulled down what, from the ring, seemed to be a dazzling feat. Constantine reported it as in reality a very easy catch from a stroke that had no power behind it and from which the flight of the ball from the bat could be easily followed. That catch was made before the ball hit the bat. And this marks Constantine's fielding at slip and short leg. He preached and constantly practised anticipation. Another superb slip, Walter Hammond, preached and practised that at slip it was a mistake to anticipate. I believe there is more to this difference than merely opposition in style. Sufficient for the time being that each master achieved in his own way mastery. You cannot ask more.

There is no need to go into further details about the famous innings, the main point about them being the strokes that make them memorable. For example there is the square cut off G. O. Allen in 1928 that sent the ball high up into the stands at Lords for six. There is another uniquely original boundary in 1933. Someone bowled Constantine a slow high full-pitch. Constantine turned, faced square leg and hit the ball for six straight behind the wicket-keeper, another of the strokes that no one remembers having seen before or seen afterwards. Yet there is a curious misconception about the last of his innings in Test cricket, the famous 79 made in the Oval Test in 1939. Of many appreciations, everyone of them in my opinion fundamentally false, the place of honour will be given to *Wisden* 1940: *Wisden* cannot possibly be affected by any sharp disagreement. This is the account of the innings.

> It was a real joy to watch the carefree cricket of the West Indies on the last day. Constantine, in the mood suggesting his work on Saturday afternoon League cricket, brought a welcome air of gaiety to the Test arena. He revolutionised all the recognised features of cricket and, surpassing Bradman in his amazing stroke play, he was absolutely impudent in his aggressive treatment of bowling shared by Nichols and Perks. While the four remaining wickets fell those two bowlers delivered 92 balls from which Constantine made 78 runs out of 103. Seldom can there have been such a spreadeagled field with no slips, and Hammond did not dare risk further trouble by changing his attack. With an astonishing stroke off the back foot Constantine thumped Perks for 6 to the Vauxhall end—a very long carry—and helped himself to eleven fours before he was last out to a very fine catch by Wood; running towards the pavilion the wicket-keeper held the ball that had gone high over his head.

The facts are correct. What I challenge is the belief invariably expressed about his innings that Constantine brought to this Test the carefree and impudent manner in which he played Saturday afternoon league cricket. That is most certainly not true. I saw Constantine year after year batting in the league. There was no air of gaiety or impudence in the innings that he played or in the thousands that he scored. There were times when he would amaze spectators by the audacity, even the daring of his strokes but it was all very seriously and systematically done: league cricket was not played for fun. At the risk of repeating myself I must give one example of this type of batting in the league.

Constantine is facing the impeccable length and direction of McDonald, the Australian who is still a dangerous bowler on a Saturday afternoon. Unable to get the ball away to a well-placed field, Constantine suddenly takes a long stride forward with his left foot and glances McDonald from outside the off-stump to long leg for four. A few balls later be brings off the same amazing stroke. Whereupon McDonald rearranges the field and

Constantine does not make the stroke again. As I have elsewhere written, "In these two strokes there was not the slightest restlessness or chanciness. The unorthodoxy was carried out with a precision and care, fully equal to the orthodoxy of Mac's classical action and perfect length."

It was in the 1939 Test that Constantine played carefree, impudent cricket. West Indies had ended on the Friday 43 runs ahead, with four wickets in hand. They had seriously planned to win that Oval Test. The runs had to be made as fast as possible and Constantine reverted to the spontaneous exuberance of 1928. But here, as always, it was business. And we get a glimpse of what he would have made of Test cricket if the early batsmen on his side had had names that began with the same letter, for example W.

Not only on but off the field this all-rounder made his mark. He is to be placed as an ambassador with Lord Hawke, Pelham Warner and Sir Frank Worrell. They travelled far and travelled wide, and where they passed the blossoms and flowers of cricket bloomed or sprouted.

And finally Constantine has written on the game as no other professional and few amateurs have written.

On bowling: "I am genuinely sorry when I hit a batsman but I know that I must have him aware that the ball can be made to do something . . . If a batsman can take my short ball and hit it round to square-leg he is a fine batsman . . . for me to put a fine leg and a bunch of short-legs and then a man on the deep square-leg boundary is to reduce cricket very nearly to a farce."

On Test cricket: "The excitement, the publicity, the material rewards, all will tend to increase and so gradually to impregnate this most beautiful of all games with the spirit which resulted in the deplorable scenes connected now, it seems inseparably, with all Test matches." This he was saying as far back as 1933.

And what to do about it? Let the last words be his.

"Conditions are such in the West Indies that we shall never be able to play cricket in the style that it is played by so many Englishmen and not a few Australians, and it is my firm belief that we can learn the atmosphere of Test cricket, get together as a side in order to pull our full weight and yet as a side preserve that naturalness and ease which distinguish our game."

He has lived to see it come true. And both on and off the field none has worked harder, all round, to make what seemed to many a wish-fulfilling idiosyncratic dream into a global reality.

1969

18

Paul Robeson: Black Star

[*This memoir of a man whom James has described as "one of the most remarkable men of the century" was first published in* Black World *in November 1970.*]

Paul Robeson was and remains the most marvellous human being I have ever known or seen. Yet this man was in his time feared by the great majority of white people in the United States, and today, although he is still alive, is forgotten by many of those who knew him. The present generation of militant young Blacks have not merely forgotten him. It is worse. They never knew him, and are not aware of him. This article is a beginning. That is all it can be of such a gigantic figure.

I went to London from the West Indies in 1932 and soon got to know Paul. He was not only a very famous man in England but he was very much loved by everybody. His reputation was legendary. The English appreciate sporting heroes and Paul, it was known, had been selected for some national football team in the United States at the end of one season. He had played in Shakespeare's *Othello* opposite to the Desdemona of one of the most distinguished young English actresses; he had even kissed her, which was quite an event in those days. He sang in recitals. He made films. But what was more than all this, there was his magnificent self. He was some six feet six inches in height and built in proportion, but he always had the silhouette and litheness of a great athlete. He was obviously immensely strong, strong enough to deal with two or three men at a time. Even in ordinary speech you were aware of his magnificent voice. He was obviously not only from his reputation and his achievements but in ordinary speech, a man of unusual intelligence. But what was most important, and this everyone knew, was that despite all these accomplishments and achievements he was as gentle a man as one could meet. He never gave the slightest impression of being aware of all that he was. He spoke a lot. But Paul was always listening to what you had to say, listening and giving it great consideration. To have spent half an hour in his company or to have ten minutes alone with him, was something that you remembered for days, and if I had to sum up his personality in one word, or rather two, I would say it was the combination of immense power and great gentleness.

I used to meet him at various places, at the houses of English people who were happy to invite Blacks as well as whites to their parties; there was not too much of that in those days because there were not too many Black people around. I wrote a play using as a basis some work that I was doing on Toussaint L'Ouverture, the hero of the revolution in the French colony of San Domingo which established the state of Haiti. Somehow—I believe through the writer Marie Seton who was a good friend of ours—the Stage Society, a very exclusive society which had given first performances of Bernard Shaw and many other playwrights who became world famous, had got hold of my manuscript. Mr Isaacs, one of their officials, said that they would play it if they could get Paul Robeson to play the leading part. It was very difficult to get him, but finally Isaacs and I ran him down at some party, told him about it and he agreed to read the script. He read it and with great simplicity and directness said, yes, he would be ready to play the role: there were not too many parts in those days which gave a Black actor, however distinguished, a role that lifted him above the servants' quarters.

The important characters in the play were played by a body of professional actors and we rehearsed many hours a day for a number of weeks. It was then that I got to know Paul pretty well. The producer was a young man, Peter Godfrey by name, who later came to Hollywood and made films. But at times Godfrey was occupied and as the author I had to rehearse the cast. It was during those days that I had a good look at Paul and got to know him well. He was here, as elsewhere, always the centre of attention, a not easy role to fill. Besides playing the lead, he was his own extraordinary self and not ony players but all who were connected with the stages where we rehearsed had their eyes fastened on him and were all ears when he spoke. Yet he continued to be that extraordinary combination of immense power enclosed in a pervading gentleness. Paul listened all the time to what Peter Godfrey or I had to say. I was somewhat naive then and was always ready to say exactly how I thought the words of the character should be said and what the character ought to do. Paul was always ready to listen and to oblige, far more so than one or two others in the cast. I remember, however, that one day we were doing a passage which I had inserted in the play almost directly from the material I had collected. I had made it into a long speech by Toussaint. If I am not mistaken, the original passage went as follows:

If self-interest alone prevails with nations and their masters, there is another power. Nature speaks in louder tones than philosophy or self-interest. Already are there established two colonies of fugitive negroes, whom treaties and power protect from assault. Those lightnings announce the thunder. A courageous chief only is wanted. Where is he, that great man whom Nature owes to her vexed, oppressed and tormented children? Where is he? He will appear, doubt it not; he will come forth and raise the sacred standard of liberty. This venerable signal will gather around him the companions of his misfortune. More impetuous than the torrents,

they will everywhere leave the indelible traces of their just resentment. Everywhere people will bless the name of the hero who shall
have re-established the rights of the human race; everywhere will
they raise trophies in his honour.

Paul was reading his part in the scene and suddenly his voice
opened up and the transition from his usual quiet undertone to
the tremendous roar of which he was capable was something to
hear. He was usually subdued but today he was giving it all he
had. When he reached ''Those lightnings announce the thunder.
A courageous chief only is wanted,'' he stopped. I and everyone
looked to him to go on. He turned to me. ''James,'' he said, ''I
don't want to go any further. I think it should stop here.'' It was
the first and last time that he made any changes in the script or in
the positions that he was asked to take. He explained later: ''I
feel that that is where we should stop.'' It seemed that he had
been reading the passage and that was why he opened out. He
was testing his ideas and he had come to a conclusion. When so
quiet a man made a definite decision you automatically agreed.

Originally, the play had not in any way given him any opening
to sing. One or two people thought that it would be a mistake for
Paul to play and not to sing. I was not too anxious for singing to
be injected into what I had written in reality for the sake of
hearing a marvellous voice, but I looked at Paul and his attitude
was: ''I am not particular but if you all want me to sing I will
sing.'' So that an opening was made and he sang a song, I
believe while he was in prison.

When the play was performed he, if not it, was a great success. For the sake of the record, I quote from two notices:

> Mr James's dialogue is informative rather than suggestive: it lacks
> suppleness, and too many of his scenes are at their best when they
> depend upon Mr Paul Robeson's almost unsupported monologues;
> but the work as a whole is sincere and unpretentious. For this
> reason, and because the dramatist, having an interesting subject,
> sticks to it, the play, in spite of woodenness now and then, holds the
> stage at the Westminster Theatre.
>
> What binds its episodes together is Mr Robeson's in-
> dividuality . . . the action is genuinely vitalised by Mr Robeson
> alone. His method is unusual and its merit hard to define. By the
> rules that apply to others it is clumsy, but his appearance and voice
> entitle him to rules of his own, justifying the directness of his attack
> upon his audience. It brings him out of the frame and, in a play
> dependent on composition, would have to be modified; but this play
> is not a composed picture—it is almost exclusively a portrait of
> Toussaint—and Mr Robeson's interpretation of him deliberately
> and rightly lays stress upon his dominance and reduces his associates
> to the background. In a play concerned with slavery, it is much that
> the tone is neither whining nor of hysterical defiance, but of
> reasoned determination. Toussaint is at once astute and guileless,

preserving through all misfortune his personal integrity and through all triumph a cautious eye for political reality as he understands it. When he is trapped, one feels that he has been mistaken in his calculations but not in his ultimate purpose, and the sympathy evoked by Mr Robeson in his prison cell is not for a tricked Negro but for a statesman paying a price for his ideal. In brief, though the obvious characteristic of Mr Robeson's acting is its gigantic vitality, it by no means depends upon this only, but has the special tension that springs only from disciplined emotion and balance. [Charles Darwin, *The Times*, 22 March 1936]

Here is one of the best known English drama critics, Ivor Brown:

Mr James's play is a careful prose-record of Toussaint's tremendous struggle against the remorseless toughness of the European exploiters and the weakness and the flightiness of his own hard-driven people . . . Probably poetry would better have honoured the great and magnanimous figure of ebony which Mr Paul Robeson presented like some tremendous tree defying hurricanes and finally overwhelmed by the small, mean blade of French dishonesty. [*The Observer*, 22 March 1936]

Paul was pleased. We agreed that we should seek ways and means to do it commercially. "I can play Toussaint and you can play Dessalines, and later we can switch, you will play Toussaint and I will play Dessalines." But at that time Paul was headed towards Moscow and I, as a trotskyist, was most definitely anti-Moscow. We knew about each other and never quarrelled, but the idea of doing the play automatically faded into nothing.

But Paul and I, as a result of the rehearsals and the play, used to talk. Before I knew him he had written a famous article in *The Spectator*, an English journal, of 15 June 1934. It should be carefully studied today. Paul believed and told me often:

No matter in what part of the world you may find him the Negro has retained his direct emotional response to outside stimuli; he is constantly aware of an external power which gudes his destiny. The white man has made a fetish of intellect and worships the God of thought; the Negro feels rather than thinks, experiences emotions directly rather than interprets them by roundabout and devious abstractions, and apprehends the outside world by means of intuitive perception instead of through a carefully built up system of logical analysis.

In this article Paul went on to say, and here again I shall use his own words:

Culturally speaking, the African Negro, as well as his American and West Indian brothers, stands at the parting of the ways. The day is past when they were regarded as something less than human and little more than mere savages by the white man. Racial tolerance and political equality of status have taken the place of oppression and slavery for the greater part of the Negro race. But the sufferings he has undergone have left an indelible mark on the Negro's soul, and at the present stage he suffers from an inferiority complex which finds its compensation in a desire to imitate the white man and his ways; but I am convinced that in this direction there is neither fulfilment nor peace for the Negro. He is too radically different from the white man in his mental and emotional structure ever to be more than a spurious and uneasy imitation of him, if he persists in following this direction. His soul contains riches which can come to fruition only if he retains intact the full spate of his emotional awareness, and uses unswervingly the artistic endowments which nature has given him.

That was an astonishing observation to make as early as 1934, and I want here to make clear what Paul was saying and what he was not saying. He used to speak to me quite often about this type of what I may call the psychological personality of the Black man. But what he always said was that he had discovered this in Negro spirituals and in the popular music and songs of various other countries. He had found a certain quality in Negro spirituals in the United States and he had found it in the songs of Africa:

As a first step I went to the London School of Oriental Languages and, quite haphazardly, began by studying the East Coast languages, Swahili and the Bantu group which forms a sort of Lingua Franca of the East Coast of Africa. I found in these languages a pure Negro foundation, dating from an ancient culture, but intermingled with many Arabic and Hamitic impurities. From them I passed on to the West Coast Negro languages and immediately found a kinship of rhythm and intonation with the Negro-English dialect which I had heard spoken around me as a child. It was to me like a homecoming, and I felt that I had penetrated to the core of African culture when I began to study the legendary traditions, folksong and folklore of the West African Negro. I hope to be able to interpret this original and unpolluted Negro folksong to the world and I am convinced that there lies a wealth of uncharted musical material in that source which I hope, one day, will evoke the response in English and American audiences which my Negro spirituals have done; but for me this is only one aspect of my discovery.

This had been written in 1934 and he was always talking about it. But he always talked about it as some information and knowledge of music and of languages which he was pursuing and which he was testing. Never did he give the impression that he was merely developing an instinct, or a political attitude that he thought was useful in the struggle against white domination.

Artist as he was, he subjected his strong feelings to a rigid historical analysis.

There was something else that he used to speak about. He was not satisfied that he as a Black man was confined to playing Othello among Shakespeare's plays. Often enough he said, "I believe that the Negro actor should be able to play Hamlet, Macbeth, King Lear, and that he should not be confined to Othello because Othello is a Black man. I am quite certain that if he played them as well as I know he will be able to play them, people will ignore the fact that this actor is Black. The play's the thing." As I think of many ideas prevalent today, it is important to remember that while Paul was insisting that the Black man had special qualities which were the result of his past in Africa and of his centuries of experience in the Western world, he was equally aware of the fact that this Black man was able to participate fully and completely in the distinctively Western arts of Western civilisation. While he was insistent that the Black man had something to contribute, something specially of his own, he did not feel it necessary to attack or to discredit or to give the impression that it was impossible for whites to understand Blacks, or Blacks to understand whites. All that was very far from Paul, and is important today.

Now I come to what makes him one of the most remarkable men of the twentieth century. A man whose history is not to be understood unless seen in the context of the most profound historical movements of our century. And, at the same time, the most profound historical movements of the twentieth century cannot be understood without taking into consideration Paul Robeson. Paul committed himself completely to the communist doctrine that only a world revolution could save society from the evils of imperialism and capitalism, in general. And, in particular, only such a revolution could assist the Black people in the United States to gain freedom and equality, and assist the white people in the United States in making America a place where all men, Black and white, could live in peace. That Paul believed completely and without reservation. In the thirties and forties I also believed the same. A whole body of intellectuals, C. Day Lewis (the present Poet Laureate in England), W. H. Auden, the most celebrated of contemporary English poets, Stephen Spender, John Strachey, André Malraux, some of the most distinguished intellectuals in Great Britain and in other parts of Europe, in those days all believed the same. Particularly after the Great Depression and the impact which the first Russian five-year plan made upon the world. Such sentiments were widespread among all the intellectuals of the day. What is notable about Paul is that he not only believed it, but all his magnificent powers, his great reputation and his impact upon the people who listened to him singing and acting, all this Paul gave completely to the idea that only the world revolution could save humanity from the crises and catastrophes of capitalism. Specifically, this world revolution was to be led by the communist parties with their ideological and organisational headquarters in Moscow.

To the extent that he expected the revolution to be led by the communist parties of Moscow he was wrong. That, here, is not important. What is important is that he gave all he had to the cause. And he had plenty to give. Nobody had more to give. And the devotion, the concentration, the complete commitment that Paul gave to his political beliefs and to the organisation which in his opinion represented it, is one of the great historical events of the period. I don't intend to go into details of his struggles with the American government, his attempts to sing at Peekskill, the long quarrel over the passport—these are details which are quite subordinate to the fact that a man of such magnificent powers and such reputation gave up everything and committed himself to what he believed was the only way for the salvation of mankind. Such is the quality which signalises the truly heroic figure. Paul had no need of a revolution to be able to participate in what modern civilisation had to offer. The exact opposite was the case. It was his devotion to the world revolution which caused him to lose the immense personal opportunities which his abilities and character opened out for him. I don't want to go into these details. Others have to do it in a way that makes people understand what Paul did and what he signified in the consciousness of world crisis which was so widespread in the thirties and forties and continues in our own time. For years Paul showed that hidden behind his friendly kindliness there was a relentless fighter who could not be moved from what he believed.

Two more points, only two, remain, because this is an article, not a biography.

I was in the United States busily noting all that was going on in politics concerning Black people, and I became certain, and all the people whom I talked to were absolutely certain, that if Paul had wanted to he would have built a movement in the United States that would have been the natural successor to the Garvey movement. Further, Paul, being what he was and his ideas being what they were, the movement would have been of a far higher intellectual quality than was the Garvey movement, which had laid a foundation for future movements. I can say, and it will be easy to prove, that people were looking to Paul to start such a movement. There were numbers of people, dozens and scores of people, who would have been ready to work with him if he had begun, and the mass of the Black population would have followed him as they were ready to follow him everywhere he went. But the plain fact is that Paul felt himself committed to the doctrines and the policies of the Communist Party. The Black movement which could have burst and swept the United States around Paul Robeson did not come because Paul did not see it that way. That is a part of the history of the United States which everybody in the United States should know. What was there, what was possible, what was missed, and why. . . .

I have one more episode concerning Paul which is strongly in my mind as a characteristic of him. When he was in England there was a singer in England whom everybody knew as "Hutch". His name was Leslie Hutchinson. He used to sing and play and was widely known and admired all over the country. It seems that "Hutch", an extremely handsome and impressive person, made an impression upon a member of the Royal Family, resulting in an association which everybody knew and used to talk about, as people gossip about these things, particularly in those days. In time the association reached a pitch when people highly placed in England thought that it should be brought to an end. Their method was quite simple and quite effective. A notice appeared in one of the evening papers in a column of society gossip to the effect that everybody was talking about the relationship between a member of the Royal Family and a popular coloured singer. That brought the thing out into the open and, from what we heard and finally saw, the lady was called and told that the matter was now a public scandal and the time was ripe for her to take a trip—to Kenya, Uganda, the Far East or the Near East, or somewhere, but she should be away for six months or so and allow this gossip to die. The lady had no choice and went.

One day I was walking up the street to the British Museum. I saw Paul's magnificent figure coming down the street and, as usual, I stopped to talk to him: it was always a pleasure to be in his company and to talk to him. He was a man not only of great gentleness but of great command; he was never upset about anything. But this day Paul was bothered. "James," he said, "you hear what all the people are saying about a coloured singer and a member of the British Royal Family? It's not me, James," he said passionately. "It's not me." I started to laugh. Paul looked at me somewhat surprised and he said: "What is there to laugh at? I don't see anything to laugh at." I told him: "Paul, you are a Negro from the United States; you are living in England and you say that people are linking your name to a member of the British Royal Family. That, my dear Paul, for you is not a scandal, it is not a disgrace. I laugh because you seem so upset about it. That is very funny." He said, "Well, maybe there is something to what you say, but you know who it is." I said, "Yes, I know who it is, and I know it isn't you, Paul, but nevertheless it is very funny," and we parted. That is many many years ago and I have seen and read about Paul and heard about him in many circumstances and in very different and more serious situations. But for some reason or other there remains in my mind his passionate denial that he was the person who was being written about in the papers and talked about as having an illicit relationship with a member of the British Royal Family. Most men whom I know, nearly all, might have denied it but in all probability would have given the impression that they were not displeased, certainly not bothered one way or the other. But for some reason or other, which I cannot go into here but which I think should be remembered about Paul, is his passionate statement: *"James, it isn't me."*

1970

Index of Names